From Reviews of Books Written by Curtis Wilkie

Of *Arkansas Mischief* with Jim McDougal, published by Henry Holt, 1998

"[Wilkie] seems to have caught every nuance and thrust of the late great raconteur's voice from the grave . . . All the usual hilarious catastrophes are interlaced with some redeeming anecdotes that needed to be preserved in print before they were lost to coming generations. Thank you, Mr. Wilkie, since Jim McDougal would never have got all this written down."—Paul Greenberg, *Arkansas Democrat-Gazette*

Of *Dixie*, published by Scribner, 2001

"Wilkie's tale ends on a grace note, not merely reconciliation with his native South, but a grateful return to it."—Jonathan Yardley, *Washington Post*

"Limber prose, self-deprecating wit, and firsthand knowledge of southern politics and society make 'Dixie' a gratifying book."—Michael A. Ross, *Times-Picayune*

Of *The Fall of the House of Zeus* published by Crown, 2010

"Reads like a John Grisham novel . . . An epic tale of backbiting, shady deal-making and greed . . . Masterful."—*Wall Street Journal*

"Fascinating, breath-holding action . . ."—Clyde Edgerton, *Garden & Gun*

Assassins, Eccentrics, Politicians, and Other Persons of Interest

Assassins, Eccentrics, Politicians,

AND OTHER

Persons of Interest

FIFTY PIECES FROM THE ROAD

Curtis Wilkie

University Press of Mississippi   Jackson

www.upress.state.ms.us

The University Press of Mississippi is a member
of the Association of American University Presses.

"Bohemia's Last Frontier," reprinted with permission
from the November 3, 2005, issue of the *Nation*.
For subscription information, call 1-800-333-8536.
Portions of each week's *Nation* can be accessed at www.thenation.com.

Other selections are reprinted with permission from the *Boston Globe* and
the *Clarksdale Press Register*.

First printing 2014
∞
Library of Congress Cataloging-in-Publication Data

Wilkie, Curtis.
   Assassins, eccentrics, politicians, and other persons of interest : fifty pieces from the road /
Curtis Wilkie.
      pages cm
   Includes index.
   ISBN 978-1-62846-126-8 (cloth : alk. paper) — ISBN 978-1-62846-127-5 (ebook) 1. Wilkie,
Curtis. 2. Journalists—United States—Biography. I. Title.
   PN4874.W57A3 2014
   070.92—dc23
   [B]   2014009130

British Library Cataloging-in-Publication Data available

To Pat and Butch Cothren, wonderful friends who helped
steer me home

To Tom Oliphant, my compatriot at the *Boston Globe*, who
personified the brilliance and irreverence of that newspaper

To Charles Overby, who has contributed so much to journalism in
Mississippi—and America

And, as always, to my dear Nancy

Contents

Part III: Covering Carter

Part IV: Covering Clinton

Part V: Middle East Interlude

Part VI: Writers

Foreword

Hank Klibanoff

Inside the *Boston Globe* newsroom, an artifact that was passed off as an innovation in the 1970s was "the blower," a recording machine into which far-flung reporters in overnight time zones or on breaking news could dictate their stories. The dispatches would be transcribed by staff assistants and sent to the national desk, foreign desk, sports desk, or metro.

Some reporters were dutiful to a fault. They painstakingly spelled every P-as-in-Paul, B-as-in-boy name and challenging word. They articulated every open double quote, open single quote, closed single quote, closed double quote. They inserted every period, comma, and, if they were truly artful writers, semi-colon. These reporters were beloved by the news assistants who were assigned to listen and transcribe their top-of-the head assemblies of words, often on deadline. Their stories sailed into the newspaper clean.

But the blower was not everyone's friend. Curtis Wilkie was certainly dutiful enough in dictating his stories. The problem was that no news assistant—oh hell, let's just go ahead and say it about our good friend—*nobody* could understand a word he was saying, especially in New England. The challenge was not simply Curtis's slow Mississippi drawl. Nor was it the combination of the drawl and Curtis's basso profundo that led baffled listeners to lean in close. It was both of those audial anomalies *and* the guttural yet gentle, molasses-soaked-marshmallows-in-the-mouth, rumbling, mumbling, rattling, tattling reverberation that accentuated the accent. Once when Curtis was speaking to a group of reporters, *Boston Globe* colleague Tom Oliphant stood beside him, interpreting Curtis in faux sign language. Another writer likened Curtis's voice to the sound of a "Mississippi Delta mudslide."

Curtis's problem with the blower came to a head when he was covering the 1980 presidential caucuses in Iowa. He covered a live debate on farm policy and raced to the phone to dictate his story into the blower. Soon after Curtis finished, a news assistant got off one call, slipped on the headphones, transcribed Curtis's tape-recorded story, and shipped it to the national desk.

It did not turn out well. The next day, in a pre-Internet world where there was no instant access to published stories, word slowly reached Iowa that while the *New York Times*, the *Washington Post*, the *Chicago Tribune*, the *Los Angeles Times*, the *Des Moines Register*, NBC, ABC, CBS, and every other news organization in the galaxy had written about the candidates' debate over *farm* policy, Curtis's story in the *Boston Globe* said the candidates had held a debate over *foreign* policy.

Curtis got deputy national editor Steve Erlanger on the phone to express his apoplexy and embarrassment. Curtis's voice came from depths previously unknown to humankind. It actually got deeper as it rose. "Stuyv, ah dint say *fawrn* policy," Curtis bellowed over the phone. "Ah said *fawrm* policy!" Even to Erlanger's ears, the words were indistinguishable.

But whatever difficulties Curtis faced in making himself understood when he opened his mouth to speak were overcome a thousandfold when he sat down to write.

Now, through this collection of Curtis's work over the past fifty years, some of it published before the Internet could make it universally available, we have the opportunity to read back in time and see why Curtis, early in his career, was identified as a unique reporter whose instincts and independent streak took him where others feared to tread, whose keen senses heard and saw what others missed, and whose clarity and coherence as a writer made him a master storyteller.

Curtis, of course, is one of the original Boys on the Bus, literally. As a reporter for the *News-Journal* of Wilmington, Delaware, Curtis caught the attention of Tim Crouse, author of that searing critique of the reporters who were covering the 1972 presidential campaign. The first time Crouse met Curtis, he had no reason to think Curtis was different from all the other reporters whose co-dependent herd instincts Crouse so decried. He described Curtis as "a thirtyish dark-haired reporter wearing a Palm Beach suit and a drooping moustache, who looked too hung over to object to my presence."

But Curtis, willing to trust his own judgment, willing to parry with editors who didn't want reporters straying from the low-risk coverage of the wire services, emerges from the pack in Crouse's book. Editors who questioned Curtis's stories when they didn't see similar accounts coming from the wires "didn't drive him back to the safety of the pack," Crouse observed. "He continued to trust his own judgment and write about whatever he himself thought was important."

Curtis got off the bus, was named an associate editor of the *News-Journal,* and the next month displayed the ultimate trust in his own judgment when he joined two other editors in walking out of the newsroom in protest of "intolerable intrusion into the integrity of the newsroom" by members of the board of directors who were associated with the DuPont Chemical Co.

Curtis landed at the *Boston Globe* at a remarkable time when editor Tom Winship was assembling a first-rate staff that could match, and often exceeded, his great ambitions for intense and sometimes obsessive political coverage, tough investigative reporting, freewheeling sports coverage, and bold writing. Curtis, as much as anyone, came to symbolize everything Winship wanted the newspaper to be.

For twenty-six years at the *Globe,* Curtis was constantly on the move as a national and foreign correspondent. He may be most closely identified with political writing from the Washington bureau, but his collection of datelines and his accumulated work shows a much broader portfolio from his assignments covering the life and times of this nation—from the road. Curtis's work, which brings you up close to people, which lets you see their distinguishing features, and almost lets you touch them, reminds me of the work of the great *Life* magazine photographer Charles Moore, who used only short-range lenses, forcing himself into the middle of the action.

There is a tilt toward the South in this book, not surprisingly. And it takes you to some of the most fascinating characters the South has produced. But it is not the hagiography you might expect or that many Southerners might want. Curtis's independence showed itself again and again. President Jimmy Carter and his band of Bubbas learned the hard way that Curtis, while hopeful that Carter would break stereotypes about Southerners, was not going to clear the path for them. President Bill Clinton and his Dixie coterie learned the same lesson. And just when it seemed that Curtis risked being typecast as the Southern reporter building his career on the Southernization of America, he moved to Jerusalem to open the *Globe*'s Middle East bureau and lived there for nearly four years before moving back to Boston, then New Orleans and, now, Oxford, Mississippi.

For Curtis, there is some risk in this book. We have the benefit of reading these stories retrospectively, from a perspective that allows us to measure Curtis's judgments, his insights, and his wisdom. What you will find is how astute he was when reporting, in the moment, stories whose outcomes might not be known for many years.

Curtis was there as these stories, these histories, unfolded in real time. But he did far more than provide a conventional, stenographic rendering of what he saw. He cast a precise and penetrating eye on the events, on the people, on the circumstances, and on the history, then told his stories—*explained them, interpreted them*—in ways that took readers to the stories behind the stories, the people behind the scenes, the circumstances no one else saw, and the history that gave everything else definition.

Hop on the bus. Curtis is behind the wheel. Enjoy the ride.

Acknowledgments

When I gathered the material for this book—some of it from yellowing newspaper tearsheets—I realized that my first newspaper job began in a smoke-filled press room, surrounded by clattering linotype machines slung with vats of boiling lead to produce "hot type." We received our national and international news on a scroll of paper churned out by a clacking, incessant Associated Press wire service. I still have the piece of paper and the terse message it delivered on Nov. 22, 1963: "KENNEDY DEAD."

I would go on to witness great stories myself, and to watch the technological transition in my profession. First, to offset, a cleaner form of printing. Then to early generations of computers, which I swore I would never be able to handle, to today's warp-speed world of communication. The progress was all fine and good, but I treasure most the personal camaraderie that I've enjoyed with countless others.

My thanks and gratitude to the hundreds of colleagues who've given me guidance and friendship from the start of my career in Clarksdale, Mississippi, to the staffs of the *News-Journal* papers in Wilmington, Delaware, and the *Boston Globe*, to the faculty at my alma mater, Ole Miss, where I continue to write fifty years after I graduated.

My love to my family—my wife, Nancy, my children Carter, Leighton, and Stuart, and my grandchildren—as well as other relatives and friends who helped me endure a lot of movement in my life.

My appreciation to Dawn Jeter, our office manager at the Overby Center, and Savannah Weider, our student intern, who provided the technical assistance I need so badly in the digital age.

Introduction

Among the rewards from a life in journalism are the fascinating stories, the interesting characters, and the exotic territories that we explore. I've been writing for publication for more than fifty years, and as I've often said, it beats working.

As a newspaper reporter for nearly four of those decades, many of my most treasured stories were set in the Deep South. Though I covered eight presidential campaigns, lived overseas, and followed a number of conflicts abroad, my interests kept turning me home. Perhaps I'm biased by my Mississippi background, but the state seems to have an inexhaustible supply of tales full of drama, poignance, and humor. It is a place where great literature somehow blossomed in a field of vast illiteracy, where we grew up reading Faulkner and Welty, Richard Wright and Tennessee Williams. When I began writing, Mississippi represented for me a veritable garden of rogues and racists, colorful personalities and outlandish politicians who managed to thrive among people otherwise kind and generous.

My career started in 1963 in the Mississippi Delta, working as a young reporter for the Clarksdale *Press Register*. A lot of journalists keep their first job for a couple of years, then move on. Because the civil rights movement dominated the news in our area, I found I was covering the biggest story in the country, day in and day out, albeit for a small daily. I stayed there for almost seven years.

But like Willie Morris, I felt pulled "North Toward Home." I went to Washington on a Congressional Fellowship, then found a job with the *News-Journal* papers in Wilmington, Delaware. My work for the

News-Journal during the 1972 presidential campaign attracted the interest of Timothy Crouse, who wound up writing about the political press corps in one of the most famous books about American journalism in the twentieth century, *The Boys on the Bus*. When the book came out, I was astonished—but pleased—to find myself "on the bus" with the heavyweights. (One friend brought me down a notch by calling it "gilt by association.") I suppose I got notice because Tim and I were younger and more irreverent than many of the reporters, and he liked my impressionistic style of writing. Still, it served as a major breakthrough for me; I'm sure it was a big reason that the *Boston Globe* hired me.

Most of the pieces in this collection come from my twenty-six years with the *Globe*. Since I was a rare Southerner on their staff, I was often assigned to cover breaking news events in the region during the last quarter of the twentieth century, stories of racial struggles and reconciliation as well as the campaigns of Jimmy Carter of Georgia and Bill Clinton of Arkansas.

It's an odd juxtaposition, but the Middle East was the other region where my work seemed to be concentrated. I lived in Jerusalem for roughly four years, and for a decade the Middle East was part of my beat—from the Israeli invasion of Lebanon in 1982 through the first Gulf War in 1991.

I retired from the *Globe* at the end of the 2000 election, but I didn't stop writing. I enjoy it too much to quit. After discovering I had the discipline to write a book with Jim McDougal, *Arkansas Mischief*, in 1998, I've had two more books published and contributed chapters for other books and occasional pieces for magazines.

Since 2002 I've been teaching journalism at my alma mater, Ole Miss, where I encourage students to develop their stories carefully, with deep reporting, rich anecdotes and quotes, descriptive detail, and relevant background information. In the stories included in this collection, I hope the same standards were applied.

In an effort to put these stories in perspective, I've added a short introduction to each—a bit of back story or an explanation of developments that took place following its publication. Virtually all of the pieces appear as they were originally published. In a very few cases, I've cut some passages or changed words for clarification.

Rather than presenting the stories in chronological order, I've arranged them in sections, starting with a set that deals with the repudiation in Mississippi of the segregated society I covered in the 1960s. Stories from that early part of my career make up the second section.

Other pieces are divided into categories. Jimmy Carter's victorious campaign in 1976 was another professional breakthrough for me; for a year I followed the winning candidate for a major newspaper and wound up as a White House correspondent. I've included stories from that period as well as a section dealing with another successful Southern candidate, Bill Clinton.

In "Middle East Interlude," I offer a few pieces where I tried to capture the frustration and despair that characterizes the conflict in the region, followed by a several profiles of prominent writers—ranging from three brilliant Israeli novelists to the infamous Hunter S. Thompson.

Of all the assignments I've gotten over the years, the most challenging involve profiles. I try to avoid pop psychology; who really knows what lurks in the minds of my subjects? But a profile invariably becomes a character study. I've included a few of these, including a couple where Trent Lott and Dexter King refused to cooperate, and I had to draw upon my previous contact with them. Another is a posthumous "appreciation" of a PLO leader I knew, Abu Jihad, who was assassinated by an Israeli commando team.

My closing section, which I call "Southern Gothic," comes from the 1990s, after I moved to New Orleans to use the South as my base as a national reporter for the *Globe*. It was wonderful to be back, to be at play again in the garden of rogues and to harvest their bizarre stories.

Part I

Redemption

"God Says Kill Them"

(*Boston Globe*, January 16, 1994)

The third trial of Byron De La Beckwith was the first major story I
covered after persuading the *Globe* to let me live and work out of New
Orleans. The case held special interest for me because, as a young
reporter, among my earliest assignments were civil rights rallies where I
met Medgar Evers.

My set-up piece before the trial was originally intended to address
the question of whether Beckwith's due process rights were being
disregarded, but his own venomous remarks—in an interview with
me—about the justification of killing blacks and Jews changed the tone
of the article.

JACKSON, Miss.—As state prosecutors prepare to bring Byron De
La Beckwith, an aging, unrepentant white supremacist, back to trial
for the murder of NAACP leader Medgar Evers thirty-one years ago,
the case is reopening a dark period of Mississippi history and raising questions of whether the notorious defendant is being denied due
process of law.

The 73-year-old Beckwith is still an unreconstructed warrior on
the race issue, but when jury selection begins Tuesday, he will be confronted with attitudes that have changed dramatically in the state.
Hailed as a hero in segregationist circles after his first two trials ended
with hung juries in 1964, Beckwith today is a virtual pariah.

The case, driven by a clamor for justice by Jackson's black community, has resurrected demons that once haunted Mississippi. As much

as any living man, the defendant is a symbol of the days when the Ku Klux Klan held the state in a vise of terror.

But protections guaranteed under the Bill of Rights are being lost in the zeal to punish a man seen as a menace to society, several legal sources here say.

A former judge who knows the case well characterized Beckwith the other day as an "evil, vicious racist." Yet the source, who asked not to be identified, said he is troubled that Beckwith was deprived of his Sixth Amendment rights to a speedy trial by the thirty-year interval in prosecutions for the same crime.

"It makes you wonder what kind of rights we would have denied Hitler," he said.

No one in the state's judicial system, he said, "wants to stand up and take flak for stopping the prosecution. The black community would come down real hard on anybody who would do it." Half of Jackson's population is black.

Beckwith is free on bond in Signal Mountain, Tenn., where he has lived for the past ten years. He said in a telephone interview that he still has the support of the Mississippi establishment. "Country-club Mississippi is tired of this crap the Jews, niggers, and Orientals are stirring up," he said.

Beckwith, who is called by a middle name pronounced "delay," said he had been told by his lawyers not to talk about his case. But he was not reluctant to discuss his racial views. He denounced Jews as "Babylonian Talmudists, a set of dogs. If you'll read in the King James Version of the Bible, a dog is a male whore . . . and God says kill them." Racial mixing, he said, "is a capital crime, like murder is a capital crime. But the Bible doesn't say 'Thou shalt not kill,' it says, 'Thou shall do no murder.'"

Beckwith has pleaded not guilty in the murder of Medgar Evers.

Days after Evers was shot to death in front of his home in Jackson in 1963, a high-powered rifle left in bushes near the civil rights leader's home was traced to Beckwith. Authorities said his fingerprint was also found on the rifle's telescopic sight. But after police officers in his hometown of Greenwood testified that they saw Beckwith 100 miles from Jackson on the night of the murder, all-white, all-male juries failed to reach verdicts in two separate trials. The case was formally dropped in 1969.

A member of a Mississippi Delta family with faded fortunes, Beckwith was originally represented by a team of politically connected attorneys and supported by a "White Citizens Legal Fund" set up by the segregationist Citizens Councils.

But there is little sympathy for him in modern Mississippi. The American Civil Liberties Union has not intervened in the case, even though there are parallels to the organization's decision to defend the right of neo-Nazis to march in Skokie, Ill., where half the population was Jewish, sixteen years ago.

"It's difficult to raise constitutional questions in this case. People want to see racists punished," said Isaac Byrd, a black trial lawyer and member of the ACLU board here. "I don't think the black community is geared to see the serious constitutional question. But we have to put these things in a larger context. I'm troubled about what kind of precedent this will set in the future for criminal defendants, 80 percent who are going to be black."

Citing due process rights as well as double jeopardy, Beckwith appealed the new 1990 indictment to the Mississippi Supreme Court.

"Our biggest problem is the time element," said Merrida Coxwell Jr., one of Beckwith's court-appointed lawyers. "Trying to locate witnesses and follow up on leads is almost impossible. Witnesses are dead. Documents are lost. And Mr. Beckwith doesn't have good recollection any more."

The Supreme Court denied the appeal, but Chief Justice Roy Noble Lee, in a sharp dissent, called the opinion "an egregious miscarriage of justice" and "the worst pronouncement of the law during my tenure on the Mississippi Supreme Court bench."

The case has inflamed passions for years. While the Ku Klux Klan carried out a campaign of church burnings, bombings, and intimidation that culminated in the murder of three civil rights workers in Neshoba County in 1964, the victim's brother, Charles Evers, acknowledged that he considered forming a "Mississippi Mau Mau" vigilante unit to retaliate against reactionary whites.

Portrait of a Racist, a damaging biography of Beckwith written by his nephew, Reed Massengill, will be published next month. In the book, the defendant is described as a misfit consumed by racial hatred. The late Mary Louise Williams, Beckwith's former wife, is quoted: "I believe De La's the only one capable of killing Medgar Evers."

Beckwith dismissed the credibility of his former wife, whom he married and divorced three times. "She died. I reckon Reed ran her crazy." The author, Beckwith said, "has been working for the Babylonian Talmudists. They gave him some money and he wrote this little book."

Beckwith was actually implicated in the Evers murder years earlier in an obscure book called *Klandestine*, which described the activities of an FBI informer, Delmar Dennis, inside the Klan. The book quotes Beckwith as telling a Klan audience: "Killing that nigger gave me no more inner discomfort than our wives endure when they give birth to our children." Dennis has been called as a witness in the trial.

After he spent ten months in custody while undergoing the two trials in 1964, Beckwith joined the White Knights of the Ku Klux Klan, a faction that led the violence in Mississippi that summer. He also ran for lieutenant governor in 1967, finishing fifth, with 34,000 votes, in a field of six candidates.

In 1973 Beckwith was arrested as he drove into New Orleans with a time bomb in his car. Police had been tipped that he was on a mission to blow up the home of A. I. Botnick, a leader of the Anti-Defamation League of B'nai B'rith.

Beckwith was convicted in state court by a five-member jury. He described the members of the jury as "five nigger bitches." He served three years in solitary confinement at the Louisiana State Penitentiary. The small jury was later declared unconstitutional, and the conviction has been expunged from Beckwith's record.

Beckwith remarried, moved to Tennessee, and dropped from sight. But he could not resist taunting William Waller, the district attorney who prosecuted him in 1964 and went on to be elected governor. When Waller appeared at a political rally in Mississippi in 1987, Beckwith materialized by Waller's side to shake his hand. "It got in the papers," Waller said. "I thought he was a little nutty."

Beckwith's appearance revived talk of renewing the Evers case. Ed Peters, the Hinds County district attorney, discouraged the move. "There is no way under any stretch of the law that this case could be tried again. Anyone having the first class in law school ought to know that," Peters said at the time.

But two years later, a Jackson newspaper, the *Clarion-Ledger*, obtained records from the Mississippi Sovereignty Commission, a defunct state agency that promoted segregation. The newspaper reported the agency had screened the jury panel for the defense in Beckwith's second trial.

An ambitious assistant district attorney, Bobby DeLaughter, investigated the hints of jury tampering and eventually won a new indictment in December 1990. The prosecutors are believed to have at least two witnesses prepared to testify that after the 1964 mistrials Beckwith boasted of killing Evers.

DeLaughter's friends say he is a conscientious prosecutor who has taken a personal interest in the case. Skeptics say he wants to run for judge.

DeLaughter has maintained that it was not politics that motivated him to pursue Beckwith, but a simple desire to see justice done.

Beckwith, meanwhile, seems to revel in the spotlight. He said he was "full of enthusiasm and adventure. I'm proud of my enemies. They're every color but white, every creed but Christian."

30 Years Later, "Justice Has Been Done"

(*Boston Globe*, February 6, 1994)

Reporters are expected to be impartial and unemotional, even when following events of high drama. But sitting for days in the courtroom balcony reserved for the press, it was difficult for me not to be rooting for the prosecution. When the guilty verdict was announced, and shouts of celebration resounded in the marble hallways of the courthouse, I could sense goose bumps on my own arms.

Beckwith died in prison in 2001.

JACKSON, Miss.—A Mississippi jury of eight blacks and four whites reached across a painful gulf of time and turmoil yesterday to convict Byron De La Beckwith of the 1963 murder of civil rights leader Medgar Evers.

When the verdict was announced at 10:35 a.m. on the second day of deliberation, there was a burst of cheers from a pocket of spectators surrounding the widow, Myrlie Evers. Within seconds, as word that Beckwith had been found guilty passed from the courtroom, cheering echoed through the halls of the Hinds County Courthouse where others were standing vigil.

The 73-year-old Beckwith was immediately sentenced to life imprisonment and led away by two deputy sheriffs. He said nothing, but waved feebly while members of his family tried to comfort his wife, Thelma, who was weeping in a front-row seat.

In the emotional aftermath, District Attorney Ed Peters said, "I think justice has been done. I'm sorry it took so long."

Beckwith was originally arrested in June 1963, days after Evers was shot in the back by a sniper lurking in a thicket of sweet gum trees and honeysuckle near the victim's home.

Beckwith, an outspoken exponent of white supremacy, was tried twice in 1964. Both trials wound up with hung juries and Beckwith was eventually released, but the case haunted Mississippi for three decades. In recent years, as prosecutors closed in on Beckwith with new evidence, the case represented a catharsis for a state with its long history of racial conflict.

Although some Mississippians disliked the idea of reopening the nightmarish period, Bobby DeLaughter, a white assistant district attorney, pursued the case relentlessly. "This case can become a focus that all races will come together to work for the betterment of our communities and our state," DeLaughter said yesterday.

Members of the Evers family and their friends, crying with joy and thanksgiving, embraced the prosecutors at the conclusion.

When the jury failed to reach a decision after five hours of deliberation Friday, Myrlie Evers expressed fears that the jury would be deadlocked. But she said yesterday that a thought had come to her in the night that "even if there was not a verdict of guilty we still would have won" merely by forcing a third trial.

After being sequestered overnight, the jury quickly came in with its verdict in the morning.

The climax came nearly twenty-four hours after DeLaughter had appealed to the jury to deliver a new version of "Mississippi justice." In his closing argument, DeLaughter said that Evers's slaying had "left a gaping wound" in the state's society and argued that a conviction was a way "to do the right thing" after all the years. "Lord knows," he said, "it's just time."

The prosecutor said that Beckwith had been undone by "his mouth. He thought he had beaten the system thirty years ago and he couldn't keep his mouth shut."

The state presented six witnesses—including two who came forward during the course of the trial—who testified that Beckwith had bragged about killing Evers after the two 1964 murder trials.

Old political statements by Beckwith were also used against him. DeLaughter cited Beckwith's comparison of blacks to boll weevils and his assertion that "they must be destroyed and their remains burned."

Beckwith's defense team attempted to minimize his racial views. "This trial is not about racial and political matters," attorney Jim Kitchens told the jury shortly before they began deliberations.

Beckwith's defenders tried to raise "reasonable doubts" about the murder scenario depicted by the prosecution. Referring to an alibi witness, Kitchens told the jury they could not disregard this testimony simply "because you don't like Byron De La Beckwith." The alibi was provided by a former Greenwood policeman who testified that he saw Beckwith in the Delta city nearly 100 miles from Jackson within minutes of the shooting.

But after thirty years, the defense case was weakened. Witnesses from the earlier trials had died and evidence was lost. Beckwith, who took the stand in both of the 1964 trials, did not testify this time.

Peters, the district attorney, said he "had at least two days of cross-examination" waiting for Beckwith.

James Holley, the most prominent defense witness, was subjected to a withering cross-examination. He admitted that even though he was a police officer, he withheld his claim that he had seen Beckwith on the night of the murder until the time of the first trial.

Prosecutors planted the suggestion that Holley and other Greenwood policemen conspired to produce favorable testimony for Beckwith. In the 1960s, the Greenwood police force was allied with the segregationist leadership of the city.

Evers, the field secretary for the NAACP, was a leading figure in Mississippi in the early days of the civil rights movement. His assassination came a few months after a bloody insurrection at the University of Mississippi that left two dead and hundreds wounded.

Beckwith has remained one of the most enduring symbols of the state's violent resistance to desegregation. He even ran for lieutenant governor in 1967, finishing fifth in a field of six.

But yesterday he was back in jail. His attorneys intend to appeal. There was speculation that he might be sent to the infamous Mississippi state prison farm at Parchman, where most of the inmates are black. Hinds County Sheriff Malcolm E. McMillin said state prison authorities may find a special cell for him "if it is determined that he has enemies in the general population of the prison."

"Your Day Of Judgment Soon Will Be Nigh"

(*Boston Globe*, July 10, 1998)

More than five years after Beckwith's conviction, the man who had orchestrated many of the Ku Klux Klan murders in Mississippi was still free. Although an investigation had resulted in the indictment of Sam Bowers, the imperial wizard of the White Knights of the Ku Klux Klan, for the fatal firebombing of Vernon Dahmer in 1966, a new and potentially critical witness feared that prosecutors were discounting the value of his testimony. Bob Stringer, who overheard the order to kill Dahmer when he was a young man working for Bowers, wanted desperately to make his story public as part of his twelve-step recovery program for gambling addiction, a step that required him to make amends to those who had suffered because of his inaction. Stringer asked Jerry Himelstein, the director of the New Orleans office of the Anti-Defamation League, for help, and Jerry, a friend of mine, called me.

We drove to the Mississippi Gulf Coast to meet with Stringer, and the anguished man laid out his remarkable tale. After several days of follow-up interviews and research, the *Globe* broke the story. Weeks later, Stringer became a key witness against Bowers.

HATTIESBURG, Miss.—For three decades, Bob Stringer has lived with the memory of a conversation he overheard in the back booth of John's Cafe, a Hopperesque hangout of the Ku Klux Klan in Laurel, Miss.

It was the winter of 1966, and Sam Bowers, a jukebox operator who moonlighted as the imperial wizard of the White Knights of the Ku Klux Klan, was voicing his frustration that Klan elements in neighboring Forrest County had been unable to suppress the voting registration efforts of the local NAACP leader, Vernon Dahmer Sr.

Stringer, in an interview, recalled the exchange the other day, "Sam said: 'Something's got to be done about that Dahmer nigger down south,' and he slapped the counter. Then Henry deBoxtel said: 'We need to put a Code Four on him.'"

In the parlance of the Klan, Code Four called for death.

Within hours, Dahmer was dead.

Bowers and his band were quickly rounded up and charged with the killing, but the prosecution of the case was inconclusive and resulted in few convictions. Bowers himself went free after two mistrials.

Authorities, at the Dahmer family's request, reopened an investigation several years ago into what remains one of Mississippi's most infamous civil rights murders. But the case lay stalled until Stringer felt his conscience jarred after seeing the Dahmer family appeal for fresh information on local television in 1994.

At the time, Stringer was enrolled in a twelve-step program of recovery for gambling addicts, and step nine called for him to make "direct amends" to those whom he had caused suffering if it was possible to do so without causing injury to others.

"It was a tough decision," Stringer said. "I wanted to make amends to the Dahmer family, but on the other hand, I didn't want to injure my old friends" from the days of the Klan's campaign of terror.

After agonizing over his knowledge, Stringer drove to Hattiesburg, the county seat of Forrest County, looked up the name of Vernon Dahmer Jr. in a telephone directory, and used a pay phone to call the son of the man killed when his house was firebombed in 1966. Stringer shared little that he knew in that first, veiled conversation, but he told Dahmer he had once been affiliated with the Klan and wanted to help.

The call led to a series of telephone talks and clandestine meetings over a four-year period that culminated May 28 with the arrest of the 73-year-old Bowers and two of his associates, Charles R. Noble and Devours Nix. Bowers and Noble are charged with murder and arson; Nix is charged with arson.

With Bowers's trial approaching next month, Stringer, the Klan leader's onetime protege, agreed to talk publicly for the first time about his role in the case. In several conversations over the past ten days, he laid out an extraordinary tale, the expressions of a 52-year-old Mississippian wrestling with guilt, redemption, and racial reconciliation.

"I just want to do right," said Stringer, who operates a landscaping business in a south Mississippi community. When he was a teenager, he worked for Bowers, typing Klan manifestos and distributing leaflets. "I never took the oath, but I considered myself part of the Klan," he said. "I never went out on missions with them, but they never asked me. If they had asked me, I probably would have gone."

Although unwilling to identify the secret witness in the case, Forrest County District Attorney Lindsey Carter confirmed yesterday that a new informant was "important because he's new evidence. He's instrumental in this case."

In a separate interview, Vernon Dahmer Jr. said Stringer provided the breakthrough in his family's long ordeal. "Bob's coming forward was the catalyst in giving us hope," he said. "He was valuable in the sense that he was the first informant who had been affiliated with the Klan who agreed to come forward and tell what he knew."

The attack on the Dahmers' farm home, on a night when the pastures were covered in frost, is a legendary chapter in the ugliest part of the state's history, and the recollections of Dahmer's widow, Ellie Dahmer, are as vivid as Stringer's own memories after thirty-two years.

"We had been gettin' threats over the phone," she said this week as she retold the story in her comfortable brick ranchhouse, built on the site of the home that was burned. "We knew the Klan was active. They would put up signs on the trees, and when Vernon would drive by, he'd stop and tear them down. They would call and ask for Vernon." The anonymous callers accused him of "wanting to be white," she said. "Then they would use the N-word and tell him he was going to get killed."

Nightriders burned down a shed full of hay on the Dahmer place, but it did not deter him from advising blacks on how to register to vote at his grocery store next door to his home. Windows were knocked out of the store several times, Ellie Dahmer said.

For several years, the couple slept in shifts to protect their home. Dahmer kept a shotgun and a pistol by his bed. But with the passage of the Civil Rights Act of 1964 and the Voting Rights Act of 1965, their fears ebbed.

"We had started going to bed like ordinary people," she said, when their sleep was interrupted on the night of Jan. 10, 1966, by the sound of gunfire and crashing glass. "I told Vernon, 'I believe they got us this time.' There were two carloads of them. One stopped by the grocery, the other by the house. They shot out the plate glass window of our house and the display window of the grocery." The raiders flung gallon jugs filled with gasoline to drench the roofs and interiors of the two buildings, then they used burning rags as torches.

While Dahmer fired several loads of buckshot at the nightriders, his wife escaped from the burning house by bundling their 10-year-old daughter, Bettie, in a coat, breaking through a back window, and falling safely to the ground. Two other children and an elderly relative who had been living in the rear of the grocery also retreated to sanctuary in a barn. After the raiders fled, Dahmer stumbled outside, but his lungs had been seared by the flames. He died twelve hours later.

Dahmer's death, which followed the assassination of Medgar Evers and the murder of three civil rights workers in Neshoba County, triggered outrage in Mississippi. Dozens of FBI officers and state investigators swarmed into the area and traced a dropped pistol to a Klansman named Billy Roy Pitts. One of the cars used in the raid was abandoned with a flat tire, and it produced more clues.

Bowers, the founder of the most dreaded unit of the Ku Klux Klan, was quickly rounded up along with more than a dozen confederates. Although thirteen men were indicted on murder and arson charges in state court, and federal charges of conspiracy and intimidation resulted in fifteen indictments, there were few convictions.

Three men were sentenced to life but none served more than ten years. Another defendant served less than two years of a ten-year term for arson after then Governor John Bell Williams, a darling of the radical right, commuted his sentence in 1970.

In exchange for his testimony against his fellow Klansmen, Pitts was given a brief federal sentence and was allowed to disappear without serving a day on his life term on state charges. But as the Dahmer case intensified recently, Pitts was found in Louisiana and is now being held in the Forrest County jail here. He is expected to again testify against the Klansmen, and law enforcement sources say Mississippi Governor Kirk Fordice has privately agreed to Pitts's release if he cooperates with the prosecution.

Meanwhile, deBoxtel, whom Stringer heard suggest a "Code Four," died after a mistrial was declared in his case. Bowers survived two mistrials in the Dahmer case, but spent six years in prison following his conviction on federal charges growing out of the Neshoba County murders. He has long been considered the kingpin of the Klan and is believed to have directed much of the violent opposition to integration that once terrorized the state.

Although he has been a free man for more than twenty years, Bowers was never forgotten by Dahmer's family.

"All we wanted out of this was justice," said Vernon Dahmer Jr.

The Dahmer case gained renewed interest following the 1994 conviction in Mississippi of Byron de la Beckwith for the murder of Evers, the state's leading NAACP official, thirty years earlier.

Encouraged, the Dahmers pressed the county district attorney's office and the state for action, and the Legislature responded by appropriating funds for a new investigation. During the 1995 election, the Dahmers asked each district attorney candidate for a commitment to pursue the case. They wound up supporting a Democrat who promised a vigorous reexamination. Carter, a Republican, was elected. But he, too, had pledged, "If it can be done, it will be done."

Unknown to the newly elected district attorney, talks between Stringer and Vernon Dahmer Jr. were already underway.

In their telephone chats, Stringer was unwilling to give his name, but a relationship of trust was growing. "We talked about his affiliation with the Klan, what he knew, and how he felt about trying to help us," Dahmer said. "These conversations continued for two years, but we never met face to face."

Then in late 1996, an intermediary for Stringer contacted Dahmer and said Stringer was willing to meet privately if his safety could be ensured.

In April 1997, six men gathered in a motel room in Diamondhead, a Gulf Coast resort: Stringer and a friend known only as "Frank," Vernon Dahmer Jr. and his brother, Dennis Dahmer, Jerry Himelstein, the director of the New Orleans office of the Anti-Defamation League, and Jerry Mitchell, a reporter for the *Clarion-Ledger* newspaper in Jackson, Miss., whose stories had helped revive the case against Beckwith.

Stringer, a towering man with graying hair and a moustache, was identified only as "Bob." He spent most of the day talking about his experiences as an "errand boy" for Sam Bowers.

Despite his reputation as a racial terrorist, Bowers was an erudite man, the grandson of a congressman. Bowers's favorite book was George Orwell's anticommunist allegory *Animal Farm*. He ran his affairs from Sambo Amusement Co., a business that distributed juke boxes and pinball machines throughout tough, gritty Jones County.

When Stringer was 14, living with his grandparents and holding down two jobs, he met Bowers. "Sam took me in like a son," he said. He handled small tasks, helped install amusement machines, and when it was discovered Stringer could type, he was enlisted to put Klan messages on paper. One of the "Klan Ledgers" carried the lines:

"Now listen, you COMMUNIST and NIGGERS and JEWS.

Tell all your buddies to spread the news.

Your day of judgment will soon be nigh,

As the Lord in his wisdom looks down from on high.
Will this battle be lost? NEVER! I say,
For the KU KLUX KLAN is here to stay!!!"

Young Stringer distributed the leaflets around Jones County. He also ferried packages. "I didn't know what I was hauling. It could have been dynamite or guns," he said. He attended Klan rallies, where Bowers always appeared in a seersucker suit. As Bowers's acolyte, Stringer was able to move with confidence among the Klansmen at John's Cafe, where he heard the discussion of the strike against Vernon Dahmer Sr.

While he discussed his past at the Diamondhead meeting, Stringer told the group about his fears for his future. After losing his job and $30,000 gambling at Mississippi's new casinos, he was trying to come back from the bottom. He and his son had taken lawn mowers and rakes and begun knocking on doors to build up a business. He had controlled his gambling addiction through group therapy. But Stringer felt he might jeopardize his family if he agreed to become a witness against the Klan.

Himelstein assured Stringer that the ADL could help him relocate, to start over with a new job in a new state.

Stringer agreed to come to a second meeting, a month later, which included an investigator from the district attorney's office, Ray Howell.

"At that meeting," Dahmer said, "Bob said he was willing to cooperate by wearing a wire and talking with the Klansmen."

A few days later, Stringer met with Carter, the district attorney, and Howell at a cafe in the south Mississippi town of Wiggins, where Stringer offered the authorities more information.

At times, the attempt to ensnare Bowers veered into a Keystone Kops routine. The county investigator gave Stringer a bulky tape recorder to wear. If someone asked about the protrusion in his clothes, Stringer said, he was supposed to explain that it was the aftermath of surgery.

During one conversation with a member of the Klan's women's auxiliary, who was unwittingly implicating the Klansmen, the tape recorder clicked off loudly. Stringer was relieved when the state attorney general's office joined the investigation and wired him with more sophisticated equipment.

He had lengthy talks with Roy Wilson, Bowers's friend who ran a truck stop in Laurel. According to Stringer, Wilson told him that Bowers had given him his memoirs, titled "Rifle in the Bush," to hold for safekeeping. "I was told it was all about Medgar Evers's killing, Martin Luther King's killing," Stringer said, and it was not to be revealed until after Bowers's death.

Stringer secretly taped two conversations with Bowers—one at the truck stop, another as they rode around Jones County in Stringer's pickup. Stringer said he asked Bowers why he had never given him a more important role in the Klan.

"Sam said: 'Because you were too young. You were needed to type up the propaganda while I was busy fighting the revolution. You were important because your propaganda caused more revolution for me to fight.'"

After their second meeting last summer, Bowers grew suspicious and broke off further contact. Stringer said he is convinced Bowers knows he has become an informant; as a result, Stringer said he was willing to be identified in this news story.

In their last meeting, Stringer said, Bowers gave him a final accolade. "He called me 'a great patriot and a good disciple.'"

"An Evil Genius" Is Convicted

(*Boston Globe*, August 22, 1998)

Bowers died in prison in 2006.

HATTIESBURG, Miss.—Sam Bowers, an imperial wizard of the White Knights of the Ku Klux Klan and reputedly the mastermind behind a campaign of terror across Mississippi three decades ago, was convicted yesterday for a 1966 civil rights murder, after three previous prosecutions had failed.

Bowers, who reached his 74th birthday this month, was then sentenced to life imprisonment. Three black deputy sheriffs led him from the courtroom.

The verdict, reached in three and a half hours by a jury composed of six whites, five blacks, and an Asian American, climaxed a long crusade to win a conviction in the murder of Vernon Dahmer, leader of the Hattiesburg chapter of the NAACP.

When the verdict was announced, members of the Dahmer family bowed their heads in blessing and wept quietly in a balcony overlooking the Bowers defense table. Bowers, who seemed to have been anticipating immediate imprisonment, had begun emptying his pockets of belongings moments before the jury filed back into the courtroom.

He was stoic when pronounced guilty, and had no comment before he received his sentence.

Afterward, outside the courthouse, the victim's widow, Ellie Dahmer, said: "I'm just filled with joy. The tears I'm shedding are for Vernon, because I know he's watching."

Her son, Dennis Dahmer, who survived the Klan attack with his mother, brother, and sister, spoke for the family: "Thirty-two years ago, Mr. Bowers and his fellow Klansmen started something. Thirty-two years later, we hope to bring some closure to this. . . . I hope today's verdict reflects that we're living in a new South and a new Mississippi."

The revival of charges against Bowers was a joint effort by the local civil rights community and by white prosecutors, and there was a celebration in the court after Bowers was led away. Attorney General Mike Moore embraced the members of the prosecuting team, as well as the Dahmer family, as they departed the courthouse.

Robert Helfrich, the assistant district attorney who led the prosecution, was weeping. "This is the Dahmers' day," he said. "They waited too long for it."

A lawyer for Bowers, Travis Buckley, said he would seek a new trial. "I can't say I was surprised," he added.

Bowers was accused of commanding his compatriots to eliminate Dahmer in the winter of 1966 to stifle Dahmer's civil rights activity in Forrest County and to send a message to Washington that the South would violently resist efforts to integrate the society here.

Dahmer died from burns fourteen hours after a firebombing on his farmhouse near here, at 2 a.m. on Jan. 10, 1966. He had been leading a voter registration drive.

According to prosecution witnesses, Bowers ordered his followers in a Klan unit in Jones County to execute a "Code Four" on Dahmer because the Forrest County Klansmen had been unable to subdue Dahmer. In a Klan structure, where Code One called for a cross-burning, Code Two a whipping, and Code Three an arson attack, the extreme penalty was Code Four—death.

In his instructions to the jury, Circuit Judge Richard McKenzie pointed out that a murder conviction was warranted if it could be proved that someone had commanded the murder even if not present at the crime. "It is as if his own hand committed the offense," McKenzie said.

Bowers, who was arrested with more than a dozen other Klansmen shortly after the attack, withstood three trials in state court in the 1960s. Each ended in a mistrial. However, he was convicted of conspiracy in federal court in connection with the murder of three civil rights workers in Neshoba County, and he spent six years in federal prison.

Federal investigators said Bowers was responsible for deploying teams of bombers and nightriders across the state in a period of violence that claimed many lives and intimidated many citizens.

A clamor to revive the Dahmer case began after authorities closed in on Byron de la Beckwith, an associate of Bowers who was convicted in 1994 for the assassination of Mississippi's NAACP leader Medgar Evers thirty years earlier. Beckwith's two trials in the 1960s had also ended in mistrials.

In the past few years, local and state prosecutors were able to produce two new witnesses to augment the testimony of three former Klansmen who testified against Bowers in the earlier trials.

Bob Stringer, an errand boy for Bowers in 1966, came forward to testify this week that he overheard Bowers and other Klansmen discussing a Code Four for Dahmer two or three days before the raid.

Cathy Lucy, the former wife of a Ku Klux Klan leader in Jackson, also provided new testimony that Bowers appeared at her home shortly after the murder with a newspaper story of Dahmer's death. "Did you see what a good job my boys did?" she reported that Bowers said, and she described his mood as "jubilant."

In his closing argument, Buckley, the Bowers lawyer, said that the case had been "worked up by political expediency and someone in the press" and charged that his client was "being offered up on their altar to be sacrificed to the media and to private, political ambition."

After the case languished for three decades, Buckley said, "along comes an attorney general who seeks political advancement," and he suggested that Bowers was being prosecuted "to appeal to racial prejudices and the bias of voters."

Moore, who lent personnel from the attorney general's office to help develop the case against Bowers, is pondering a run next year for governor in a state where one third of the voters are black.

"We brought this case at the request of the Dahmer family," Moore said. "I'm proud we were able to turn up new witnesses and stronger evidence to see that justice was done." Moore called Buckley a "Klan lawyer" and said his remarks about politics "did not warrant comment."

In his final remarks before the jury retired to deliberate, Buckley also compared the prosecution to the work of an "evil genius," Adolf Hitler, charging that prosecutors had orchestrated a drumbeat of propaganda to make Bowers the "scapegoat," just as Hitler had targeted Jews in Germany.

After Buckley completed his rambling remarks, Helfrich, the prosecutor, turned the Hitler analogy on Bowers.

"Let's talk about an evil genius, sitting right there," Helfrich said, pointing at Bowers. The people who killed Dahmer, he said, "were nightriders and henchmen who attacked a sleeping family, and they did it because one person told them to do so."

Recalling that Billy Roy Pitts, one of the key prosecution witnesses, had testified that he heard the voice of a man "in distress" inside the burning Dahmer home on the night of the raid, Helfrich suggested that Dahmer's "voice is in distress because Sam Bowers is still walking the street."

"A Stigma on State Government"

(*Boston Globe*, November 19, 1994)

For nearly twenty years, the Mississippi Sovereignty Commission existed as a state agency created to spy on its own citizens. Triggered by the U.S. Supreme Court's *Brown v. Board of Education* decision in 1954, segregationist leaders used public funds to deploy investigators and collect information and rumors in order to develop files on those who were considered a threat to the status quo.

The agency conducted some outrageous work, as insidious and reprehensible, in its own way, as the activities of the Gestapo. After Gov. Bill Waller terminated funds for the commission in 1973, it went out of business—but was not forgotten. In the 1990s, a clamor arose among some of those who had been spied upon to open the old files of the agency. Others—though unsympathetic to the commission— opposed the move because they felt damaging falsehoods and other material that had been gathered should be kept sealed. There were good arguments on both sides.

JACKSON, Miss.—An intriguing struggle, involving accusations of spying and collaboration inside the civil rights movement, is approaching a climax in Mississippi, following a federal court order to open the files of a defunct state segregationist agency that have been sealed, like scar tissue over an old wound, for two decades.

Records of the Sovereignty Commission could contain information implicating members of a surveillance operation that tracked

"Freedom Summer" activity in 1964, the year three civil rights workers were murdered in Neshoba County.

But some of those who were spied upon by the agency express countervailing fears that innocent people could be embarrassed or falsely accused by the release of unfiltered gossip collected by the commission between 1956 and 1973.

During a long legal battle to open the files, two classes of plaintiffs have developed: an "access" group demanding full public disclosure of the papers, and "privacy" advocates who argue that the files should be edited. Meanwhile, the state has fought to suppress the information for years, and officials face the prospect of a contempt citation after the legislature recently refused to appropriate funds to index the records in compliance with court orders.

With the state now under a deadline to notify individuals named in the files and to have the records ready for inspection by the middle of next year, the dispute is intensifying.

A well-known black politician in Jackson has been publicly identified as "Agent X," a Sovereignty Commission operative, and others who were active in the movement are being privately branded as informers. Charges of betrayal, madness, and paranoia were flung back and forth by former allies in the civil rights movement during a series of interviews conducted here by the *Boston Globe.*

"Our focus is to protect the victims, not the perpetrators," said Ed King, the principal "privacy" plaintiff. King, a white Methodist minister, once served as chaplain at black Tougaloo College and ran for lieutenant governor on the Freedom Democratic Party ticket in 1963. Nevertheless, he said, he has been accused of conspiring with state officials and intelligence agents to limit access to the files.

Moreover, said King, "I am smeared with charges of bribery and of being involved in the murders of my friends and brothers, from Medgar Evers to Chaney, Goodman, and Schwerner in Neshoba."

Ken Lawrence, who worked for the Southern Conference Education Fund here in the 1970s, said King is trying to provide cover for those who informed on the movement. "He's crazy. He wants to disclose paid agents, but not the unpaid agents," said Lawrence, a plaintiff on the other side of the issue.

Lawrence said the records will show that commission agents infiltrated civil rights groups, broke into offices to steal lists of names of sympathizers, and carried on a campaign of intimidation in the state.

As an original plaintiff, Lawrence was given access to the papers and is believed to be one of the few persons who have read the entire file, which fills six cabinets in the state Department of Archives and History.

Lawrence said some of those who will be "exposed as collaborators" are black educators who were on the public payroll, and black journalists.

Over the years, Sovereignty Commission documents have been leaked to the press, identifying Percy Greene, a late black newspaper editor in Jackson, as a commission ally who published stories that were damaging to civil rights activists.

A few years ago, the Jackson *Clarion-Ledger* obtained Sovereignty Commission documents indicating the state agency helped defense attorneys for Byron De La Beckwith investigate potential jurors before Beckwith's second trial for the 1963 murder of Medgar Evers, the head of the NAACP in Mississippi. Armed with charges of jury-tampering, prosecutors reopened the case against Beckwith, who had so far escaped with two hung juries. He was finally convicted of murder last February.

Others are expected to be drawn into new controversy if the files are completely opened. In a telephone interview from his home in Pennsylvania, Lawrence said the files identify R. L. Bolden, a black man, as "Agent X," a principal informant for the commission in 1964. Bolden now works for U.S. Rep. Mike Parker, a conservative Mississippi Democrat.

"On his first day on the job, 'Agent X' went to a CORE meeting in Ohio in February 1964, and reported back the tag numbers on cars," Lawrence said. One of those vehicles, he said, was a station wagon belonging to Michael Schwerner. CORE is the Congress of Racial Equality, a civil rights group.

Bolden, contacted recently, said, "I've decided not to talk to anybody about it. Too much false information got out." Earlier, Bolden confirmed to Bill Minor, a local political columnist, that he had worked for Day Detectives, a Jackson firm that was retained by the Sovereignty Commission. Bolden said he was simply an investigator in divorce and domestic affairs cases.

Although Erle Johnston, former director of the Sovereignty Commission, said, "There is no point in my talking about Bolden," he acknowledged in an interview that the commission had a contract with Day Detectives "to find out things about plans for confrontation and violence" from civil rights activists. He said the information was passed on to law enforcement officials.

He also acknowledged that a state legislator from Meridian had asked the commission to investigate Schwerner, a civil rights activist in east Mississippi. "We got a report on Schwerner. Our investigator went over to talk to him," Johnston said.

In June 1964, Schwerner's station wagon was found burned. Weeks later, the bodies of Schwerner, James Chaney, and Andrew Goodman were discovered. A group of Ku Klux Klansmen, as well as the sheriff and deputy sheriff of Neshoba County, were eventually charged in the case.

Johnston said it is "a helluva lie" to suggest that the Sovereignty Commission was involved in the case. "The FBI will tell you Schwerner was a marked man by the Ku Klux Klan from the day he got to the state."

While ghosts of the Neshoba County murders, a dramatic turning point in the civil rights struggle, still stir, fresh charges and countercharges are spilling from the period.

Lawrence said the files will show that Ken Dean, a prominent figure in civil rights circles, had improper contact with the Sovereignty Commission.

In a long telephone interview from his home in Rochester, N.Y., Dean said, "All I know to tell you is that this is crazy."

Dean, who has sided with the group that wants complete disclosure, said a full inspection of the files would clear his name. As director of the biracial Mississippi Council on Human Relations, Dean said, he tried to maintain a proper relationship with all sides, including Johnston of the Sovereignty Commission, during that turbulent period.

He said he once passed on to Johnston a report that a black man had been targeted by white extremists. "I wasn't reporting on a civil rights group," Dean said. "I was reporting a racial confrontation in Oxford" in an effort to ward off violence.

Johnston insists that the Sovereignty Commission's role during Mississippi's years of conflict is being blown out of proportion. Johnston said he and Dean had both worked "to keep down tension and confrontation. I was on the segregationist team, he was on the integrationist team."

The commission was created by the legislature in 1956 with a mandate to guard Mississippi "from encroachment by the federal government." In its early years it was controlled by the White Citizens Council and blamed for bizarre activities.

According to court records, the commission once conducted an investigation into the family lineage of a Mississippian and "prepared to arrange for the young man to be drafted into the armed services should he be found to have a sufficient number of nonwhite ancestors."

Others familiar with the agency say it was largely a toothless, inept operation and contend that most of the files will consist of old newspaper clippings. Bill Waller, the former governor who vetoed funds for the Sovereignty Commission in a 1973 action that led to the death of the agency, said he considered the commission "a sinister thing. They didn't do much but clip newspapers and lobby for conservative legislation. It was Mickey Mouse, but it was a stigma on state government."

The State That Couldn't Spy Right

(*Boston Globe*, September 21, 1997)

U.S. District Judge William Barbour ultimately delivered a Solomon-like decision that opened the Sovereignty Commission papers but allowed "victims" to review their own files and restrict information about themselves. I applied for a look and was pleased to learn that the commission considered me sufficiently subversive to keep a record of me in Mississippi in the 1960s. But after seeing my file and talking with friends whose names showed up in the papers, my suspicions were confirmed: the investigators were basically incompetent fools attempting to do the devil's work.

In a piece for the *Globe*'s Sunday opinion section, I followed my earlier story on the squabble over the files with a first-person assessment of the Keystone Kops quality of the investigation.

JACKSON, Miss.—After I obtained my personal file from the records of the old Mississippi Sovereignty Commission and perused the pitiful contents, I was not sure whether the documents were a commentary on my insignificance or the incompetence of the defunct state agency that once spied on its people to try to preserve segregation.

Probably a bit of both.

But after reviewing a few of the "secret papers" released last month under a federal court order, I've concluded that the Sovereignty Commission agents were about as useful to the forces of segregation as the German guards on *Hogan's Heroes* would have been to the Third Reich.

The commission was created in 1956 as an official wing of the white Citizens Councils. The agency was responsible for some insidious activity involving informers and for attempts to discredit civil rights workers by planting false stories in the press. Yet much of its work seems to have been incredibly inept.

Although I was one of a small group of white liberals who worked to subvert "the Southern way of life" in my home state during the 1960s, my activity was reduced in the commission files to two references concerning an integrated Democratic delegation that unseated Governor John Bell Williams's all-white group at the Chicago Democratic National Convention in 1968.

Instead of a dossier that took note of my meager donations to such subversive organizations as the American Civil Liberties Union, the NAACP, and U.S. Senator Eugene McCarthy's presidential campaign, or my efforts with Aaron Henry, the late NAACP leader, to promote black candidates for public office in Coahoma County, I discovered that I was glowingly described in the commission files as a newspaperman, with a wife and a child, who had won a couple of awards and had graduated from the University of Mississippi. On closer inspection, I realized that the dope sheet was actually a press release from the Democratic Party that somebody had stuffed in the commission files.

My name was also on a list of insurgent delegates. One of the commission gumshoes had made notations on the list. There was handwriting beside Henry's name, suggesting that he was "NAACP." That was a brilliant deduction, since he was in the news every day as state president of the organization.

Under the terms of the court order, I am officially classified as a "victim" of the commission. At least my name showed up. More than 700 persons who suspected they were spied upon applied for their files; half of them were chagrined to learn that their names were not recorded. For many, it was like being left off President Nixon's enemies list.

Since we were about as popular as the plague in those days, a lot of us left the state. I moved in 1969. My friends Patt Derian and Hodding

Carter III, who were well-known activists, left a few years later. They both went on to become assistant secretaries of State in President Carter's administration.

When I called to see if they had gotten their files, Derian laughed. The concept of the commission, she said, was "quite foolish and totalitarian," but the records were "really pretty funny."

Carter forgot to apply for his file, but Patt had hers. The most comic piece of evidence in it is a 1969 letter from W. Webb Burke, the commission director, to the state attorney general concerning the bogus use of a Sovereignty Commission envelope.

It seems that two of my friends and fellow Mississippi journalists at the time, Lew Powell and Ed Williams, had somehow gotten the envelope and used it to mail to Derian in London a copy of the *Mississippi Freelance*, an irreverent monthly publication that regularly lampooned state officials. Powell failed to put sufficient postage on the missive, so it was returned to the commission office. Headquarters was not amused.

According to the report, the director and an investigator descended upon Greenville, where "it was learned that both of these men do some work for the Delta Democrat Times," which was then run by Hodding Carter. The agents conducted an interrogation in which the suspects "expressed the feeling that Derian would get a big laugh at receiving the paper in a Sovereignty Commission envelope." The report added that Powell and Williams "refused to indicate how or from whom they had obtained the envelope."

The director reported that he warned the pair that although they had broken no laws, the commission might bring suit.

Williams was described as belonging to "a very fine family in Dundee, Mississippi"; Powell was said to be from Missouri. The director had it backwards. The director also reported that Powell was "obviously the 'smart alec' of the two." He got that right.

Powell is now a columnist for the *Charlotte Observer*, where Williams is editor of the editorial page. They were delighted when I informed them that the incident had been preserved in the commission files.

It can finally be revealed that the culprit in the envelope caper was Luther Munford, now a prominent lawyer in Jackson. Munford was a student at Princeton at the time, and he snitched the envelope from a trash can while he was at the commission office interviewing the director.

The minutes of one commission meeting attended by eight members—white men true to the cause of segregation—also make wonderful, if dim, reading. Investigators reported that:

—"Four acres of land in Leflore County has been purchased by a Michigan corporation which is known to be a front for the Republic of New Africa."

—"A black student boycott of classes was staged at Coldwater Attendance Center, protesting school officials' 'unequal enforcement' of a school dress code after a black student was told to shave his beard."

—"At the University of Mississippi, the Black Student Council has not made any demands; however, a white group called the Coalition for Progress is pushing for open visitation in dormitories and the legalization of beer on campus."

The members agonized over whether to deny a newspaper report that the commission was investigating the gubernatorial campaign of Charles Evers, who was then a civil rights leader and is now a conservative Republican legislator.

One member "stated that the last thing we want to do is get into a fight with the news papers [sic]. Sometimes it is better to let them get on to another subject rather than to pick up the bate [sic] . . . As far as Evers and his group, I would forget them. All they want is to give them some attention."

Mississippi—Now. And Then

(*Boston Globe*, May 17, 1978)

I flew to Oxford with Ted Kennedy for his commencement speech.
It was a natural assignment for the lone Southerner in the *Globe*'s
Washington bureau. Since many of the parties are now dead, I feel free
to make a couple of confessions. To tweak Kennedy on the flight down
I gave him the copy of the old advertisement attacking his brother. But
I didn't know he would then use it to tease Sen. Eastland. On our way
home, both Kennedy and I had several drinks as we waited for our
commercial flight in a VIP room in the Memphis airport. He was in an
expansive mood, and when he told me of his wish that a photographer
had been there to capture the moment between Aaron Henry and
Eastland, he exploded in laughter.

OXFORD, Miss.—The sun was brilliant Sunday, and across the campus little knots of graduates—many of them black—posed for pictures with their families in the old grove at Ole Miss. The air was heavy with the rich fragrance of magnolia blossoms and honeysuckle vines. Sixteen years ago the same plot of land reeked for days with the smell of tear gas.

Memories: Oxford. September 1962. Crowds of students line the streets to watch a confrontation at the campus gateway, where state officials, backed by scores of highway patrolmen, are prepared personally to block James Meredith from registering. Attorney General Robert Kennedy, fearing violence, pulls Meredith and the federal marshals back to Memphis. Lt. Gov. Paul Johnson, triumphant, patrols the street with a bullhorn. "Go back to your dorms," he tells the students. "The nigger isn't coming today."

Robert Khayat was a football star at Ole Miss in the early 1960s, a popular figure who was voted "Colonel Rebel," the equivalent of Mr. Ole Miss. He is now a law professor, and Sunday he was talking in proud wonderment of the changes that have taken place at Ole Miss. "We've still got a way to go," he said. Because of the school's relatively small size and endowment, he said, "it is hard to compete for blacks."

But there are now 700 blacks in a student body of 9,600 and several black professors. Another Ole Miss football player, Ben Williams, was named Colonel Rebel a couple of years ago. Ben Williams is black.

A scholarship program to support needy law students is being established in the name of James O. Eastland, the retiring senior senator from Mississippi who once served as the behind-the-scenes leader in the fight against integration. And it was Eastland who invited Sen. Edward Kennedy to come to Oxford Sunday to lend prestige to the school and the scholarship. "Things have certainly changed," Khayat said. "I think the people here are going to be very supportive of Kennedy." That was not always the case in Mississippi.

It was John F. Kennedy who ordered the military occupation of Ole Miss in 1962 to protect the first black student enrolled there, an event almost as traumatic as Reconstruction. It was Robert F. Kennedy who concentrated national exposure on the plight of the hungry in the Mississippi Delta in 1967 after Gov. Paul Johnson had declared that there was no hunger, that the black women were "so fat they shine."

There was the image of Edward M. Kennedy as the playboy. He never directly intervened in Mississippi, but his Catholicism, accent, wealth, and glamour, like his brothers', made him seem foreign to the Mississippians who earned their living from the soil. The Kennedys were despised in Mississippi, and on the afternoon of Nov. 22, 1963, bands of Ole Miss students cheered and waved Confederate flags when they heard the news from Dallas.

But passions have ebbed in the long interlude of years since then—

after the murders of Bobby Kennedy and Medgar Evers and the three civil-rights workers in Neshoba County. After all of the night-riding, church bombings, burnings, and beatings, it is as though the violence finally served as a catharsis, and the state is now becalmed.

Ole Miss chancellor Porter Fortune was joking when he formally declared a "truce" between Mississippi and the last of the Kennedy brothers as he welcomed Ted Kennedy to Oxford to deliver the commencement address.

Memories: Oxford. September 1962. There is a snowy vision of President Kennedy on a black and white TV set, telling the nation that desegregation has finally come peacefully to Ole Miss. Even as he talks, fusillades of bullets and tear gas are being exchanged in a pitched battle that will last all night. Before the first campus riot of the 1960s is over, two will die, hundreds will be wounded, and thousands of troops will occupy the campus.

Sunday afternoon, one of Kennedy's hosts at Ole Miss took him to the Lyceum building, where 400 federal marshals were under siege that night in 1962. The old red brick building had served as a Civil War hospital, and its halls were bloodied again a century later. The university official, George Street, pointed out the bullet holes and described the scene for Kennedy and his nephew, Robert Kennedy Jr. Shouting imprecations at the Kennedys, wave after wave of rioters attacked the building with bricks, a fire truck, a bulldozer, and bullets. There were snipers in the trees, raining fire on the embattled marshals until President Kennedy airlifted a division of paratroopers to the rescue.

Ted Kennedy took his cigar out of his mouth as he heard the story. "My God," he said.

Memories: Jackson. August 1963. Paul Johnson, running for governor, successfully tars his chief opponent, J. P. Coleman, with being a "Kennedy man." One Johnson ad, with a picture of a bed in the governor's mansion, says "Jack Kennedy Slept Here" when Coleman was governor before. "Remember," the ad says, "J. P. Coleman would turn Mississippi over to the Kennedys—lock, stock, and barrel." A Republican candidate has also lined the Mississippi highways with billboards with the message "KO the Kennedys."

After he arrived in Oxford, Ted Kennedy borrowed a yellowing copy of the "Jack Kennedy Slept Here" ad from a reporter who brought it along on the trip. Kennedy was amused by it, and he showed it to Eastland. Eastland looked at it, grunted, and handed it back to Kennedy. He was not amused.

Eastland's powerful political organization had backed Johnson in the race and had been responsible for the ad. However, through the years, Ted Kennedy had gotten along with Eastland while serving in the Senate Judiciary Committee, which Eastland heads. Despite Big Jim Eastland's reputation for intransigence, Kennedy said, "He has a standard mode of conduct which you can deal with."

On Sunday, Kennedy was wearing an Ole Miss "Colonel Rebel" patch and a "Big Jim" label pin. It was, said Champ Terney, Eastland's son-in-law, "a classic example of politics making strange bedfellows." Said Terney of his father-in-law, "I never heard him say a bad word about Kennedy."

Memories: Oxford. March 1966. Despite an outcry by state politicians over the "liberal-leaning" Ole Miss law school, the law students have dared to invite Robert Kennedy to speak on campus. The state politicians, Kennedy says, felt his presence at Ole Miss was "like putting a fox in the chicken house." He looks out over the crowd. "I feel like a chicken in the fox house." He disarms his audience.

"I am here today on a long overdue mission of apology," Ted Kennedy told his Ole Miss audience Sunday, "to concede that, on one of the most crucial political issues of an earlier time, a Massachusetts president was wrong and the people of Mississippi were right." A smattering of applause broke out. "But wait," Kennedy cried. "I speak of John Adams," who appointed a Yankee governor for the Mississippi territory nearly 200 years ago. The crowd broke out into laughter.

Memories: Cleveland, Miss. April 1967. Robert Kennedy is touring a neighborhood of shanties in this Delta town. In one house he stops to stroke the face of a crying little black child whose belly is distended. The editor of the local newspaper confronts Kennedy outside the house and criticizes his mission. "There are no hungry people here," the editor says. Kennedy's eyes bristle. "Step over here," he replies, "and I'll introduce you to some."

Following commencement exercises Sunday, a reception was held for Eastland at the Oxford Country Club. Blacks mingled with whites. Many of the prominent leaders of the community pressed into a circle to try to get to talk to Kennedy.

Aaron Henry, the venerable leader of the NAACP in Mississippi, was sporting a gold peanut for Jimmy Carter in his lapel and wearing a tiepin denoting his membership in Gov. Cliff Finch's honorary colonel's staff. He was so overwhelmed by the occasion that he planted a kiss on Eastland's cheek. "I'd like to have two pictures of that," one spectator said. "One of Aaron kissing Eastland. The other of Eastland when he realized somebody had taken a picture of Aaron kissing him."

Memories: Neshoba Fairgrounds. August 1967. Ross Barnett, the former governor who fought the Kennedys in 1962, is trying for a comeback. At this old-time political and revival meeting, he is waving his arms wildly and warning the crowd about his rival, John Bell Williams, an archconservative who has been in Congress for twenty years. "He's been up in Washington, getting closer to the left-handed side. He's been up there fooling around with LBJ, Bobby Kennedy, Ole Katzenbach and Kowatski."

Barnett is one of the few who won't let go. He still fulminates these days against "Teddy Kennedy, that grrreat driver, that grrreat swimmer." He is out of politics now, but his son, who is considerably more moderate than his father, was elected to the legislature. Barnett showed up at the Neshoba County Fair a couple of years ago, and one acquaintance asked him if he was "going to talk about the niggers again this year." "Naw," Barnett replied, "I can't do that anymore. Ross Junior's got a bunch of 'em in his district."

Memories: Marks, Miss. March 1968. In two weeks, Martin Luther King will die in Memphis. In two months Bobby Kennedy will be dead. It is King's last journey, preparing for the Poor People's Crusade in the Mississippi Delta. He is speaking to a congregation of black women, who stir the air in the little church with hand fans from a local funeral home. Suddenly a white man lurches to the pulpit and presents King with a $100 bill. He introduces himself as "Money Mobley" and is behaving erratically. "God bless you, Brother Mobley," King says. "Any brother who gives one hundred dollars can say a word." Money Mobley takes the microphone and shouts, "There ain't no hungry people here." As King's lieutenants wrestle him off the podium he is still shouting about "the goddamn Kennedys."

H. M. Ray has been U.S. attorney for the northern district of Mississippi since the Kennedy administration. He was at the Eastland reception Sunday, reflecting on the change in Mississippi. "It was the law" finally passed by Congress after Kennedy died that brought the state around, he said.

Fred Banks, a black civil rights lawyer from Jackson, used the law to battle in the courts for change, fighting the white power structure, bit by bit. Sunday, he and his wife were hobnobbing with the establishment. He said he really didn't feel surprised to be there. It hadn't happened overnight, after all. "It's been a long, gradual process."

Banks was chatting with Ed Perry, a state legislator who was a student at Ole Miss during the Meredith era. Perry said that most of the animosity toward the Kennedy family had dissipated. "It was mostly directly at John and Robert Kennedy, anyway," he said. "Things," he said, in the refrain that was heard so often Sunday, "have really changed around here."

REDEMPTION

Part II
Out of the Delta

In the Heat of Freedom Summer

(*Clarksdale Press Register*, August 13, 1964)

"Freedom Summer," conducted in Mississippi in 1964 by a few hundred college students who came to take part in the civil rights movement, helped serve as a dramatic introduction for a young reporter to the top story in the nation. The struggle spanned the seven years (1963–69) I spent on my first newspaper job and remained a frame of reference for me throughout my career.

At the time, I was roughly the same age as the college volunteers and got to know most of those who worked in Clarksdale. We developed a tenuous sort of friendship, though they felt that the *Press Register* was part of the enemy establishment. I admired the students' courage and very quietly sympathized with their activities, but when I wrote about them I knew that I had to maintain a neutral position. There was a great deal of resentment in the white community over their presence. Sometimes, the editor-publisher-owner, Joe Ellis, would pencil in a bit of negative commentary in stories under my byline. (Looking back, I see Joe's hand in this piece in a parenthetical insert and the assertion about "strong evidence" of good educational opportunities for blacks.) Joe was smart and a decent man, and I believe he knew that segregation was wrong, but he was under all sorts of pressures from peers at the country club and advertisers. And I was not exactly a profile in courage, myself.

At least the *Press Register* covered the movement. Most newspapers in the state chose to ignore it. (Back then, the term "Negro" was the accepted racial reference used in newspapers.)

With all its scrambled syntax and clumsiness, I offer this story
as an early example of my coverage during that epic period. It was
written during a low moment for the student volunteers. The bodies
of their three colleagues had just been found in Neshoba County,
their time in Mississippi was winding down, and they told me privately
that they had failed to make the breakthroughs they had hoped to
achieve. Though I felt the story was an honest reflection of their
discouragement, several of them left town disappointed in me.

They sat in a circle in the still heat of the Silent Grove Baptist Church.

The group was discussing the recent strife in Harlem. It was a roundtable discussion of current events—apparently the dominant feature of the "Freedom Schools."

In all, there were fourteen students and three teachers. The students were Negroes, ranging in age from elementary school children to a middle-aged woman. The teachers, all white, were college students, part of about two dozen persons here this summer in connection with the Council of Federated Organizations' "Mississippi Project."

A young girl was asked her opinion of the racial violence in Harlem.

"Well," she drawled, "what I heard over the radio—this colored woman came up to this policeman . . . and she asked him to help her. So he shot her."

This was the only comment the girl made, but it represented one of the problems confronting the COFO workers this summer.

There is very little middle-ground. While they encounter hostility and disdain from most of the white community, they face apathy and ignorance with many of the Negroes. And there is distrust on both sides.

(For example, there was an obvious predisposition on the part of the girl to remember only a report that a policeman shot a Negro woman without provocation. There was no allowance for the doubtful source of the report, which was never confirmed. White people listening to the same report—the entire news broadcast—would be much more likely to remember the reports of brick-throwing and looting by Negroes.)

The first summer project workers arrived about June 20. Their program will continue until about Aug. 21, at the end of nine weeks. There is some talk of a sort of follow-up program through the fall and winter months, but nothing definite seems to have been developed.

The number of workers has varied from about fifteen to about twenty-five, the latest arrivals having come into the city this week. Several have departed. Two-third or more are white. Lafayette Surney of Ruleville, a SNCC worker who has stayed in Clarksdale in previous civil rights activities, is project director, but observers outside COFO are uncertain who wields the main force in the local group.

What are these "Freedom Schools" accomplishing?

"Not as much as we had hoped," one of the summer volunteers said and went on to explain that despite all the orientation before he came to Mississippi, he found it hard to comprehend the complexity of the programs here.

Some are discouraged, and as Joe Youngerman, 21, a recent Yale graduate from Champaign, Ill., said, "The other night we just sat around and had a depression session."

But he believes that whatever little they have accomplished, if just one thing, it will be something that was not here before they came.

The "Freedom School" at Silent Grove Baptist Church in Riverton resembles a Daily Vacation Bible School without the emphasis on religion.

The classes are held in the sweltering basement of the building, where the ceilings are barely head high.

It is, for the most part, disorganized. Classes are held daily, but at varying hours.

Usually, the first order of the day is Negro history. Ostensibly, its purpose is to instill racial pride in the pupils.

"Invariably, we get off on current events," said Youngerman, who was more-or-less moderating the discussion, querying individuals for their views.

The talk ranged from Harlem to Coahoma County. However,

the response was so poor that Les Johnson, 20, a COFO worker from Glendora, Calif., and a student at the University of California, launched into a ten-minute talk on the merits of demonstrations.

The speaker carried on as if he were chatting with his classmates instead of this group predominantly composed of teenagers. He used big words and soon the younger pupils were squirming restlessly in their seats. Only the older Negro woman and a couple of others seemed to be following what he was saying.

The speaker was finally interrupted and the discussion returned to its previous plane.

"Les just gets so frustrated he finally feels he has to say something," one of his fellow workers explained.

The third "teacher" was Kathryn (Kate) Quinn, 20, of Steilacoom, Wash., a student at the University of Washington.

Dissension is evident among some of the COFO personnel. Everyone has a different idea about how the summer program should be conducted, and because there is no one here to coordinate the group, a mild form of anarchy exists.

However, the ultimate goal is the same as far as the "Freedom Schools" are concerned—to give the Negroes an education the COFO students believed is being deprived them in Mississippi society, despite strong evidence to the contrary.

Apparently they feel the deficiencies are rather general. Besides civil rights discussions, the schools offer classes in typing, algebra, simple mathematics, science, and other miscellaneous subjects, including literature.

There are four "Freedom Schools" in Clarksdale. They are held at varying times at various churches and generally seem to operate on a very haphazard basis.

After the general roundtable discussion following a session Negro history, the Silent Grove assembly split up into groups of five or six each for instruction in mathematics and other subjects.

A total of about fifty people, mostly children, have been enrolled in the "Freedom Schools."

A "Freedom Library," a sort of adjunct to the schools, is available at the "Freedom House"—the COFO headquarters. (Freedom seems to be the catchall term for all civil rights activities.)

There are about 1,000 volumes on hand. One shelf is primarily for children, but most of the books probably are donations from college students, judging from the titles.

There are bestsellers from a few years ago and, incongruously perhaps, books on Zen Buddhism and existentialism.

Youngerman was asked about this.

"I know. You'd think they wouldn't be interested in that kind of stuff. But this one girl picked up a book on existentialism and she took it home and read it. And she came back and asked if we had any more on the subject."

Did the girl, who was about 18 and appeared to be a college student, understand the book? Youngerman seemed convinced she did.

Then with a grin, as if that "one thing" had been accomplished, he said, "And this is good."

Robert Kennedy Meets Hunger

(*Clarksdale Press Register*, April 12, 1967)

Big stories occurred repeatedly in our backyard, which was encouraging for a small town reporter. Robert Kennedy's brief trip to Mississippi, a year before his presidential campaign and assassination, was considered a seminal event in his crusade on behalf of the poor.

During a break in his schedule, Kennedy engaged in a conversation with a few reporters. I remember asking him how he had enjoyed his visit to Mississippi the year before, when he spoke at Ole Miss. His eyes twinkled in recollection. "Were you there?" he asked. I said I had covered the event. "I was astonished," Kennedy said, describing it as one of the warmest and most unexpected receptions he had ever received.

A Clarksdale mob scene over Sen. Robert F. Kennedy provided a chaotic climax Tuesday afternoon for a hectic day spent in the Mississippi Delta by two members of a Senate subcommittee studying poverty.

Kennedy accompanied fellow Senator Joseph Clark of Pennsylvania, chairman of the group, on the tour. But it was the junior senator from New York who upstaged Clark throughout the trip.

The senators, along with a troop of staff members, newsmen, and federal and state pistoleros, swept into Clarksdale at the end of a frantic series of stops along U.S. 61 between here and Greenville. The largest crowd of the day awaited them here, with more than a thousand persons—mostly Negro schoolchildren—congested in front of the Clarksdale Neighborhood Center.

Clark mounted a car to beg off from a press conference that had been planned here. "We're in a terrible rush," he said, explaining that their plane for Washington was to leave Memphis in less than two hours, "and I'm going to catch that plane."

However, Kennedy took advantage of the gathering to make a short speech atop another car. He said that he was glad to be in Clarksdale and in Mississippi and said that his visit to this area had been "most helpful."

"The problems of poverty are problems of all United States citizens," Kennedy said, emphasizing, as both he and Clark had at each stop Tuesday, that poverty woes were just as acute outside Mississippi. "We all need to make an effort together," he said.

Directing his attention to the children, he urged them to "stay in school and get as fine an education as possible." When Kennedy asked for a show of hands from the best students, a forest of arms shot up. He laughed that Clarksdale must have the "smartest students" in the country.

He was then engulfed by persons seeking handshakes and autographs, even as the car he stood on backed through the melee and onto the highway. When the way was finally cleared by local police, the senators drove north toward Memphis. They were here only about twenty minutes, but it was by far the most tumultuous welcome of the day.

Their tour had begun in Greenville Tuesday morning with visits to anti-poverty programs there and to nearby "Tent City" established by striking farm workers nearly two years ago.

After lunch, the group embarked on a fast-paced motorcade at speeds of more than 80 mph in a harrowing race against limited time. They stopped at hand-picked locations in Cleveland selected by NAACP attorney Miss Marion Wright of Jackson and Amzie Moore, a Negro anti-poverty administrator in Cleveland.

The first home visited was a wretched little shack where fifteen persons lived. A group of Negro children were huddled in front of the house, bewildered at the commotion. "What'd you have for lunch?" Kennedy asked one of the children. The boy murmured a reply. "You haven't had lunch yet, eh?" Kennedy remarked, patting his head. "What'd you have for breakfast?"

"Molasses," the boy said.

Kennedy and Clark were then directed to a neighboring hovel virtually bare of furniture. The front room was completely empty, the second room housed a bed where an infant lay sucking on a bottle. In the back, Mrs. Annie White, the occupant of the house, was washing pieces of clothing with a scrub-board and a zinc tub. Her 20-month-old son sat on the floor beside her in the middle of a scattered meal of corn bread and rice. Flies were swarming.

Kennedy knelt by the child and gently stroked his face for about two minutes without saying a word. The boy just looked at him with wide eyes. The senators stepped through the rear of the house where an open toilet without plumbing stood, and Clark was moved to call instances of poverty like this "a national disgrace." Kennedy also lamented that Americans "spend $3 billion each year on dogs."

In the only sharp exchange between the two senators and a Mississippian, Cliff Langford, editor of the weekly newspaper in Cleveland, carped about the selection of Mississippi for the subcommittee's visit. Langford also charged that they had picked the worst situations to observe here.

"Don't worry," snapped Clark. "We've been brainwashed from the other [more attractive] side."

Langford said that he was disturbed over allegations of persons starving made in subcommittee hearings in Jackson Monday. He said that he knew of no one starving.

"Step over here and I'll introduce you to some," replied Kennedy, referring to a clutch of children huddled nearby.

Clark stressed that the subcommittee had not come to Mississippi to "find fault," but rather "just to see if we can do anything about it." He said that there were similar poverty plights in his home state of Pennsylvania and in Kennedy's New York.

During the quick rounds in the Cleveland Negro neighborhood, Kennedy kept insisting that he wanted to see a plantation. So the group was led down a dusty road to a farm cabin just outside Cleveland. They went inside to find a mother nursing her child. Undisturbed, she calmly answered questions.

At one point in Cleveland, the senators considered bypassing their stop at Clarksdale because time was running out. However, Oscar Carr of Clarksdale, a prominent Democrat who attended the luncheon in Greenville and accompanied them on their swing up the Delta, intervened to urge them to make the stop.

The caravan sped towards Clarksdale, but Kennedy called for another impromptu visit at another farm home between Mound Bayou and Winstonville. There they confronted a 39-year-old Negro, Andrew Jackson, who smiled in wonderment when he realized that he was talking to "Mr. Bobby Kennedy."

Jackson's home had a tattered ceiling. A photo of the Glorybound Singers and a calendar hung on the wall. His wife apologized, "This house sho' ain't clean," adding that she had been working in the garden and had not been expecting company.

Mrs. Jackson said that her family of six children had had sausage for breakfast and "light bread" for lunch. Her husband said that he had lost his job to farm mechanization and his only income in the last two months had been $24 given him by a reporter to buy food stamps. A cat roamed the house.

"How do you feed the cat?" Clark asked.

"Oh, we do," Mrs. Jackson said.

"Stew, eh?" Kennedy said with a smile.

The group then continued to Clarksdale for their wild welcome here.

Clark, when asked about the subcommittee's findings in the state, said that the anti-poverty program needed better-skilled personnel and improved local cooperation. He said that the poor also needed food. He agreed with Kennedy that the amount of federal money going to the "war on poverty" was inadequate, but said that the problem was not that simple. Clark said that "we need a reawakening of a conscience."

Peppery Politics at the Fair

(*Clarksdale Press Register*, August 3, 1967)

The 1967 Neshoba County Fair was my first. I was covering the last of Mississippi's openly racist gubernatorial campaigns and struck by the color of the unique event and the oratory. (As Yeats put it in "The Second Coming": "The best lack all conviction, while the worst are full of passionate intensity.") Over the years I would occasionally return as a reporter. Little did I know in 1967 that forty years later I would "marry into the fair" when I wed Nancy, a member of the vast Williams family of Philadelphia, Miss. A weekend at the fair has become part of our routine each summer.

NESHOBA FAIRGROUNDS—Six thousand persons lunched on hot dogs, fried chicken, roast turkey, and demagoguery at the year's biggest political spectacular here Wednesday.

Four serious contenders for governor slugged it out in an oral fight for votes while a fifth candidate, Vernon Brown, appeared as an anticlimax. Dressed in an old blue suit, red tie, black brogans, and a straw hat, Brown noted that "they usually save the best for last, so I must be the best." But the crowd exited from the open-air, tin-roofed pavilion even as Brown assured them he "hadn't sold out to nobody."

Brown, who took it upon himself to run for governor after many years of county service in Wiggins, had some hard acts to follow. Preceding him were Jimmy Swan, Bill Waller, Ross Barnett, and William Winter, all jousting for support at this historic den of noise.

It was Winter who stole the show with a rousing display of allegiance by his backers. It was like a carefully organized demonstration at a convention where presidents are nominated. Cheers and sustained applause washed over the tightly packed forum when he first appeared, interrupting the presentation of the outstanding Neshoba County schoolboy.

Although many of his most vociferous supporters were under voting age, the loud, long receptions he repeatedly received highlighted the afternoon.

Winter had been pasted by Barnett and Waller before he spoke, so he opened by stating, "I haven't come to get elected on my ability to vilify and assassinate the character of anybody in this race." He was engulfed by applause.

Meanwhile, Barnett went packing to Clarksdale after one of his typically colorful campaign addresses. Waving his arms wildly and rocking back on his heels to laugh at his own jibes at Winter and John Bell Williams—who will get his licks in here today—Barnett was spurred on by a whooping pocket of fans. He also drew at least two choruses of boos—the only ones of the day.

Barnett thumped the rostrum as he praised his industrial program while governor, then turned the closing minutes of his speech to attacks on Williams—"He's getting closer to the left hand side. He's fooling around with LBJ, Bobby Kennedy, Ole Katzenbach and Kowatski"—and Winter—"He's like one of those scorpions you see sitting on fences and changing colors."

Waller, who preceded Barnett, suggested that "if they're going to call me the underdog, then I'll call William Winter 'Heckle,' John Bell Williams 'Jeckle,' and Ross 'Mr. Magoo.'"

Waller also wondered about the "sympathy club" for Williams, the "job promise club" for Barnett, and the "high society club" for Winter. He said Winter had promised "six chickens in every pot," adding that he had mapped out a "Winter plan for harmony among tom cats" in jesting reference to Winter's eighteen-point program.

Swan led off the barnstorming with a denunciation of his fellow candidates for conducting a "three ring circus." Swan said he didn't come "to sling mud" but, instead, "to preach truth." His "truth" included the observation that "so-called federal judges have ordered the destruction of our children . . . They have already taken the prayer of God from the mouths of our little children."

Swan said that "so-called federal judges are thieves and outlaws" worshipping at "the filthy, atheistic altar of integration."

Swan, a slight man almost hidden by a Medusa's head of microphones atop the Gomillion Marble Works pulpit, also promised a "counter-revolution" to stop the communist revolution in order to "take the free-loading politicians' heads out of the trough."

Swan was accompanied by his crowd of right-wing beatniks, and after his speech he hob-nobbed with sympathizers in Hawaiian shirts and one chap in a bright yellow and green outfit labeled "Hamasa Clowns."

The afternoon's speech-making began as rain spit on the sprawling carnival panorama. Skies gradually cleared as the day warmed with the oratory.

Surrounding the pavilion is a square of bungalows where it's always open house. Bunting and posters cover many of the cottages. Huge throngs milled through the area and onto the adjacent midway throughout the speeches.

After the politics ended, the crowd adjourned to the dirt racetrack for more sport. But the horse racing was not nearly as competitive.

The Last Days of Martin Luther King

(*Clarksdale Press Register*, March 20–22, 1968)

The first days of spring 1968 would be the last in Dr. Martin Luther King Jr.'s life, and as he traveled in the Delta to rally support for his Poor People's March on Washington, I followed him. Strangely, at most events I was the only reporter present, even though King was a world figure and recipient of the Nobel Peace Prize.

He had been in and out of Clarksdale over the years, and through the good offices of the local NAACP leader Aaron Henry I usually got some time to talk with Dr. King.

His final visit produced four pieces from me: a column dealing with his tenuous relationship with other civil rights forces in Mississippi; an account of a series of speeches he delivered in one day; a bizarre confrontation with a white man in Marks; and an analysis based on an interview about King's plans for masses of poor people to take their grievances to the nation's capital.

Following his encounter with "Money" Mobley in Marks, I asked Dr. King if he was ever frightened during these visits to rural Mississippi.

He told me he was not, in part, because "the climate of violence is gradually decreasing in the South."

Two weeks later he was shot dead in Memphis.

Not the King in Mississippi

Dr. Martin Luther King, the Messiah of civil rights activity in America in the '60s, was due in Clarksdale today for one of his infrequent appearances in Mississippi. Although he is in and out of the state occasionally, his visits are usually quiet, and today's scheduled stop here has provoked a minimum of advance notice. This seems to be playing it low-key for a man of his prominence, but then that's the way it almost always is in Mississippi.

Actually, Dr. King is only a name in this state and does not command a real power base here. As the leader of the Southern Christian Leadership Conference, an organization that has thrived mostly in Georgia and Alabama, Dr. King's influence is mitigated by the fact that the National Association for the Advancement of Colored People controls civil rights business in Mississippi instead of SCLC. This is not to say that there is a great conflict between the two groups. Both follow generally the same philosophy, but both organizations covet their positions of influence in these Deep South states and are unwilling to yield it to another outfit.

"We're happy to have Martin here anytime," state and local NAACP president Aaron Henry said Monday.

However, when you consider all of the civil rights trauma in Mississippi in this decade, Dr. King has not been here often. He invited himself to the Mississippi Delta today, although local Negro leaders allied with the NAACP have been happy to help him arrange speaking engagements. Dr. King is currently trying to marshal troops for the April 22 poor people's march on Washington, an event that the NAACP has not embraced with zealous support. The NAACP favors the principle of the march, but is wary of the tactics that might be employed.

As Henry says, he is willing to go to Washington for one day to join in a mass demonstration for additional help for the impoverished of this country. But he says he does not approve of a prolonged sit-in at the nation's capital, nor of plans to clog up normal governmental process. Henry is also wary of the role that black power chieftain Stokely Carmichael might play in the march. Henry's statement is a good summation of the NAACP approach to achieving civil rights action—employing relatively orderly and moderate methods. Dr. King's civil disobedience strategy carries the movement a step further to the left, while Carmichael and H. Rap Brown theorize in anarchy.

The splits in the disparate civil rights groups are especially apparent these days, and there is little likelihood that they will ever meld into a viable joint venture like the Conference of Federated Organizations (COFO) of 1964 again. This amalgamation of NAACP, SCLC, Student Non-Violent Coordination Committee (SNCC), and Congress of Racial Equality (CORE) spawned Freedom Summer that year, but the group finally broke up after it was the midwife of another rump group, the Mississippi Freedom Democrats. The organization of organizations was rent by disagreement over moderate policy, represented by Aaron Henry, and more radical elements from the Delta Ministry bloc.

They have gone their separate ways since then, and are united at best very loosely. The NAACP still pushes for more civil rights progress through legislative and judicial means, and voter registration drives have been mounted to grab control at the polls. But their efforts are made through legal channels.

Dr. King, meanwhile, has lapped his pacific philosophy over into programs to end America's involvement in Vietnam, and now to seek greater aid for the poor in this country. None of this represents a departure from the principles he has advocated through the years. The emphasis is just in different places.

As for Carmichael—who I remember as a virtual unknown COFO worker in overalls who used to put his two bits' worth in at rallies here in 1964—his star has risen fast and the concept that he and his confederates stand for strikes unrest not only among whites, but among the old guard Negro leaders. Dr. King's position is between the moderate left of the NAACP and the far left of the black power structure.

He will probably always be welcome in Mississippi by his cousins in civil rights activity—the NAACP—as long as his ideas are not too far from their own. But the NAACP will never be willing to hand over to Dr. King the control of the strength in numbers they have worked so long to organize.

Rallying the Poor in the Delta

Dr. Martin Luther King drummed through the Delta Tuesday, denouncing poor living conditions as "criminal" and calling for Negroes to converge upon Washington in a demonstration that would "upset this nation."

Dr. King spoke at Batesville, Marks, Clarksdale, Greenwood, and Grenada during the day before flying to South Mississippi last night to continue his campaign.

Traveling in a dented white station wagon crowded with his lieutenants, the Rev. Ralph Abernathy and Hosea Williams, and several of his Southern Christian Leadership Conference (SCLC) partisans from Grenada, the civil rights leader moved far behind schedule all day. But he still attracted hundreds of spectators in hot, teeming churches at every stop. The trip went peacefully, with local law enforcement and FBI agents maintaining surveillance along the way.

Tuesday's tour officially opened Dr. King's drive for recruits and money for a poor people's march on Washington beginning next month. The open-end demonstration is designed to dramatize poverty in America, he said, and he wants to shake the conscience of the capital and the country. "This is a stay-in movement," he said in Clarksdale. "We're going to have freedom schools every day and black culture schools."

He suggested that farm shacks should be loaded onto flatbed trucks and transported to Washington to be dumped at the Smithsonian Institute.

Dr. King also spoke of a "mule train" emanating from Mississippi to help ferry followers to Washington. He promised that there would be plenty of places to live, enough food to eat, and medical attention available to assure the longevity of the demonstration.

"We'll keep these issues before the Congress," Dr. King pledged to a crowd in Marks. "We're going to Washington to demand—not to beg—that something be done immediately to improve the lives of the poor," he said. "All of God's children have got to have a nice house to live in . . . We need jobs, and we need jobs that will pay us something. We're tired of working on full-time jobs for part-time pay.

"We're going to go there and demand that they seat us and hear us and tell us what they're going to do about it," Dr. King continued, referring to Congress and government agencies including the Departments of Health, Education, and Welfare and Agriculture.

"Some of you unemployed can take off and come on up there," he said. He said that he wanted to take a group of poor Negro children to show Sargent Shriver, head of the Office of Economic Opportunity.

Dr. King stuck to generally the same theme in all of his talks; however, in Clarksdale he also struck at the Vietnam War in lamenting that "things are not right in this country."

"I am angry about the war in Vietnam . . . black and white boys are dying there in dedicated solidarity, but then they come home and can't even live on the same block," he shouted to prompt a thumping, yelling response from approximately 400 persons wedged into the Chapel Hill Baptist Church here.

Dr. King kept his Clarksdale audience waiting nearly three hours. Some persons defected during the long, hot wait, but their places were quickly taken up by others milling around the church as local Negro figures bided their time with speech and song. Fire-eating oratory by Hosea Williams, Dr. King's companion, immediately preceded the key speech here.

The schedule was thrown out of order from the beginning when the SCLC entourage arrived an hour and twenty minutes late in Batesville. Dr. King said that meetings in Memphis in connection with the garbage strike and a proposed Negro work stoppage and march there Friday had delayed his arrival in Mississippi. He was an hour and a half late in Marks, and spoke to a church gathering there and then went to a Head Start center to hear complaints from Negro women concerning living conditions.

The group arrived in Clarksdale shortly after 3 p.m., but Dr. King first went to Aaron Henry's Fourth Street Drug Store where he stayed for about half an hour using the telephone, sipping a glass of water, and thumbing through a *Sepia* magazine before moving on to the waiting crowd here. Henry was at the church.

Afterwards he left for Greenwood, where he cut his visit short in an attempt to pick up lost time. However, some 700 persons at Hattiesburg had the longest wait of the day. The meeting there began at 7 p.m., but Dr. King didn't arrive until 11:45 p.m.

Money Talks

W. B. (Money) Mobley, a white Marks farmer, lived up to his nickname Tuesday.

He donated a fresh $100 bill to Dr. Martin Luther King and then became involved in a curious exchange of words in the closest thing to an incident during Dr. King's Delta tour.

Mobley, who was described by one Marks resident as "wealthy enough to do it," interrupted the beginning of Dr. King's speech before about 200 persons at the Silent Grove Baptist Church by walking up to the pulpit and presenting him with the big bill.

Dr. King appeared astonished at first. Mobley then whispered something to the Negro civil rights leader while the crowd murmured. "Brother Mobley says he's been here thirty years and he's got more colored friends than white ones," Dr. King announced. The crowd cheered.

"Any brother who gives one hundred dollars can say a word," said Dr. King. Mobley said that he didn't necessarily want to make a speech but that he had "just wanted to make a donation."

However, he eventually took the stand and announced, "Ain't nobody hungry down here in Mississippi."

That provoked an outburst. "We are too hungry," shouted several women sitting up front. Mobley then started to say something about "Kennedy," and amid more shouts from the audience, Dr. King, who was by this time wondering about Mobley's altruistic motivations, stepped in. Using diplomacy, he thanked Mobley again and invited him to shake hands with his associates, the Rev. Ralph Abernathy and Hosea Williams, before leaving.

Mobley addressed the Rev. Abernathy as "boy," to which the Rev. Abernathy snapped, "I'm not a 'boy,' I'm Rev. Abernathy."

After another minute or so of confusion, Mobley walked out of the church. A Marks policeman who had been watching Mobley warily from the time he appeared on the scene before Dr. King arrived said afterwards that the donor had been removed from the church area but not arrested.

Speaking later to the crowd, the Rev. Abernathy said, "We appreciate this one hundred dollars from this white brother, but we've got to get him straight . . . He owes us more than a hundred dollars." Asked about the incident, Dr. King said, "I don't know him so I can't comment on him as a person . . . But he was generous."

The most colorful events of the day occurred in Marks, where Dr. King also heard several Negro women castigate the anti-poverty program in Quitman County at a Head Start Center. Shouting over the wails of many restless pre-school age children, Mrs. Ruth Fig took the spotlight in a scene being filmed by a Public Broadcast Laboratory team to declare that "Mid-State [the anti-poverty agency in Quitman County] has never done anything but starve us to death." She said that a preacher connected with the program was walking around "lying to us night and day."

The PBL show will be telecast the week of Dr. King's mobilization of the poor in Washington. The National Education Television network has already shown two PBL programs on the Delta. Dr. King said that he was "deeply moved" in Marks, promised the people that "we're with you," and indicated that he would see what could be done.

Washington's D-Day Nears

Dr. Martin Luther King has a dream.

In it, he envisions "waves of people" descending upon Washington. They are arriving aboard buses. Some are riding horseback. Others via a "mule train" that will make the journey from Mississippi in three weeks. Many more will make the pilgrimage on foot. Finally, their ranks will swell to such size that the nation's capital will be bulging with poor people. The gears of government will be gummed up by the masses.

Then, theoretically, the situation will become so acute that some-body—presumably President Johnson—will be moved to do some-thing.

Dr. King is not specific about his goals. He speaks of a guaranteed minimum income for all families. He says that his followers are going to demand new rights, better jobs, and additional funds for anti-pov-erty projects that will be channeled to the needy, not to the project personnel. But he talks about these objectives generally.

The poor people's march on Washington still seems disorganized at this point, but Dr. King defends the timing. In his speech in Clarks-dale earlier this week he intimated that if he waited several months to plan it, Negroes would soon be arguing among themselves. He said that his Montgomery bus boycott and his Selma march had been de-scribed as ill-timed, but he noted that they achieved their purpose.

Dr. King's Southern Christian Leadership Conference was called "only the architect" of the coming demonstration, and Negroes not affiliated with SCLC—as most Mississippi Negroes are not—were in-vited to join up. However, a large delegation from this area appears doubtful, and participation by other civil rights organizations may be no more than token.

Elucidating on his proposed march on the capital while eating a fried chicken leg during a brief wait in Marks, Dr. King said that while April 22 was D-Day for the invasion of Washington to begin, the ac-tual movement would not be culminated until a mass demonstration sometime in June.

A vanguard of approximately 3,000 will move into Washington next month. He said, "We want it small enough to be manageable in the early weeks." From that number, he wants the crowd to steadily grow as the day's move into the summer.

Dr. King said that the country's largest civil rights group, the Na-tional Association for the Advancement of Colored People, had not yet sided with the plan. But he said he would be talking with Roy Wilkins, the NAACP's executive secretary, and other moderate Negro leaders next week. "I expect they'll all eventually support it," he added.

What role will Stokely Carmichael and the black power advocates have? "No role as far as leadership is concerned," Dr. King replied. They will be welcome to participate, he said, "but everybody must follow the discipline of non-violence."

Although throwing around such terms as "demand—not beg—demand" and "going to do battle" in his speeches, Dr. King insists that it will be a non-violent demonstration.

His pitch in Mississippi has been made solely toward Negroes. He acknowledged that there were poor whites in Mississippi too, but said that he expected no enlistments from them. Most of the white members of his poor people's army will probably come from Kentucky and West Virginia, he said.

Dr. King is urging entire families to move into Washington. "You'll be better off there than here," he says. He wants to establish a shanty town, composed of rickety, makeshift dwellings in the heart of the District of Columbia, thus creating an additional tableau of poverty in a city already festered with slums.

Two hundred doctors have pledged their professional aid for the encampment, Dr. King said. In addition, local labor unions will supply food. The length of the demonstration is indefinite. Dr. King says he is prepared to stay through the summer in order to arouse action from somewhere—Congress, the president, or existing departments.

Dr. King made seven stops in Mississippi this week promoting the march on Washington. He collected greenbacks and silver at every point, but few promises to accompany him.

Is he frightened in Mississippi? "No, I'm not frightened," he answers in his calm, Baptist minister's voice. "I move without fear because I know I'm right. I'd be immobilized if I were afraid. Besides, the climate of violence is gradually decreasing in the South."

The climate in Washington this spring is unpredictable, though. Yet Dr. King is resolutely moving toward his latest attempt to reshape history regardless of the minimum of enthusiasm shown by his former compatriots in civil rights.

Gadfly Payoff

(*Mississippi Freelance*, February 1970)

Shortly after I moved to Washington in 1969, the investigative journalist Seymour Hersh enlisted me to write for his Dispatch News Service, which gathered enough expense money to send me back to Oxford to do a piece on the Ole Miss Law School's attempt to get rid of a couple of troublesome professors. It was the latest example of efforts to purge the school of voices challenging the status quo.

My story, timed to appear just before a meeting of the Association of American Law Schools, was published in a number of major dailies around the county. I wrote this updated version for *Mississippi Freelance*, an upstart, muckraking monthly that was run by Ed Williams and Lew Powell, a couple of Ole Miss grads and staffers for Hodding Carter's *Delta Democrat-Times*. The *MF* folded in 1970, but Ed and Lew went on to illustrious careers with the *Charlotte Observer*.

The Ole Miss Law School eventually broke its political shackles, recruited a number of progressive faculty members, and began producing many of the state's prominent black attorneys.

A $20,000 bribe.

It sounds like the Mafia, but actually it was a last-ditch maneuver by the University of Mississippi this winter. Its law school, in the throes of transition from Dean Joshua Morse to the status quo ante posture of new Dean Joel W. Bunkley, had just lost a 5th Circuit Court ruling reinstating renegade professors Mike Trister and George Strickler. As a result of the case, the Association of American Law Schools was conducting an investigation into infringement of academic freedom and the institution's accreditation was in jeopardy. So someone came up with a solution: offer Trister $20,000 to drop his case.

Trister, a member of the corps of young Yale Law School professors imported to Ole Miss during Dean Morse's progressive movement in 1966, was apparently viewed as the most immediate threat. After he and Strickler were ousted from the university payroll for their participation in a legal aid program for the poor in 1968, Trister stayed on in Oxford to run North Mississippi Rural Legal Services and become a gadfly to the Ole Miss administration. Strickler, meanwhile, moved to a civil rights organization in New Orleans.

They finally won their faculty posts back in a federal court appeals case in October 1969, and panic set in through the groves of academe in Oxford.

"I think it's astounding that they were so frightened about my teaching there again," said Trister. He characterized the $20,000 offer as "a payoff to keep me away." After some soul-searching, he turned down the money.

Dean Bunkley, questioned about the unusual offer, confirmed that it had been made in an attempt "to settle the federal court case." He refused to elaborate. In the lawsuit, Trister and Strickler simply sought their jobs back—not a cash judgment.

An offhand remark he made to a friend still on the law school faculty may have instigated the offer, Trister speculated. It was at a party after he had won the 5th Circuit appeal.

"I said, half-joking, that if the price were right, I'd drop things. Not much later Bunkley called me up and said he heard I was interested in a settlement. I said, 'Fine. Get a contract.' He said, 'No, a monetary settlement.' So I mentioned a preposterous figure—$50,000. He said, 'That's outrageous!' I said, 'Oh, I don't know . . .' That was Monday. On Friday, he got back in touch and talked about 15 to 20 thousand and asked if he could pursue it. I told him I'd give it serious thought. On Sunday [Dec. 14] he called back with a firm offer of $20,000 and said, 'You're going to accept it, aren't you?' He was very upset when I told him I wasn't. He seemed to feel it was bad faith on my part."

Bunkley may have also been put out that all his efforts had been in vain. It was at his suggestion that he and Chancellor Porter Fortune flew to Hattiesburg the day before to approach college board chairman M. M. Roberts about the deal, one university source said. Members of the college board were reportedly polled about the idea on the phone and agreed to it—although no one who is talking knows where the money was to come from.

"Bunkley had convinced everybody this was the thing to do," the source said. "So when it fell through, he looked pretty bad."

Trister said he did not consider accepting the offer. "Probably the more radical position would have been to take the money and use it for scholarships for black students or for this free breakfast program we're sponsoring . . . But it came down to a real feeling that what we were fighting for would not be gained by letting the school off the hook."

Of the university's negotiating, Trister said, "They weren't very skillful about it."

Strickler, 400 miles removed from the campus, was not offered any cash. After the 5th Circuit decision, Strickler said he was contacted by Bunkley. The dean, Strickler related, asked what he wanted. Strickler told him he wanted to come back to teach at Ole Miss next September.

"Bunkley said he would talk with the chancellor and be back in touch," according to Strickler. He heard no more. "I don't worry them as much as Trister," he mused.

During this same period Trister said he "tried to discuss it [his rehiring] with the chancellor and he wouldn't even talk to me."

The administration is not so reticent now. The Trister-Strickler affair got a full airing before the Association of American Law Schools' convention in late December, and formal charges were brought against Ole Miss. The unprecedented action threatened the school's accreditation. Chancellor Fortune and the law school were cited for "the clear impairment of academic freedom."

In a move to redeem the school, the Mississippi college board on Jan. 15 voted to let the university rehire the two professors.

The $20,000 fiasco was just one of several factors weighing against the law school after the purge of liberalism began in 1968. An earlier *MF* article by law school professor Ken Vinson rankled the university establishment, and he and ex-Dean Morse were two of only four Ole Miss faculty members denied a routine salary raise last year. An AALS report on the incident noted "the Vice Chancellor (Alton Bryant) explained the non-raise in part in terms of abrasive personalities."

Vinson and Morse both moved on to Florida State University—Vinson on a "leave of absence." Vinson said he asked Morse to find out the reason, if he could, for the salary freeze. But he never heard anything official before departing last September. Concurrent with the announcement that Trister and Strickler would be offered their jobs back, Chancellor Fortune said Vinson would be offered a salary meeting AALS standards "when and if" he returns.

To avoid AALS sanctions, the Ole Miss law school may also offer a faculty position to a black professor. Franklin D. Cleckley, a 29-year-old teacher at the University of West Virginia Law School, applied for an assignment at Ole Miss last June. He was told no positions were available, but was informed that his application would be kept on file. Two new professors were subsequently hired—both white.

The law school's black student body, which composes about 10 percent of the enrollment, petitioned Dean Bunkley to hire a Negro professor last November. Cleckley has indicated he is still interested.

Otherwise, change will be token at best. Trister plans to return for second semester and Strickler may join him next fall, but neither is prepared to spend the rest of his professional life at Ole Miss. Vinson expresses no interest in going back.

Heavy still hangs the political hand over the university. And while a victory was won in the courts and through the AALS, Ole Miss's grudgingly turned new leaf may prove as transitory as the Josh Morse era.

Part III

Covering Carter

Carter's Problems Back Home

(*Boston Globe*, January 25, 1976)

As the "house Southerner" at the *Globe*, I was assigned to begin covering Jimmy Carter, an obscure candidate for president, in the fall of 1975. I quickly learned that behind his big smile lay a fierce drive and little sense of humor. Within a short time, I fell into disfavor with him, especially after this piece about his inability to get along with the Georgia legislature when he was governor. The story led a Sunday edition of the *Globe*, widely distributed in New Hampshire a few weeks before that state's critical primary. That evening the candidate—wearing a forced smile and sarcastically calling me, "My friend"—literally got in my face to tell me of his other "friends" whom he believed were sources for my story. They were hack politicians, he said, who had for years "been eating out of the trough of the state treasury."

Despite Carter's objections, I think the piece foreshadowed his difficulties in Washington. He seemed to hold Congress in the same contempt he had for the Georgia legislature, rarely recognizing that there were some very wise and wily people on Capitol Hill—many of them Democrats who had looked forward to working with a Democratic president before his tactics alienated them.

ATLANTA—Tuesday morning, hours after Jimmy Carter finished first in the Iowa caucuses, a friend considered introducing a congratulatory resolution in the Georgia Senate. He drew back, it was said, for fear that the roll call would reflect an embarrassing number of dissenting votes.

This is the paradox of the Carter campaign for the Presidency. While the former Georgia governor is gathering strength around the country, he is unpopular with many politicians back home who profess to be mystified by his success.

Indeed, the picture of the Carter years (1971–74) that emerges from conversations around the State House is often in contrast to the image of an efficient state government with a streamlined bureaucracy that is portrayed by the Carter campaign.

There is no dispute on some points. The Carter administration was scandal-free and provided unprecedented opening to blacks and other political have-nots.

But it also was marked by conflict and a bookkeeper's nightmare in the state's largest department—Human Resources—that still has not been untangled.

The adversaries Carter developed during his term as governor remember him as a headstrong, stubborn administrator who bankrupted his credibility with the Legislature.

"I supported him both times he ran for governor and we ended up at each other's throats," said House Speaker Thomas B. Murphy. "There was nearly total conflict during his entire term. Jimmy has no compromising ability at all. It's his way or no way. When you've got 100 House members and 56 senators with varying opinions, there has to be compromise. But with him it was no compromise. He liked to run the state like he was still commanding a submarine."

Says State Sen. Julian Bond: "I have never seen a man so rigid, and it was not on a question of principle. Carter just wouldn't give in."

Stubbornness. This is a characteristic often attributed to Carter, along with intelligence, ambition, a capacity for hard work, and a strain of opportunism.

All these traits came together in his victorious campaign for governor. He traveled the state tirelessly after running third in 1966, and by 1970 established himself as the principal opponent to former Governor Carl Sanders, a liberal by Georgia standards.

Though he had once stood up for blacks among his Baptist congregation, and had rebuffed the White Citizens Councils in his hometown of Plains, Carter ran a campaign that appealed to the Georgia segregationists.

Carter was blamed for the wide distribution of pictures of Sanders celebrating, over champagne, with black basketball players following an Atlanta Hawks victory.

Carter often invoked the name of Alabama Gov. George C. Wallace. He also embraced politically his running mate, Lester Maddox, the fried chicken and axe handle entrepreneur.

Maddox, who had been elected governor after chasing blacks from his restaurant, was prevented by law from running for re-election and was seeking the job as lieutenant governor at the time.

"I didn't like his campaign," says Atlanta lawyer, former congressman, and liberal Charles L. Weltner, who nevertheless likes Carter now. "He decided he wanted to be governor. He felt he could be a good governor—and he was. He carefully looked at the situation, assessed the weaknesses of his opposition, surveyed the potential support, and said the things that engendered support. I don't think it was necessarily evil."

After Carter was elected, however, many people feel he turned on his constituency.

Carter immediately fell out with Maddox and failed to reappoint an arch-segregationist supporter, Roy Harris, to the University of Georgia's board of regents.

In a Legislature that included many old-guard politicians, there was a sense of betrayal. Relations with the governor would further deteriorate over the next four years.

"His word was not his bond," says one longtime senator whose seniority goes back to the period when Carter served in the State Senate in the early 1960s. "After he was governor it was hard to believe what he said." After Carter claimed his position had been misrepresented by legislators, the senator said, they began sending delegations to meet with him so they could vouch for each other.

The major battles were over the plan to reorganize the state bureaucracy, and its merits are still being debated. One view holds that it made the government more responsive and accountable. The other view is that it created a monstrosity, in which all welfare, health, and vocational rehabilitation programs were molded into one Department of Human Resources, which employs half the state's workforce.

The department is so unwieldy, critics say, that services are not properly delivered, morale is shot, and bank statements cannot be reconciled.

Rather than cutting the number of workers, the state payroll went up by 10,000 employees during the Carter years.

And critics scoff at Carter's present claim that he eliminated 278 of the state's 300 agencies during the reorganization.

"There weren't anywhere near that many," said one state official. "They were a lot of default organizations which just existed in the statute books."

In spite of the problems with the Department of Human Resources, Carter left the state with a surplus and the best bond rating available.

In December, Carter was claiming he had the support of "every civil rights leader who has endorsed a candidate," when he knew that Mississippi NAACP president Aaron Henry was working for Sargent Shriver and that Julian Bond had made a derogatory crack about Carter. Carter said he had since talked with Bond and promised, "Julian will be with me."

Bond says that is not exactly the case. The Georgia legislator says he prefers any one of four liberal presidential candidates to Carter. "But if it looks like Florida is a contest between only Carter and Wallace, I'll be more than pleased to campaign for him there," Bond said.

How liberal is Carter?

Neither Bond, who describes Carter as a "moderate conservative," nor Benjamin Mays, the black president of the Atlanta Board of Education, has any criticism of his handling of the race issue.

Carter's position vis-à-vis another major component of the old Democratic liberal coalition—organized labor—is less clear.

An opponent, Rep. Morris K. Udall of Arizona, has complained that he is regularly assailed by pro-labor audiences for a vote against the overthrow of right-to-work laws. "The press is giving Carter a free ride," Udall said in an interview last week. "Nobody ever asked him about right-to-work."

Actually, the subject seldom comes up in Carter's appearances, but he was asked about it in an interview with the *Globe* last month.

Georgia has a right-to-work law that forbids a closed union shop, and during his term as governor Carter said he met with labor leaders who wanted to overturn the law. "I told them if they were successful in getting the legislation passed, I would sign it," Carter said. "But I told them I would not take it on as a crusade."

It was a safe position to take in Georgia, because labor is so ineffectual politically here that the measure had no chance for passage.

But now that he is a serious contender for the Democratic nomination, Carter must deal with the AFL-CIO power brokers, just as he must face other new questions and investigations into his record and rhetoric.

It is the price he is paying for early success.

Carter's Black Neighbor Displaced

(*Boston Globe*, July 28, 1976)

I spent much of the summer of 1976 in Plains, Ga. One day, as I caught
a ride from a gathering at the home of Carter's mother, Miss Lillian, at
her "Pond House," my driver, a local woman, remarked as we passed
the candidate's home, "You know, they're tearing down that old nigger
house across from Jimmy's." No one there seemed to think much about
it, but I did.

PLAINS, Ga.—They are tearing down the wooden shack across the
street from Jimmy Carter's house.

It had been the home of a black family, Mr. and Mrs. A. Z. Pittman
and seven of their children. Now the Pittmans have become the first
displaced persons of Plains, victim of the sudden growth in interest in
the little town.

There are conflicting accounts of why the Pittmans were forced to
move. Their landlord, Marlin Poole of nearby DeSoto, "told us Mr.
Carter was going to be President and didn't want a house like that
across the street," Mrs. Pittman said.

Carter said yesterday that neither he nor any member of his family had asked Poole to evict the Pittmans. "I hate to see them go," the
Democratic presidential nominee said.

Carter apparently became aware of the family's move when workers began demolishing the ramshackle house a few days ago. The
house stood behind a clump of trees in a field directly across from the
Carter home.

At that time, Carter expressed his regrets to Pittman, a 67-year-old retired laborer.

Pittman is still permitted to work in the garden he cultivated in the front yard, a plot that produced peas, tomatoes, collard greens, butterbeans, squash, okra, and green peppers and was said to be the nicest garden in town.

He sometimes sold bunches of greens and okra to Carter's 8-year-old daughter, Amy, who would be sent by her mother to buy fresh vegetables. The garden also helped to feed the Pittman family, who paid $16 a month rent for the house and the land.

"We could raise things there," Mrs. Pittman said. "If you don't raise for your own you can't have nothing."

When the season is over, however, Pittman will have to give up the garden forever.

The welfare department found a $39-a-month apartment for the Pittmans in a housing project in nearby Americus, but they can't grow vegetables there.

Every day now, Pittman drives out to Plains to pick vegetables and to slop the one pig he has left, which he moved to another lot across Highway 280.

He was dressed in a straw hat and neat, inexpensive brown shirt and pants as he fed the animal yesterday afternoon, and he broke down and wept as he discussed the move.

"I don't like it, to tell the truth," he said. "I have to drive ten miles a day over here to work this land and feed my little pig."

"I might have been a little mistreated in the deal, but I love Mr. Carter as a white man. I know he don't know nothing about it. He's a Christian gentleman. I hated to leave, to tell the truth. Mr. Carter wasn't an associate of mine, but he had my sympathies."

Pittman had lived on the property for three years. The house was dilapidated and had an outdoor toilet, but he preferred it to the housing project.

He said Poole, the owner of the property, had told him he would replace the house with a "double-wide trailer."

"After a while he come again and said it would cost too much so I'd have to wait until he sold some of his land. Then he come back and said we had to move."

That was in April, Pittman said, after "I had already planted my crop. I spent thirty sure hard dollars for seeds."

"He [Poole] told me the house had to be tore down," Pittman said. "He said the Democratic Party came to him, but to tell you the truth I don't know about that."

Poole is in Canada and could not be reached. His 24-year-old son, Michael, said they had been planning to tear down the house for about a year but had no plans to develop the property.

Was there community pressure to tear down the house?

"I don't know, I've been out of town," he said and referred questions to Poole's lawyer, Anthony May of Leesburg.

In a telephone interview, May said he'd "rather not make any comment" when asked about reports Poole had been asked to tear down the house because it was an eyesore.

Billy Carter, the candidate's younger brother and manager of the Carter enterprises in Plains, vigorously denied that any member of his family had a role in the Pittman's eviction.

He said he had bought land in the area from Poole, but said Poole wanted to hold on to the property immediately adjacent to the candidate's house.

As Carter rose politically the property skyrocketed in value.

Another property owner in the area has petitioned the town to change his lot from residential zoning to commercial in order to build a souvenir stand. Poole has made no such move yet, but other developers are at large in the town. Two men from Americus are installing a delicatessen on Main Street. A professor is selling guided tours of the town.

"This is the very thing Jimmy talked about," Carter's press secretary Jody Powell said yesterday, "that he didn't want Plains changed."

But Pittman, the first to be pushed out of Plains, said he had not asked Carter to intervene on his behalf.

"He was traveling miles and miles around the country. He was busy trying to help the working man, and I just felt like he didn't need none of my problems," he said.

The Next President Returns in Tears

(*Boston Globe*, November 4, 1976)

It had been a long, grueling year for all of us, and with a sense of relief we boarded Carter's charter to fly from his home in southwest Georgia to Atlanta to await election night returns. Strolling through the plane, Carter was confident that he would win and dismissed polls that indicated a close race. But later in the evening the atmosphere grew tense at the convention center, where thousands of Carter's followers had gathered; after midnight, their candidate still lacked the few electoral college votes he needed for victory. Finally, Mississippi reported that Carter had won the state and he was over the top.

Before dawn, we prepared to fly back to Carter's home. As he walked down the plane's aisle again—as president-elect—I said to him, "Governor, congratulations! I didn't have to labor to deliver Massachusetts, but I had to work like hell to get you Mississippi." Instead of responding to my intended humor, he chose to remember our clashes. He fixed me with a glare and snapped, "If it weren't for people like you, this election would have been over at 9 o'clock last night." And he turned his back and marched to his first-class compartment. His reaction seemed surprising for a man just elected president of the United States, but it was impossible for me not to appreciate the drama when he got to Plains.

PLAINS, Ga.—At last it was over, the campaign that was entering its third winter, and Jimmy Carter had come home the victor.

On the ride from the Albany, Ga., airport to Plains the sun had begun to light up the bayous and pecan orchards, and by the time Carter's motorcade moved into town a large crowd was waiting for him in front of the railroad depot.

At that time, 7 yesterday morning, the President-elect of the United States began to break down a little.

It had been a campaign that had first labored through the bitter cold of New Hampshire and Iowa; a campaign that had suffered an ignominious primary defeat in Massachusetts and had known much loneliness before blossoming.

Through it all his townspeople, his fellow Georgians, and Southerners who supported a native son had stuck with him.

And he acknowledged it in his homecoming, with a rare public display of humility and emotion.

He gave his maverick brother, Billy, whose eyes were red from drinking all night, a bear hug as he mounted the platform.

Then he said to the crowd, which included many people who were crying with joy and exhaustion, "I told you I didn't intend to lose."

"I came through twenty-two months and I didn't get choked up until . . ." then his voice broke and he could not continue because he was weeping, too.

He turned and embraced his wife, Rosalynn, whose face was streaked with tears. He borrowed a tissue to wipe his tears away. Then he was able to continue.

". . . Until I turned the corner and saw you standing here and said that people that foolish [to stay up all night] . . . you can't be beat."

"I had the best organization any candidate ever had," he said.

"I had the best family any candidate ever had."

"I had the best home community any candidate ever had."

"I had the best supporters in my home state any candidate ever had."

"And the only reason we were close last night was because the candidate wasn't quite good enough as a campaigner. But I'll make up for that when I'm President."

And so, a Southerner had been elected President, and yesterday the little town of Plains was winding down from the biggest night it had ever experienced.

While the ubiquitous tourists continued to prowl the one main street, many of those who had made the long march with Carter sprawled on the grass beside the railroad tracks under a warm November sun, reflecting on the end of the campaign and the beginning of a Carter administration.

Even in the final twenty-four hours they had seen the different facets of Carter's personality:

- The cockiness early Tuesday when he flew to Atlanta expecting a ringing mandate and criticized the pollsters for predicting that it would be close.
- The flat victory speech before thousands of supporters at 4 a.m. yesterday in the World Convention Center in Atlanta.
- The impatience an hour later when the buses carrying his staff and the press became separated from his motorcade to the Atlanta Airport, forcing him to wait on his plane thirty minutes before they arrived. Two of his close aides prevailed upon him not to leave the rest of his party, but when the boarding of the passengers took too long, Carter strode to the rear of the plane to expedite the departure home.
- And finally, in mid-afternoon yesterday, the presidential Carter, who returned to the depot platform to read a brief statement to tourists and newsmen.

President Ford had called at 11:04 a.m. to deliver what Carter described as a "gracious expression of congratulations and cooperation."

Because of Ford's hoarseness, the message was read to Carter by Ford's chief of staff, Richard Cheney.

Carter said he told Ford of his admiration for his "strong, well-planned, and effective campaign."

He said he was grateful for Ford's willingness to cooperate during the transition period, and disclosed that members of his staff were already meeting with Fords' aides to facilitate the transfer of executive power from a Republican to a Democratic administration.

Mayor Billy Carter?

(*Boston Globe*, December 6, 1976)

During my many months as a part-time resident of Sumter County, Georgia, while covering Carter (I still remember my mailing address: Best Western Motel, Room 220, Americus, Ga.), I became friends with Billy Carter. I think he liked me because I was Southern. Billy resented members of the press corps who looked upon the South and the little town of Plains with condescension. (One Washington-based reporter actually strolled around in coveralls with a piece of straw in his mouth.)

Most of my colleagues went to church regularly with the candidate; I preferred to drink beer with Billy at his service station, where he gave it away on Sundays because Sabbath sales were illegal in Georgia. Billy decided to run for mayor during the period when the Carter press corps was still stuck in rural Georgia while his victorious brother chose his cabinet. Billy's zany—and ultimately unsuccessful—campaign became an amusing break in our routine.

Billy lost the election, but the Christmas tree mysteriously disappeared shortly afterwards.

PLAINS, Ga.—Billy Carter's first official act—if he is elected mayor of Plains today—will be to cut down an artificial Christmas tree just erected on public land across the highway from his service station.

"In fact," the brother of the President-elect said Saturday morning, a can of beer in hand, "me and the boys were thinking about getting together tonight and chopping the goddamn thing down then."

He looked scornfully at the tree, a thin, towering green plastic monstrosity, which was shimmering in the late autumn sun. It was donated to the town and is a symbol of all the things Billy Carter thinks are wrong with Plains these days.

Two weeks ago, he decided to challenge Mayor A. L. Blanton, a quiet man who works at Albany Airport, about forty miles from Plains, during the week and cuts hair in Plains on Saturdays.

Blanton, like Billy Carter, professes to be opposed to the exploitation of Plains, so the real issue seems to be personality. "Hell, I just don't like him," says Carter.

About 300 residents are eligible to vote. The challenger said he expected "CBS to project a winner fifteen seconds after the polls close."

Although he anticipates drawing much of the community's black vote, Carter conceded he is the underdog because most of the voters are white Baptists unamused by the doings at his service station.

A few years ago he was elected to the town council, succeeded in passing an ordinance permitting the sale of beer in Plains, obtained the first beer license for himself, and was voted out of office in the next election.

In defiance of the prohibitionists, Billy Carter threw another of his periodic barbeques Saturday, what one of his supporters claimed was "the start of a victory celebration."

It was, in fact, a convention of professional good old boys who play their roles as well as any of the characters in Plains.

In the backyard of the service station, a rack of chicken parts was broiling over a bed of charcoal while a kettle of deer stew boiled. Six feet away was a pool of stagnant rainwater, rusted tire rims, gunk, and empty beer cans.

"Billy believes in ecology," said Randy Coleman, a Carter employee at the peanut warehouse. He belched and pitched another beer can into the water.

"That's the only river in Plains," Carter said. "There's a big catfish in there that comes up for air about every thirty seconds."

Coleman is "finance chairman" for the campaign. Last week he sold a bunch of T-shirts printed with "Billy Carter for Mayor" for $3 each.

They were snatched up, not by potential voters, but by the droves of tourists willing to pay any price for a Carter artifact.

Flushed by that financial success and plenty of beer, Coleman was charitable at the barbeque. "Naked women get to eat free," he kept shouting.

Leon Johnson, Billy's "campaign manager," appeared with two more packs of beer and announced that the funds were "down to $4.15, about enough for a pint of whiskey."

Johnson, a contractor who is installing a sewer line in Plains, lives in a trailer outside town and can't vote. However, Billy indicates that Johnson will be in line for a Plains cabinet post if the candidate wins.

Also under consideration for a ranking job in the Carter town administration is Bud Duvall. Carter has designated him his "press secretary—because nobody can understand him."

Duvall, a bachelor, is touted as a "good catch" to women visitors because he is alleged to have money buried all over Sumter County.

In the middle of the revelry Saturday afternoon, the next President of the United States arrived at the barbecue. Stepping gingerly to avoid the debris, Jimmy Carter said he planned to vote for Billy Carter.

For Brother Billy, the Tab Comes Due

(*Boston Globe*, March 11, 1979)

With some sense of guilt, I made a sad return to Plains to retrace some
of Billy Carter's manic behavior. I had been a party to some of it myself.
He had invited me to fly on his chartered jetliner to Washington for
his brother's inauguration, so I chose that route, giving up my seat on
the final flight of the president-elect's own charter, "Peanut One"—on
which I had logged tens of thousands of miles.

On Jan. 19, 1977, as we prepared to board the "First Brother's
plane" in nearby Albany, Ga., I treated Billy and his retinue of good
ole boys to early morning Bloody Marys at the airport bar. One of
them viewed a stalk of celery in his drink with suspicion and demanded
to know, "Who put the goddamn cabbage in my drink?" We drank
our way to Washington, and when we arrived, Billy put his wife and
children into a limousine and climbed into a bus with me—because I
had a pint of Jack Daniel's that we could sip on the way to the hotel.

It would be the last time I ever saw him. As reports of his self-
destructive antics piled up during the Carter presidency, I concluded
that I—and other reporters who had helped make him notorious—had
created our own Frankenstein's monster. Billy eventually expelled his
demons and quit drinking. But he died a decade later of pancreatic
cancer.

PLAINS, Ga.—For more than two years he was on stage, the merchant
of foolishness in his theater of the absurd.

He gave outrageous quotes to reporters for free publicity and peddled outlandish behavior to promoters for as much as $5,000 a performance. For awhile, excess was success for the President's brother, Billy Carter.

But recently his string began to play out, and last Tuesday night he was admitted to the Alcoholic Rehabilitation Center at Long Beach Naval Hospital in California to begin a stern regimen that will last six to eight weeks.

Back home in Plains, his friends and members of his family hope the treatment will restore Billy Carter, for in recent weeks he has been beset by many problems, his health has deteriorated, and he has become a public embarrassment.

He had fallen under the shadow of a Justice Department investigation of a $3 million line of credit that Bert Lance's National Bank of Georgia extended to Carter's Warehouse in 1976, and he had created problems for the president with his comments about Jews. There have also been recent revelations that Billy Carter took out large personal loans after his brother was elected—at a time when he was bragging that he was making twice as much as the president's $200,000 salary.

He has been so troubled, a close friend said, that before he was first hospitalized in nearby Americus two weeks ago, he had begun drinking as soon as he arose each morning. "He was not eating anything. He was smoking four or five packs of cigarettes a day, and I mean inhaling them deep down. The last time I saw him he could hardly breathe," the friend said.

As he was collapsing physically, his problems were compounded by a sudden reduction in his income. The market for his antics had shrunk to nearly nothing.

"It was after he talked about the Jews," said Leon Johnson, who helps run Billy Carter's Service Station. "After that he got cancelled by the *Hollywood Squares* and everybody else."

Carter's agent, Tandy Rice of Nashville, confirmed Friday that demands for Billy Carter had dwindled to "just about zero" after he was linked with Libya.

Rice said he did not learn of Billy Carter's involvement with Libya until Billy called him from Rome last fall on the way to North Africa, indicating that the President's brother was approached directly by Libyans. Since that time Billy has acted as a goodwill ambassador for the radical Arab nation, which harbors terrorists.

During a recent visit to the United States by a Libyan delegation, Carter declared them to be some of his best friends and suggested that they had been unfairly tarred by "the Jewish media."

He also observed, "There's a hell of a lot more Arabians than there is Jews."

The incident set off protests by Jewish organizations and forced the president—who has his own problems with the same politically important groups over his Mideast policy—to disassociate himself from his brother's remarks.

Billy Carter's response to the criticism from the Jews was to tell a radio reporter: "They can kiss my ass."

Following that episode, the president again disassociated himself from his brother's remarks. But he added: "Billy is my brother. He is seriously ill at this point. I love him . . . and I know for a fact he is not anti-Semitic."

If it was not anti-Semitic, it still showed an insensitivity toward Jews that is probably related to the fact that Billy Carter comes from a little town where there are no Jews. And, to begin to understand Billy Carter, it is important to understand the subculture that he has chosen for his environment.

It is a male-dominated society whose members make their living from the soil or from hard work at assembly lines. They are more concerned about the price of seed than AT&T stock. They play poker instead of polo. They do not read John Kenneth Galbraith.

In the evening, they do not slip off to fashionably dark bars with their secretaries, but they like to congregate at roadhouses to drink and tell stories and play jokes among themselves.

In Plains, their temple is Billy Carter's Service Station.

He bought it a few years ago to establish a sort of clubhouse for himself and his friends, winning a seat on the town council, siring an ordinance to permit the sale of beer in Plains, and then obtaining the first license for himself.

When the service station was threatened by a fire in the summer of 1976, Billy Carter had to be restrained from endangering himself in his attempt to save the building. He began crying and shouting that it was "all I've got in the world." And when a photographer attempted to capture his grief on film, Billy Carter tried to fight him.

It was an early warning signal that he lacked the strong self-discipline that is a characteristic of his brother, and, as the months in Plains passed under the heavy scrutiny of an international press corps, Billy Carter became the "best copy" in town.

Rather than remain in the background of his brother, Billy Carter relished his role as an errant prince. He regaled reporters with irreverent stories about Jimmy Carter and the Baptists.

The afternoon that his son, Earl, was born, he left the hospital shortly after the birth to play softball with the usual gang of reporters and off-duty Secret Service agents. A television crew caught him for an interview. "And how big is the baby?" the correspondent asked. "Eight and a half pounds," Billy Carter responded proudly, adding that the infant's genitals accounted for eight pounds. Only he did not use the word genitals. "Cut!" a CBS producer shouted. Billy Carter cackled.

During the interregnum before his brother was inaugurated, Billy Carter ran for mayor of Plains, and his chief campaign promise was to chop down a tall, ugly plastic Christmas tree someone had erected on the town's greensward. He lost the election, but within hours nightriders tied the tree to the back of a car and dragged it down the highway out of Plains.

On the eve of the inauguration, Billy Carter chartered a jetliner for a hundred of his friends to go to Washington. The group celebrated all the way, and by the time they reached their hotel Billy was drinking boilermakers, barely conscious and drooling copiously.

There was a time, when he was still managing the Carter family's peanut warehouse, that Billy Carter rose before dawn and put in a ten-hour day at work before he went to his service station. He drank from seven-ounce cans of Pabst Blue Ribbon, hobnobbed with his buddies for awhile, and went home for dinner with his wife and six children.

By all accounts, he was a good family man. "Billy is as good as gold," one store owner in Plains said last week. "He'd give you the shirt off his back. I really hope this treatment brings him around, because he had gotten downright embarrassing. The problem was that he didn't have anything to discipline himself with. When he had that warehouse, he knew he had to get up every morning and work."

Since Jimmy Carter owned the controlling interest in the warehouse, he had his peanut business put into a blind trust after he became president. Atlanta attorney Charles Kirbo was in charge of the trust, and he leased the warehouse and the Carter land to outsiders, spurning Billy Carter's bid to take over the operation. It earned him bitter accolade from Billy later. "Charlie Kirbo is about the dumbest bastard I ever met."

In lieu of his daily duties at the warehouse, it was easy for Billy Carter to turn to a career as a human spectacle, appearing as an honored guest at belly-flop contests, hot-air-balloon rides, and rodeos. He was paid handsomely, and he hired a couple of friends from Plains to travel with him so that he would not be lonely.

Tales of his experiences on the road were always awaited at the service station. The more outrageous the story, the better it was received. He and his friends could come home with stories of wild, all-night stands in Nevada bars that dwarfed mundane accounts of getting "knee-walking drunk" in Georgia and escaping arrest for public drunkenness.

"Billy is a highly intelligent person who was shoved into a situation where everywhere he goes he was expected to be a showman and to make a blatant statement," one friend of his said.

There was no surcease.

"Tourists would come down here," said a Plains businesswoman, "and they'd say, 'What's wrong? We just saw Billy and he didn't have a beer in his hand.'"

So he would invariably put a beer, or something stronger, in his hand.

He began to pick fights.

Larry Flynt, who claimed to have been religiously converted by

Carter's sister, Ruth Stapleton, started a newspaper in Plains and said he wanted to use Carter's mother, Lillian, as a centerfold in his better-known publication, *Hustler*.

Billy Carter subsidized a rival publication, incongruously called the *Plains Statesman*. The contract was written on a brown paper bag. Carter's partner in the enterprise "was so sorry [a Southern expression for worthless] that he went up the road and lost all the money the same night," according to Johnson. The paper is not a success and Carter is no longer associated with it.

Billy Carter also declared war on his first cousin, State Sen. Hugh Carter, who sells "antiques" in a store across the railroad tracks from the service station. Billy has denounced him as a "self-made son of a bitch."

Last year, the gang at the service station sponsored an opponent to run against Hugh Carter. Their candidate was a friend of Billy's, known around town simply as "Chicken."

Mounted on the wall of the service station are four snapshots of the challenger in various stages of drunkenness—in the first urinating on an automobile tire, in the last passed out. It passed for a campaign poster for "Chicken."

Hugh Carter won re-election, despite the efforts of his cousin, and last week he said he would not talk about Billy "because he's family."

The incidents in Plains, once faintly humorous, had taken on an ugly aura.

"Standard Idiot Behavior"

(*Boston Globe*, July 20, 1980)

I was at the Republican convention in Detroit when I got word that Hodding Carter, a friend from our Mississippi Delta days, would be willing to talk to me, on the record, about his disillusionment with President Carter. Hodding had been a high-profile spokesman for the State Department and left the government earlier in the year when Secretary of State Cyrus Vance resigned following an abortive attempt to rescue American hostages in Tehran.

The *Globe* immediately dispatched me on a three-flight journey, which I completed in a small prop plane that landed at little Owl's Head airport in Maine. I found Hodding, who had been seething over the White House's treatment of Vance's departure and his perception of the president's disdain for the State Department, quite ready to talk. Our conversation lasted for several hours and I took pages and pages of notes. When it was over, we played tennis and had a good "off the record" dinner.

I flew back to Boston early the next morning, going through my notes on the way. The more I read, the more I thought: My god, this *really* is some good stuff. I wrote the story that Saturday afternoon. It led our Sunday paper and had national repercussions.

CAMDEN, Maine—Former State Department spokesman Hodding Carter 3d says that some of the measures taken by President Jimmy Carter to control foreign policy leaks were offensive and demoralizing, and he blames Zbigniew Brzezinski for convincing the president that the State Department was the source.

Carter, who left the administration this month, was critical of Brzezinski's National Security Council operation and said it was responsible for the "most substantive leaks."

In an interview Friday at his summer home in Camden, overlooking Penobscot Bay, Carter also said the administration had a misconception about the way reporters work in this country.

The White House, he said, "sees the press as the enemy.

"There are some people there, who are major leakers themselves, who think the only way reporters get a story is through a leak. They think reporters are clods and animals, and that you simply feed them," said Carter, who is no relation to the president and who has spent much of his life as a journalist.

He left the government two weeks ago—not long after the resignation of his friend and boss, Cyrus Vance, as secretary of state—and retreated to the quiet of Maine after three and a half years at the heart of the action in Washington.

However, he was pitched back into the maelstrom last week by a series of news stories involving leaks and bureaucratic strife. As he sat on a large rock rising out of the back lawn of a "castle" he purchased with part of the proceeds of the sale of the Mississippi newspaper his father founded and he once ran, Carter reflected on the in-fighting of the nation's foreign policy apparatus.

Carter's remarks came after reports that he had refused to sign an affidavit declaring that he was not responsible for leaks that led to a news story about a debate within the administration over increased military aid to Morocco.

The article appeared in the *Washington Post* last October. It reportedly angered the president so much that he sought affidavits from such high-ranking officials as Vance, Brzezinski, and CIA director Stansfield Turner in which they professed their innocence

Carter said he was approached by FBI agents. "I talked to them quite willingly. I told them it was not a story in which I was involved."

Shortly before he left the State Department—he announced his intention to resign shortly after Vance quit—Carter said he was presented with an affidavit to sign. "I was led to believe that it came from the highest levels of the White House. I refused to sign a presumptive statement that says I'm a good boy."

Asked if he had been offended by the affidavit, Carter said: "Of course I found it offensive. But I found it sillier than offensive. It was also counterproductive."

He said the president had depressed many members of the State Department hierarchy in an earlier attempt to stop leaks.

Vance and sixteen other State Department officials were summoned to the White House in February 1979 for a dressing down after a report by CBS that U.S. officials believed the Iranian government of Shapour Bakhtiar would soon fall.

The president, who was enraged over the story, according to accounts of the incident, threatened to fire any officials who had leaks coming out of their divisions at the State Department, even if the officials themselves were not directly responsible.

Carter, who was assistant secretary of state at the time, said he was "heartsick" after the meeting.

"I was mad. I felt it was a bum rap. I felt that the procedure amounted to a kangaroo court. It was a humiliation to Vance and destructive to the loyalty of those who had to sit there and be told: You are untrustworthy. You are my problem."

The Bakhtiar government fell within days of the meeting.

Carter is married to Patricia Derian, an assistant secretary of state in charge of human rights. She was also singled out in a *Washington Post* story last week as a prime suspect for leaks. "We start with Patt Derian and then we add to the list," an investigator of leaks was quoted as saying.

"Patt is articulate, and she opposes policy openly," Carter said. "Some of the idiots who work in government are not used to people speaking up. In a town which shoots from ambush, they can't believe anybody will look them in the eye and disagree."

It has been reported that there are fifteen criminal investigations of leaks of military or diplomatic information, and that another ten investigations were closed last year. Carter said he had not been aware of any of them until the FBI discussed the story of the Moroccan aid with him.

As for his wife, Carter said she was "demonstrably" clear of guilt because not a single case had been proved against her.

Carter acknowledged that the State Department "leaks—and leaks like a sieve," but said that other government agencies, including the NSC, the White House, the CIA, and the Defense Department, also leaked stories "for self-serving reasons and for policy reasons."

"I think that one sad thing that happened was that the president, over time, became convinced by Brzezinski—who is doing it for a reason—that it's the State Department" that is responsible for most of the leaks.

"The most substantive leaks come from the White House," where Brzezinski's NSC staff works, Carter said.

Carter was especially critical of the relationship between Brzezinski and Richard Burt, a reporter who covers national security issues for the *New York Times*.

"You don't have to read anything less juvenile than Richard Burt to see Zbigniew Brzezinski's lips move while Burt writes," Carter said. "Burt is notorious for being an open wound on the National Security Council. They turn on the arterial flow and he transmits it to the *New York Times*."

If the leaks do not come directly from Brzezinski, Carter said, "it's from his aides. I have no idea if the President is aware of it, but everybody else in town [Washington] surely knows."

In an article in the *Times* last week, Burt wrote that a spirit of cooperation was prevailing between Brzezinski and the new secretary of state, Edmund S. Muskie. One of the reasons cited by the reporter's sources for the "relative absence of rancor" was the departure of some of Brzezinski's "fiercest critics" at the State Department, such as Carter and Leslie H. Gelb, former director of politico-military affairs.

The *Times* story followed by a week an account in the *Washington Post* in which sources close to Muskie—widely believed to be Washington lawyer and longtime Muskie associate Berl Bernhard—complained of Brzezinski's attempts to upstage the former Maine senator.

During the president's European trip last month, Brzezinski appeared on television repeatedly and the White House distributed texts of his interviews.

"Because the president allows him to do it, and because Brzezinski loves to do it, you have a highly visible national security adviser," Carter said.

After the *Post* article critical of Brzezinski appeared, Carter said, Burt "went over [to the NSC] and got his tap turned on."

Burt, reached for comment in Washington yesterday, said that Muskie had told a *New York Times* group prior to the publication of his article that the situation vis-à-vis the NSC was "working harmoniously."

The *Times* reporter said he felt Hodding Carter's comments were "unfair" because he had talked to State Department officials, as well as the NSC staff, before writing the story.

Burt also pointed out that it was one of his stories about a possible site for an electronic listening post in Norway to verify Soviet compliance with the strategic arms limitation treaty that triggered one of the government investigations into leaks.

Hodding Carter's attack on Brzezinski in the interview with the *Globe* represents one of the sharpest and most open criticisms in the history of disputes between the State Department and the NSC.

The conflict between the State Department, which lies in Foggy Bottom, and the White House's NSC will continue, Carter said, "until the president brings one to heel."

Several times during his administration, the president has ordered the State Department and the NSC to stop sniping at each other. It has created truces, but Carter said that eventually "somebody from across town would throw a knife into us."

He said the State Department was repeatedly branded for being "soft on the Russians," which he called "reprehensible" conduct by "guys on that [NSC] staff, starting at or near the top."

He also called it "standard idiot behavior in a bureaucracy with overlapping turf."

Carter said that Vance often differed with Brzezinski on approaches to foreign policy, but would accept the president's decision even if he lost.

"It is a fact that Brzezinski does not easily take no for an answer, or accept it when a decision goes against him," Carter said. "Vance would often think an issue was decided and then look over his shoulder and see Brzezinski nibbling away."

During his years as State Department spokesman, Carter was popular among the diplomatic press corps. Asked if he had ever leaked a story himself, the 45-year-old Carter grinned and answered cryptically: "I think I felt an intense loyalty to the Secretary of State and the President, to policies as I understood them."

Carter became well known to the nation as the administration's chief spokesman on the Iranian crisis in the first months after the hostages were seized. He said he agreed with the president's handling of that issue.

However, he said the president's remark in which he called Muskie a more effective Secretary of State than Vance—whom the president described as "bogged down in details"—was "a sad and unfortunate misuse of words."

"What he said could only hurt the man who bent over backwards to keep from hurting him."

The Democrats' Odd Couple

(*Boston Globe*, August 14, 1980)

The struggle between President Carter and Ted Kennedy had been a great political story, reaching its climax at the Democratic convention where Kennedy delivered his valedictory "The dream will never die" speech. I drew upon my contacts in both camps to write this piece, but lost a bet I made with Dick Moe, Vice President Mondale's chief of staff. I felt the animosity was so intense that Kennedy would not appear on stage with Carter. He did.

NEW YORK—After nearly a year of conflict in which hatreds were honed to a sharp edge, it had come at last to a desperate effort to reconcile Sen. Edward M. Kennedy with President Jimmy Carter, to bridge the gulf between liberal and pragmatist, Catholic and Southern Baptist, Boston and Plains. For all their contempt for Kennedy, the President and his men came to New York wanting his endorsement, and after his electrifying speech Tuesday night, needing it even more.

Like occupants of the White House before them, they have a "Kennedy complex," born out of envy at his wealth and the ease with which he reached prominence. But it is not an inferiority complex, and like good Calvinists, they are proud of their own hard work, and believe that they are superior to the Kennedy crowd.

Yet there was an underlay of apprehension among them yesterday. Jody Powell, a character out of Faulkner, with eyes like a predator and wit like a sabre, found it necessary to praise Kennedy, the candidate he once ridiculed as a "fat, spoiled rich kid."

"I thought it was a fine speech," Powell said yesterday, a smile betraying his understatement.

Carter, himself, called it "one of the greatest speeches I ever heard" before going into seclusion shortly after arriving in New York.

And in the Carter headquarters at the Sheraton Centre, a tower of New York kitsch, they waited for word from the losers, sequestered in their own retreat four blocks away in the Waldorf-Astoria, that symbol of cosmopolitan luxury so foreign to Sumter County, Ga.

For the first time this year, Kennedy held the high card, and he was holding out for every concession he could extract from his adversary, the president he has derided in private as a weird, mean little man.

On Tuesday night, in the flush of the drama his speech had created, Kennedy gathered several acquaintances at his suite. The discussion soon turned to the decision he faced—whether to appear on the podium with Carter tonight.

It was an eclectic group outside his immediate staff, including New York Gov. Hugh Carey, Massachusetts Atty. Gen. Francis X. Bellotti, historian Arthur Schlesinger Jr., Rep. Edward Markey of Massachusetts, and Kennedy's sister Jean Smith.

Carey, another Irish Catholic from the East, was said to have spoken, with incredulity, of how he considered Carter strange and naive. Because Carey had supported the unsuccessful move to free the delegates from Carter's grip, the decision to land Air Force One in Newark instead of New York was interpreted as a rebuke to the governor. Carter was not smart enough, Carey said, to know that the jurisdiction of the Port Authority of New York and New Jersey extends to the Newark Airport.

Schlesinger, the quintessence of Eastern liberalism, was said to have recommended to Kennedy that he endorse Carter this week, in order to free himself of the burden of campaigning for a man he did not like in the fall.

It was said to have been a refined conversation, like a scene out of

O'Hara, with Jean Smith making a forceful argument for Kennedy to join Carter for the sake of party unity, and with Markey also encouraging him to do so for the sake of his chances in 1984. Kennedy had resurrected himself by the force of his speech, and to fail to appear at the podium would probably dash his political future.

Bellotti, according to a source in the room, advised Kennedy that he should not feel compelled to pay fealty to Carter just because it was traditional to present a tableau of unity on the convention's closing night.

Away from the air-conditioned splendor of the Waldorf, in sweltering Madison Square Garden corridors lit by television klieg lights, the talk was cruder among some of the Kennedy loyalists.

They wore Brooks Brothers suits, but their language came from McSorley's saloon. They denounced Carter in the vilest terms, and one friend of Kennedy's said he hoped the senator would strike Carter if an attempt was made to get Kennedy to raise the President's hand in the gesture the victor usually enjoys.

Among those who worked for the man who expressed gratification that he had not had to "kiss Kennedy's ass" in winning the nomination in 1976 and vowed "I'll whip his ass" in order to win renomination, the mood was sober, in spite of their triumph.

Instead of rubbing it in, as they longed to do, they actually had to console Kennedy in an effort to keep him from bolting to Cape Cod before the convention ends.

In the first telephone call between the two campaigns following Kennedy's withdrawal from the race Monday night, a Kennedy aide had only one request. There were many Kennedy workers in the city without tickets to the convention galleries, and they wanted to see their candidate's appearance Tuesday night. The Carter campaign obliged by turning over many tickets they controlled to Kennedy for the evening.

To avoid antagonizing Kennedy when he spoke, the Carter delegates were instructed by their whips to greet him civilly and warned not to boo him, despite the catcalls that were being heaped on spokesmen for the administration during the debate over a commitment to public jobs that Kennedy wanted.

It was uncommon conduct for the same people who underwrote the television commercial that implicitly attacked Kennedy's troubled marriage.

But they were determined this week to make their own political marriage between two enemies, the millionaire's son from New England and the driven self-achiever from the rural South.

Plains Knew When Carter Wept

(*Boston Globe*, November 5, 1980)

Written on Election Day 1980, this piece could serve as a bookend with the one I wrote from the same spot four years earlier. Jimmy Carter cried both times. But this time, the story was far more painful.

I found myself in an interesting position that day. On the press plane during our pre-dawn flight from Seattle back to Georgia, I had been quietly informed by a ranking member of Carter's staff that their latest poll, completed a few hours earlier, showed that the president's support had collapsed almost overnight. I was told that Carter, who felt he was leading, would surely lose the race with Ronald Reagan. "We're going to have to tell Jimmy on the way home," the aide said. "I'm glad I'm not on Air Force One."

Later that morning, it was my turn to be the pool reporter, so I accompanied the president to the polling place. I knew that he knew he would lose, but I was sworn to secrecy until after the polls closed, so Carter had no idea that I knew of the poll. I asked him a couple of lame questions. He seemed downcast, his replies as weak as my questions. I awkwardly tried to prompt him, telling him I hadn't heard his usual, confident boast: "I don't intend to lose." So he delivered that line, for the last time, almost grudgingly. Then he walked over to the old depot to address his followers, and he broke down.

PLAINS, Ga.—After a final, punishing campaign journey of more than 6,000 miles, President Jimmy Carter made a melancholy return to his hometown yesterday. He struggled to keep from crying as he told his followers of the "difficult" and "politically costly" decisions that he felt were costing him his presidency.

Even though the polls had just opened, he appeared exhausted and disheartened by the grim word from his staff—based on their own polling data—that the election appeared to be irretrievably lost.

Carter had learned the worst a few hours before on the long overnight flight from Seattle to Georgia, news his aides had kept from him until he could complete, in a confident and fighting manner, the last of seven stops on both sides of the continent that they had scheduled for him on the final day of his campaign.

He had not known of it in Seattle, where he rallied a late-night throng in a cavernous airport hangar and blew kisses at a young heckler who held a sign that said: "Carter Blew His Four Years of Time." He had not even lost his composure as another man bearing a sign that read, "Carter's Maternal Grandmother Is a Mulatto," attempted to storm the stage and had to be dragged away. As the hour approached midnight on the Pacific Coast—it was nearly 3 a.m. back home and seventeen hours since he had first set out—Carter delivered one of his finest speeches of the campaign.

But outside the hangar his longtime associate and press secretary, Jody Powell, stood despondent on the airport tarmac, washed by a gentle autumn rain. Powell had heard of Patrick Caddell's latest poll findings over the sophisticated communication system aboard Air Force One on the leg between Portland, Ore., and Seattle. The information showed that Carter had slipped further behind in the target states, and as the president basked in the cheers of the crowd, Powell turned to another Carter aide and said simply, "It's gone."

And Carter, himself, was told before his plane descended at dawn yesterday to the funereal southwest Georgia landscape that was shrouded in a heavy ground fog, the leaves a dull and dying brown in the pecan groves and little calves awaiting slaughter for veal tethered in a field outside Plains.

The president went first to the old red brick schoolhouse he had attended as a boy. Joined by his wife, Rosalynn, he stood with a group of thirty other Plains residents in a foyer where the ceiling was exposed by a gaping hole in the plaster and the paint on the walls was drab and peeling.

He showed little of the old Carter confidence. His complexion was ruddy, and the splotches were visible under the pancake makeup he wore to make himself look healthier on television.

He was asked if he felt he would win. "I hope so," he said. "We'll see." When it was suggested to him that he did not seem confident, he said, "I always think I'll win." He was told he was not using one of his favorite expressions: "I don't intend to lose." So he smiled wanly and spoke up: "All right, I don't intend to lose. Right on."

From the school he went to the old railroad depot that served as his local headquarters in 1976. A crowd was waiting, and he mounted the same platform where he stood triumphantly four years and one day ago, the morning after the 1976 election. He had broken down and wept that day before a cheering mass of his townspeople who were themselves weeping tears of joy over the success of their native son.

This time, Carter's appearance was just as dramatic, though the crowd was smaller and more subdued, as if they sensed that defeat was enveloping the man from Plains.

At first, as he began speaking to the crowd of familiar faces, Carter's voice seemed strong, but by the end, his chin was trembling and his eyes filled with tears.

He recalled how he had gone proudly out from the South four years ago to make profound judgments at the White House "in a time of crisis or a time of solitude." Always, he made these decisions "with the memory of my upbringing here in Plains, the fact that I'm a Southerner, the fact that I'm an American."

It seemed as though he were developing a rationale for his own defeat.

He told the gathering he had "made some difficult decisions. Some of them have not been politically popular." But he insisted that they had been right.

"We've tried to deal fairly with all people, with black people, with those who speak Spanish, with women, for those who've been deprived in life. We've done this in every instance. Sometimes it's aroused the displeasure of others, and sometimes it's been politically costly," he said.

Carter cited the Panama Canal treaties—vilified by conservatives as a giveaway—as another "courageous judgment" by his administration that proved to be damaging politically.

Talking with reporters outside the school, he also said, "The concern about the hostages, the frustration that all Americans have felt, I think has obviously been a negative political factor."

Now he was nearing the end of his last campaign speech. He recalled how many of his neighbors from Georgia, "people from Plains, from Americus, from Richland, from Preston, from Schley County, from around this area have gone all over the nation to speak for me and shake hands with people in other states, to tell them that you have confidence in me and that I would not disappoint them if I became president."

Now it seemed that Carter feared that he had disappointed them, and his jaw quivered.

"I've tried to honor your commitment to those other people," he said, and it became a struggle for him to get the words out. "In the process, I've tried to honor my commitment . . ."—and he had to stop altogether, biting his lips as tears welled in his eyes, before he could finish the sentence—". . . to you."

He collected himself and called out in a voice hoarse from the many speeches in the past twenty-four hours: "God bless you. Thank you. Don't forget to vote, everybody."

And he sprung down from the platform to await what he called "the judgment of the American people."

The Other Version of Carter's Memoirs

(*Boston Globe*, October 17, 1982)

Before I decided to write this first-person piece, which appeared in the *Globe*'s Sunday opinion section, I conducted an internal debate with myself before concluding—perhaps it was a rationalization—that I would not really be breaching an "off the record" agreement. Several anecdotes from our dinner had already been published, and I was prepared to argue that Carter finally broke the embargo with his new book.

Needless to say, after this story was published, Carter was indignant at me again—just like old times. So were some members of his staff—as well as a few of my colleagues who felt I had unfairly scooped them.

Time heals. When I spent a week in Atlanta in 1990 to do a magazine story on Carter's work at his Carter Center, the former president could not have been more gracious. His brother, Billy, had recently died, and we had a good, private conversation about him. While I was there, Carter allowed me to accompany him to classes at Emory and to a couple of luncheon appearances. When he introduced me, he would say, "Curtis knows as many people in Plains as I do."

He went on to write many books. I saw him infrequently over the years. When I did I would usually ask him to sign my copy of his latest book. He always did, as "your friend, Jimmy Carter."

But I never asked him to sign *Keeping Faith*.

WASHINGTON—Just before he left office, Jimmy Carter went home to Georgia for the last time as president, already prepared, he said, "to spend the rest of my life in Plains, to die and be buried here."

At a small dinner party the press corps arranged for Carter and his wife, Rosalynn, at a French restaurant located—of all places—on a highway outside Plains, Carter also talked about how he expected to spend much of the next year or so of his life writing his memoirs.

He said he was pleased to learn that a former president could command a lot of money for a book, and he intended to use the income to pay off debts that, presumably, had accrued after his peanut business fell on hard times when he went to Washington.

He originally planned to write two books—his memoirs as well as a book on the Mideast—but his agent discouraged him, telling him he could "make just as much from one book as from two."

Now, nearly two years after his defeat by Ronald Reagan, Carter has produced that book. It is called *Keeping Faith*, and it is obviously written by Carter himself.

In it, he expounds on some of the themes he merely touched on at dinner that night in Plains, but the book is not nearly as interesting as his private conversation with the eight of us who had covered his presidency. It was a fascinating evening. Afterwards, the reporters compared recollections of quotes and made records of his remarks. I filled twenty pages in my notebook with details. In the months that passed, some of Carter's remarks seeped into print. He has addressed many of the same subjects in his book in a style that one close Carter aide describes as "uh, well, call it presidential."

I remember saying to Carter that night that I felt his old campaign biography *Why Not the Best?*—which had been written in 1975 in his quaint style—was the single most valuable and revealing book about Jimmy Carter. I said I hoped his new memoirs would be as candid as his comments over dinner. They are not. Since Carter has now put his thoughts on these subjects into the public domain, it is interesting to compare some of the things he said on Jan. 10, 1981, with passages in *Keeping Faith*.

Carter's annoyance with the "inertia" of the State Department bureaucracy comes across in his book, but he was much more pointed in his criticism when he talked with us.

The State Department, he told us, "had not produced a new idea in twenty years." They were burdened by a mentality, he said, that made them overly protective of their own areas of expertise and overly cautious about making mistakes.

He said that former Secretary of State Cyrus Vance, who left his administration in the spring of 1980, had been too "reticent." Carter said that he had dispatched Vance to China in 1977 to formalize relations with the People's Republic of China, and that Vance had come home without accomplishing his mission. He said that he had to send his national security adviser, Zbigniew Brzezinski, to get the job done.

(In his book, Carter says that Vance was sent for "exploratory discussions" and attributes the lack of progress to the fact that the Chinese government, in a period of transition, "was still not well acquainted with me or my policies, and probably needed a few more months before deciding how far to trust us on the major discussions.")

Carter defended Brzezinski and said that his National Security Council staff came up with far more suggestions for innovative approaches to foreign policy than the State Department. He also said that Brzezinski was, unfairly, being painted as a "scapegoat."

Hodding Carter, who had quit as State Department spokesman after Vance's resignation, had just written an article in *Playboy* that was critical of the president's foreign policy apparatus and, especially, of Brzezinski.

I asked Carter if he had read it.

"It really pissed me off," Carter said. Then he fixed his eyes on me with a baleful glare—he knew Hodding was an old friend of mine from Mississippi—and declared, "I think Hodding is a creep."

The president said he had only read excerpts of the article in the *Washington Post*. "I marked twenty-five errors in it . . . I was going to send it to him, but I finally just threw it in the trash can," he said.

In this spirit of candor, I asked his impression of Vance's predecessor, Henry Kissinger.

"Brilliant and devious," Carter said.

"He's a liar and everyone in the Mideast knows he lies. [Syrian President Hafez] Assad, [Jordan's King] Hussein, [Egyptian President Anwar] Sadat, they all know he lies," Carter said. Kissinger, he said, could not be trusted.

(In his book, Carter complains that Kissinger undermined his efforts to resolve the Iranian situation, but recalls that "the first one" to call after the abortive rescue raid in Iran was Kissinger, "full of praise and approval of our attempt and offering to help me in any way.")

Discussing his upcoming memoirs, which would run 600 pages, Carter suggested that Kissinger was such an egomaniac that he was supposed to have covered his eight years in the Nixon-Ford administrations in 600–700 pages, but had already spent a thousand pages on the first four years. He said Kissinger had sent him a copy of his latest volume, but that he had not read it.

Of Reagan's Secretary of State–designate, Alexander Haig, Carter was especially biting. Carter said he "made a mistake" when he retained Haig as commander of NATO. "He was political, and I always had the feeling he was running for president." Carter also said that Haig had not been loyal to the Democratic administration.

(In his book, Carter simply observes that Haig, as well as Reagan's first national security adviser, Richard V. Allen, refused to be briefed on Iran during the transition by Carter officials. "A guy named Fred Ikle is the only one that's been designated for a briefing," he writes.)

Carter was reluctant to take shots at Reagan that night, ten days before he would yield the White House to him, but he warned that Reagan's Interior Secretary James Watt "could be a catastrophe." Carter said he was counting on Democratic congressional leaders to rein him in.

Like most American presidents, Carter was obviously charmed by his own image as a world leader. The vast majority of his book deals with foreign affairs.

At the dinner twenty-one months ago, he was asked to give thumbnail comments about other leaders he had known.

Israeli prime minister Menachem Begin was the most "difficult" person he had to face, he said, which was not surprising to those of us who had covered his ups and downs with the Israeli leader.

(In his book, Carter repeatedly expresses exasperation with Begin during efforts to work out a Mideast peace treaty.)

In a humorous moment, Carter said that he hoped two things would endure during the Reagan presidency—that Begin would stay on as prime minister and that Sam Donaldson of ABC (who was at the table) would continue to cover the White House.

Carter was not completely negative, however, and characterized Begin as "a gutsy little guy." He used the same words to describe Joe Clark, who served briefly as prime minister of Canada.

When asked about West German chancellor Helmut Schmidt, with whom he had well-publicized differences, Carter said Schmidt would be friendly in face-to-face meetings, "then he would go home and stab you in the back."

(In his book, Carter describes "an unbelievable meeting" with Schmidt in Venice in which the German leader was "ranting and raving. . . .")

Carter said his favorite leaders were Sadat and former British prime minister James Callaghan. He recalled a summit meeting on the Caribbean island of Guadeloupe when Callaghan was peeved by the seat he had been given at a table underneath a cabana. Behind him, Carter said, "the women were walking around with nothing but little bikini bottoms on," and he gestured below his waist. Callaghan, he said, was quite unhappy that he did not share the view of the other leaders.

He also described the late Japanese prime minister Masayoshi Ohira as "a good buddy of mine." Carter said that he and Ohira had worked together at the Tokyo economic summit in 1979 to prevail upon the leaders of the other industrial nations to cut oil imports, and he said that he hoped his long, lonely trip to Ohira's funeral—which was taken against the advice of White House aides—would help solidify U.S.-Japanese relations.

(In his book, most of these characterizations are repeated, including Carter's sympathetic recollection of Soviet president Leonid

Brezhnev as a peaceful man who did not want a military confrontation with the United States.)

Carter also recalled a state dinner in Caracas (this is not in the book) where the president of Venezuela delivered a forty-five-minute toast. Carter could not remember his name (it was Carlos Andres Peres), but he said the speech was so long that he waived the translation. "It was terrible," he said, one of the ceremonial things about serving as president that he would not miss.

Looking back on his administration, Carter praised his deputy secretary of state, Warren Christopher, as its "finest public servant." Christopher, he said, was better than the president himself. He said he did not choose Christopher to succeed Vance because he needed a prominent figure such as Edmund S. Muskie to command respect overseas.

The chief White House domestic adviser, Stuart Eizenstat, was ranked second most valuable.

Carter had his difficulties with Congress, and concluded that the best ally anyone could have on Capitol Hill was Rep. Jack Brooks (D-Texas), chairman of the House Government Operations Committee. "He is a tough son of a bitch and a mean in-fighter," Carter said admiringly.

(In his book, Carter has high praise for Christopher and says of Brooks, "It was better to have Jack Brooks on my side than against me.")

Carter was considered a proponent of public education, so it was surprising when he talked about his efforts to find a new school for his daughter Amy and revealed that he would have pulled her out of the public schools of the District of Columbia if he had been re-elected.

Asked if he had a commitment to public schools for his children, he answered, "Not really."

He said that White House aides Jody Powell and Frank Moore had already felt compelled to take their children out of the D.C. schools and to enroll them in private schools, and that he would have done the same thing.

(In his book, Carter writes, "We had always been strong supporters of public education, and so Amy was enrolled in District of Columbia schools.")

As the conversation lightened near the end of the two-hour dinner, Carter was asked to tell the "real truth" about the "Killer Rabbit"—the incident that had brought him so much ridicule.

"It's funny," he replied, "I was just looking at a picture of it today. It's a good picture."

Ed Walsh of the *Washington Post* and I teasingly threatened to file a Freedom of Information action to obtain the photo.

Carter said he had been fishing from a small boat in his pond when he heard a splash near the bank and saw a rabbit swimming toward him. "I thought it might be rabid," he said, and spelled it R-A-B-I-D. So I got a paddle and splashed some water toward him."

He said a Secret Service agent shouted to make sure he was all right, while the rabbit turned, swam back to shore and scampered up a hill. A White House photographer, he said, captured the picture of him slapping the water and the rabbit's two ears were clearly visible in the photo.

Afterwards, he said, the Secret Service agent expressed wonder that rabbits could swim. "This one did," Carter said. He said that he had often seen rabbits swim in swamps when they were pursued by dogs.

Part IV
Covering Clinton

The Making of the Candidate

(*Boston Globe*, June 3, 1992)

Bill Clinton is the most gifted, natural politician of the hundreds I covered. A word I used to describe him was "protean"—he tried to please everyone. Blessed with a brilliant mind, an instinct for cunning, he had an ability to escape from the direst of dilemmas. He's also a charming conversationalist. I can remember interviews with him that turned into informal chats about college basketball, books, junk food, mutual friends, and the scourge of tornadoes in the South. I first met him a few weeks after he had been elected governor of Arkansas in 1978, and thought he looked too youthful for the job. I got to know him much better during the course of his 1992 campaign. During that period, one could see Clinton fine-tuning his centrist patterns and developing his ability to reach compromises with competing interests—an approach that became known as "triangulation" in his administration.

When I mentioned my admiration for his political skills to journalists in Arkansas, they warned me of his capacity for smooth talk and deceit. Paul Greenberg, a Pulitzer Prize–winning Arkansas columnist, had already branded Clinton "Slick Willie." (Years later, some of the same Arkansas guys told me I would be sorry Ole Miss hired Houston Nutt for football coach.) After months of exposure to Clinton on the campaign, this was the first of two long pieces I wrote about him as he closed in on the nomination.

LITTLE ROCK—As he has risen from the backwaters of Arkansas politics to the brink of the Democratic presidential nomination, Gov. Bill Clinton has carried with him several riddles.

He would be the first presidential nominee produced by the sex, drugs, and rock 'n' roll generation, a stigma he has borne throughout his campaign. But he seems cut from an earlier, simpler time when a gift for oratory and the power of personal persuasion were the trademarks of a successful politician.

By surviving a grueling set of challenges so far this year, Clinton has established a reputation for toughness and cunning. Yet he is so conciliatory that, as a youngster, he gave up his own name to promote tranquility in his family.

As a voice for national reconciliation, he has straddled so many issues that his convictions seem blurred. But his formative political years were spent in a peace movement where waffling was unacceptable.

He is driven by his desire to be known as a unifying figure, and his political heroes are Abraham Lincoln and Rev. Martin Luther King Jr. But he has created doubts about himself because of unspoken parallels with King, whose moral leadership was made vulnerable by alleged dalliances outside his marriage and whose commitment was questioned when he refused to make the sharp left turn taken by many of his allies.

Political analysts have difficulty classifying Clinton as liberal or conservative, and during the 1992 campaign Clinton has performed rhetorical acrobatics that landed him on opposing sides of issues. He boasts, for example, that his health care proposal is "liberal" because it extends public services to people; in the same breath, he calls it "conservative" because it cuts bureaucracy.

His remarks often sound disingenuous, crafted to please all. His evasive response concerning his use of marijuana at Oxford—"I have never broken the laws of my country"—and his subsequent claim—"I never inhaled"—seemed the quintessence of Clinton Speak. By failing to give straight answers, he has raised further questions about his reliability.

But those who have known Clinton the longest say there is nothing enigmatic or contradictory about him. At Clinton's core, they say, is a yearning to be a friend of all humanity. His instincts are essentially liberal, but he is so determined to sweep everyone up in his embrace that he finds wisdom in conservatism, too.

"His basic philosophy is that there is good in every person," said Betsey Wright, Clinton's chief of staff in the governor's office for many years. His disposition translates into his penchant—frustrating to those who want an ideological edge—to take divergent views and use them like tent poles to build a consensus.

His search for a middle ground is also believed to be a product of his early role as a peacemaker in his troubled childhood home as well as the moderating experience during his first term as governor, when he sought to shake up the state with innovation and was beaten for reelection.

As the fall campaign approaches, Clinton's allies say it is crucial for him to give up trying to represent all things to all people, to stand up again for difficult causes, and to establish his character as strong and genuine. If he can project the concerns he voiced on the racial issue at the time of the Los Angeles riots, his strategists say, and show he is guided by the same sort of beliefs that drove him to oppose the Vietnam War, then he may be able to overcome the negative perceptions that have hurt his image.

"He's not Camelot. He's not perfect. He screws up sometimes. But his heart is unbelievable," said a friend of forty years, David Leopoulos, a Little Rock salesman. Once, when they were in elementary school, Leopoulos said, "He came home Thanksgiving Day with a boy he had met at the store. The kid had a bag of potato chips. Bill told his mother, 'This is Bobby. He wasn't going to have a Thanksgiving dinner.'"

Even though he has become a celebrity, Leopoulos said, Clinton is still considerate in private, personal ways that are never publicized, and maintains close friendships with the people with whom he grew up.

Richard Stearns, a Massachusetts superior court judge who studied at Oxford with Clinton, calls him "the most empathetic person I've ever met. He has a genuine interest in other human beings. If Bill has any weakness, he's too sympathetic to others. He collects stray cats. That was part of the Gennifer Flowers problem. Sometimes it overwhelms his judgment." When Flowers claimed to have had a relationship with Clinton, he denied it, but acknowledged he found her a state job when she sought help.

It is a measure of Clinton's following that when his campaign floundered over charges that he committed adultery and dodged the draft, hundreds of his friends rallied behind him. Comparing Clinton's crisis with the ill-fated campaign of Gary Hart, with whom they both worked for George McGovern in 1972, Stearns said: "Gary's problem, when he got in trouble, was that he had no friends, nobody to defend him."

In many ways, Clinton is an avatar of Lyndon B. Johnson, whose style Theodore H. White wrote "was shaped in the Old South where one runs man against man, with victory going to the man who can out-shout, out-dramatize, out-campaign, out-smile and out-entertain the raw voters until they feel in their hearts that . . . he understands them, he is one of them."

To watch Clinton campaign is to see a natural politician in his habitat. He speaks extemporaneously with the fervor of an evangelical minister. In crowds, he moves gracefully, shaking every hand extended to him. Stopping to talk to individuals, he fixes his eyes on their faces. Listening to their plaints, he clutches their arms as if it were part of a healing process.

Sometimes, Clinton's zeal to reach common ground creates misunderstandings; even the most compromising figures cannot deliver for every special interest. In his first term as governor, members of the education lobby were delighted because Clinton spoke their jargon. "It was a trap we fell into," said Sid Johnson, the president of the Arkansas Education Association. "Because he understands your problem, you think he agrees with you. You begin to think he's bought in."

Despite their natural alliance, the governor and the organization were estranged for years because of his demand that teachers submit to competency testing as part of an education package.

He has disappointed other supporters by avoiding some statehouse fights because he was unwilling to invest his political capital. As a result, Clinton has been criticized because Arkansas has not passed a civil rights bill and has remained a right-to-work state for the twelve years he has been governor.

"Liberals are kind of piously disappointed in Clinton because they want to refurbish Arkansas in their image and he hasn't done that," said Mike Gauldin, a long-time aide in the governor's office. "They are chasing the ideal, while we're trying to get the whole kit and caboodle moved toward that ideal—not in one term or one decade. Arkansas is slow to move. In Arkansas, we are reluctant to take risky moves or to change our past, because we love it so."

And it is against the backdrop of Arkansas, an impoverished and peculiar state, that measurements of Clinton must be taken.

On the surface, his childhood in rural Arkansas sounds as innocent as a scene from *American Graffiti*. As a little boy, he lived for a time with his grandparents in a town called Hope, then he moved with his mother and stepfather to Hot Springs where he attended public school.

Hot Springs was different from other places dominated by Southern Baptists scornful of vice. In those days, the city had a racetrack, a resort, and open gambling. Big-time entertainers performed at a local nightclub, the Vapors. But Clinton, by all accounts, was untouched by this demimonde on the fringe of the Ozarks.

He was, he says, a "straight kid" who played saxophone instead of football. He hung out at an ice cream parlor and sang folk songs such as "Blowin' in the Wind" with a group called the Wayfarers. He ran for school offices, he said, "But I didn't always win because, for one thing, I lived in a culture where athletes were more popular than musicians and if you were big like me and you weren't on the football team, it was sort of a handicap."

Clinton considered becoming a jazz musician. "I remember thinking then: the lifestyle demands, up half the night, sleep half the day and all that sort of stuff, leave your family, travel around the world," he recalled. "I didn't want to live like that unless it could totally consume me, and I could be really wonderful at it."

The wholesome picture of his boyhood is tarnished in at least two places by the turbulence in his own home, and by conflict over race in the region.

When he lists his heroes, Clinton always mentions his mother, Virginia Kelley, who still lives in Hot Springs. She made "inordinate sacrifices for me," he said, as "a working woman and a widow." When he was born in Hope on Aug. 19, 1946, it was four months after his father, Bill Blythe, was killed in an automobile accident.

After entrusting him to her parents for several years while she completed nursing school, Virginia and her second husband, Roger Clinton, took custody of the child and eventually moved to Hot Springs when he was in the third grade.

The Clinton household was the scene of terrible clashes between his stepfather, an alcoholic, and his mother. The boy often interceded in the disputes. He was a big youngster and once, he said, he broke down the door to their room during a fight to protect his mother. He also tried to defuse the tensions. When he was 15, William Jefferson Blythe 4th went so far as to change his name to Bill Clinton as a gesture to his stepfather. Friends say it was entirely in Clinton's character that the two grew close before the older man died while Clinton was in college.

Clinton never talked publicly about the strife until the stories were drawn out of him during the presidential campaign. In an effort to explain his "character" to a New York group this spring, he said: "I grew up in an alcoholic and sometimes violent home, and I carried some of that baggage around with me for a few years." He rarely drinks and tries desperately to avoid unpleasant confrontations. Recently, he has talked openly of how he hated conflict among those he loved, and how he learned to "express disagreement without being disagreeable."

Leopoulos calls his old friend "a fairly internal guy. The first time I ever heard of the abuse in his household was five months ago. He never thought it was anybody's business, his family troubles or his smoking dope."

Leopoulos said Clinton "never talked" about the problems with his half brother, Roger Clinton Jr., who was arrested by state police in 1983 for dealing cocaine. Clinton, as governor, authorized the arrest, but supported his half-brother through court appearances, a jail sentence, and treatment that broke his drug addiction. While Clinton's values were nurtured by his mother—who lamented the inequities suffered by poor people she saw in her job—it was his grandparents who had a profound impact on his thinking about race.

"There's that poor white Southerner phenomenon where some of them were the most racist of all because they needed somebody to look down on," Clinton said in an interview. "But a lot of other poor whites in the South were real sympathetic with blacks because they knew them, and they knew what it was like to be discriminated against . . . and that's basically where my grandparents were coming from."

They ran a "little country store where half the customers were black," he said. "It was not any great political cause to them, it was just second nature. It was, you know: 'Why aren't we letting these kids go to good schools? Why aren't we letting these people have decent jobs?'

"I remember my granddaddy's store was next to the cemetery where my daddy was buried, and I used to go to the cemetery all the time. And behind the cemetery was one of the black neighborhoods of Hope, and for the longest time the streets weren't paved, and I noticed that and I asked about it, and my grandparents said: 'It's not right.'"

In 1957 an epic battle over school integration took place in Arkansas, and President Eisenhower deployed federal troops to ensure that blacks could attend Little Rock Central High School. The event, Clinton recalled, "galvanized and riveted our whole state, it was all anybody could talk about for months and months. I have a very vivid memory of sitting at a table with my grandparents and having them tell me that someday we'd have to integrate the schools" and that the change should be accepted.

The civil rights movement reached its peak during his high school days. Talking about that period, Clinton reflects regret that he was an observer instead of a participant. "I was just a straight kid who was involved in his own life growing up. I wish in a way . . ." His voice drifted off, then he resumed: "But I was not a political activist in that sense as a kid. I wasn't a high schooler who went to demonstrations in the '60s. I don't know anybody in my high school who did."

Despite his tendency to tolerate any side in a dispute, Clinton said he never saw merit in the libertarian argument, led by Barry Goldwater, that owners of hotels and restaurants should be free to determine their own customers during the debate over the Civil Rights Act of 1964. "That was a no-brainer for me," Clinton said. "It was easy. I never had any sympathy for that argument. I thought it was nutty. I thought black people ought to be able to go where they wanted to go."

He calls Martin Luther King "the great American of my life" and expressed sadness that he never saw him. Their destinies were finally joined in the days after King died and Washington burned. Clinton, a senior at Georgetown, took the 1963 Buick LeSabre convertible his parents had given him, slapped a Red Cross sticker on its side, and used it to deliver provisions to poor people in the riot zone in Washington in the spring of 1968. Clinton discounts the theory that he set the White House as his goal when he was a boy, but he acknowledged, "I've been fascinated by politics since I was a little kid." When he was 8, he handed out cards at a polling place for his uncle, who was running for the state Legislature.

The seminal event for Clinton was the coming of television and the coverage of the 1956 conventions. "I remember just literally sitting transfixed in front of the television, watching the Democratic and Republican conventions," he said, and he gives a clue to his early role models.

"I remember Frank Clement giving his speech," he said, "and I remember Kennedy's gracious speech" after a dramatic roll call in which Estes Kefauver defeated John F. Kennedy for the Democratic vice presidential nomination.

Clement was the "boy wonder," elected governor of Tennessee when he was 32. He delivered a keynote address, lush with Southern rhetoric, that excoriated the Republican administration for policies of division and neglect, and ended with a cry, "How long, O America, shall these things endure!" To a generation of aspiring Southern politicians, the speech was an oratorical marvel.

By the time he was 16, he said, "I liked and believed in politics passionately, and decided it was something I would like to do with my life. I was interested very much in medicine at one time. I was really, really good in math, but not all that great in science, and I thought, I'd be a good doctor, but maybe not a great one. I loved music, and I was really good at it, but I wasn't great. I wasn't prodigious. I wasn't a genius at it. . . . And I just thought that I would try to get as good an education as I could and go into politics if I could."

In the summer of 1963, before he entered his senior year, Clinton was selected by the American Legion to go to Washington to attend Boy's Nation. He shook hands with President Kennedy in the Rose Garden. He was determined to come back to the capital, even after Kennedy's assassination.

"The economy was booming, the issue was civil rights, it was exciting to me, and I wanted to go to Washington to school so that I would be there as this Great Society unfolded," Clinton said. "Johnson was a Southerner, and at that moment the whole country had very high hopes for him, and I did, too."

He picked Georgetown University because of its academic reputation and its school of foreign service. "Even though I never intended to be in the foreign service, I thought that by the time I came of age, America would be much more involved in the rest of the world, and I would get a very rigorous education."

He applied to no other school. He was accepted late, and given no scholarship. "It was a pretty good lick to hit my parents," he said, "but my high school counselor and my folks finally persuaded me to go.

They said they would make the financial sacrifice, and they thought maybe I could get some scholarship or help after I'd been there a year."

Clinton, a Southern Baptist from an unsophisticated state, arrived at the Jesuit school and made two impressions on a classmate, Thomas Caplan: "He was very gregarious, and there was a sense of place about him." Clinton obviously impressed others. He was elected president of his freshman and sophomore classes at Georgetown.

Caplan, a novelist living in Baltimore, said Clinton "has an amazing ability to imagine himself as someone else" that is abetted by his reading of fiction and history. "If you read, it forces you to give your concentration over to some other life, and for people in public life, that's kind of enriching."

In his junior year, Clinton obtained a job with Arkansas Sen. J. William Fulbright, and it changed his life as surely as had his brief encounter with Kennedy. The war in Vietnam was escalating, and Fulbright, the chairman of the Senate Foreign Relations Committee, was its most prominent critic.

"One of my jobs was to read six newspapers a day and to clip the papers for the senior staff of the committee," Clinton said. "I read the *Washington Post*, the *Washington Star*, the *Baltimore Sun*, the *Wall Street Journal*, the *New York Times*, and the *St. Louis Post-Dispatch*. Those six papers. Every day for two years. So I became fairly well informed. I remember at the time that McGeorge Bundy once said that anybody that read six good newspapers a day would know as much as he did. I don't know if I did, but I knew a lot because of that, and I think it was the reason I won a Rhodes Scholarship."

He set off for Oxford in the fall of 1968. Stearns, his classmate, said: "I knew within an hour of having met him that his location was politics and his ambition was to be president of the United States. Back then, the time was not that far removed from JFK and RFK, and it was not considered unseemly that public office was what you aspired to."

Clinton and Stearns went to Spain together the following spring. "Bill was determined to get the most out of it," Stearns said. "He had collected six or eight books on the Spanish Civil War, and we began touring Spain with a heavy presumption toward the cause of the Republicans," the leftists who battled the fascists and monarchists.

"As we traveled, we learned that the savagery was not confined to one side." It was characteristic of Clinton to weigh both sides in the conflict. "Nothing is as simple as it seems when you're trying to make it ideological," Stearns said. But there was no equivocation over the conflict in Vietnam.

While a Rhodes scholar, Clinton participated in one of the teach-ins against the war at a London campus and led a demonstration at the U.S. Embassy, timed to coincide with the moratorium marches taking place in Washington in October 1969. "I remember Paul Newman and Joanne Woodward came," Clinton said. "They happened to be in London at the time and they demonstrated."

Stearns recalled that he and Clinton spoke at an antiwar service, and Clinton remembers attending another "huge antiwar demonstration in London," a protest that was believed to have been sponsored by Trotskyites.

It was during this period that Clinton wrote his letter, revealed during the New Hampshire primary, thanking an ROTC officer for "saving me from the draft." He said he hated the war.

Clinton has described himself as "thoughtful and conflicted" at the time. His experience with the Foreign Relations Committee was buttressed by his contemporaries. He particularly remembers a gathering, in the summer of 1969, of students who had worked in Eugene McCarthy's campaign.

"They were some of the brightest and most interesting people of my generation," Clinton said, "and I was honored to be invited to be with them." Even though he had not worked for McCarthy, Clinton said he was asked to come "to fulfill a higher quota of Southerners at this meeting." The only other Southerner was a Georgian, Taylor Branch, now a successful writer. The party was held at activist John O'Sullivan's family home on Martha's Vineyard. Prominent antiwar leaders such as Sam Brown and David Mixner were on hand, as well as James Johnson, who would run Walter F. Mondale's 1984 presidential campaign.

The following summer, Clinton worked in Washington for Project Pursestrings, a lobby to support the McGovern-Hatfield amendment to cut off funds for the war.

By the time he entered Yale Law School that fall, Clinton was involved in the senatorial campaign of Joe Duffey, an antiwar minister who challenged the Democratic establishment in Connecticut and won the party's nomination. Duffey lost in the fall.

Now president of American University, Duffey is a prototypical member of the prestigious network of Clinton's friends. Clinton stays in touch, Duffey said, and they often talk about books and politics. "Of all the people I know in politics, Bill has read more and thought more about American society than almost anyone."

In 1970, Duffey said, "There was real division over how to oppose the war." Some took to the barricades. Others, he said, "felt it was important to use the political system. Bill was very much a part of that group."

Clinton, Stearns, and Branch were reunited in McGovern's antiwar crusade for president. Stearns, McGovern's deputy campaign manager, dispatched Clinton to Texas for the fall campaign. Clinton's girlfriend from Yale Law School, Hillary Rodham, accompanied him. They shared an apartment in Austin with Branch.

"It was a difficult cause," said Branch, the prize-winning author of a biography of Martin Luther King. Conservative Texas was not fertile territory, and there was bickering among the outnumbered liberals who supported McGovern. "We spent a lot of time refereeing disputes between blacks and Hispanics," Branch said. "I thought Bill was truly gifted at taking angry people he didn't know and making a quick reading and solving their antagonism. And he wasn't always finding the lowest common denominator." With the end of the McGovern campaign and his graduation from law school, Clinton went home to Arkansas to enter politics. As a young faculty member at the University of Arkansas Law School, he challenged a popular Republican congressman, John Paul Hammerschmidt, in 1974.

David Matthews, a law student at the time, remembers being swept up by Clinton's personality. "I was working at Perry's Jewelry Store in Fayetteville and he came in shopping. I had a ring on he admired, a

Demolay ring," Matthews said, referring to a high school organization that is linked to the Masons. "He had been a Demolay, too, he mentioned this to me. But as he got older, he realized that their attitudes were segregationist and he quit fooling with them. He told me he was going to be a professor. I didn't know him from Adam, but it was a very pleasant visit."

Matthews enlisted in Clinton's campaign and drove him around the district that summer. "It was a vigorous campaign. Not ugly. He was hitting on Watergate and calling for confidence in government. He was the best speaker I ever heard. He had a pure oratorical style."

Hammerschmidt, who escaped with 52 percent of the vote and still serves in Congress, said the other day he has already warned Bush that Clinton is a "very formidable" opponent. "He brought in a lot of McGovern people to campaign for him." To Hammerschmidt, there is no question of Clinton's ideology. "He's a McGovernite. He's a liberal."

Another Arkansas politician who encountered Clinton that year was George Jernigan, a self-described "old guard conservative." He saw a youthful Clinton deliver a speech in Russellville he still remembers as "outstanding." They clashed two years later, when Clinton was running for attorney general and Jernigan was pushed into a contest against him by the conservative forces in the state.

"They said he was a liberal kid who had never practiced law," Jernigan said. "They convinced me, and I foolishly filed. I found out Bill had spent the last year traveling the state. Some of my close friends were already committed to him. McGovern? I brought that up. I brought up his lack of military service, too. Plus, the fact that I was licensed to practice before the Supreme Court and he wasn't. It didn't do any good. At political rallies, I'd be up there speaking, and I'd look out and he'd be in the crowd shaking every hand. He's the best campaigner ever. He beat the hell out of me."

Jernigan refused to support Clinton for six years. Then, in 1982 Clinton sought him out as a campaign cochairman. Today, Jernigan is state Democratic chairman at Clinton's behest.

In 1978, Clinton was first elected governor. He was 32. His goals for Arkansas were boundless and so was his ambition.

Arkansas was near the bottom of almost every socioeconomic rating: employment, education, income, health. "He decided to cover the whole waterfront, and he brought a lot of bright, young idealistic people in to the state who felt they could fix it," said Betsey Wright, who later joined Clinton's staff. "Their problem was they didn't bother to explain to people that they were raising the price of their car tags so they could fix their roads."

The people of Arkansas voted Clinton out of office at the end of his first two-year term. He took defeat hard. Looking for a way to resurrect his political career, he considered running for chairman of the Democratic National Committee in 1981. Charles Manatt, who had the inside track for the job, diverted Clinton with an honorary title and a role as a roving party spokesman.

Clinton was bored by the task, according to a party official, and concentrated on winning back the governor's office.

Ten years ago, he was elected again and he has served since that time. This part of his career is well documented, as he began his political climb using his talent as a mediator to build powerful coalitions in Arkansas. At the same time, Clinton gained national recognition through his high-profile work with the bipartisan National Governors Association. He was able to work closely, for example, with John Sununu to develop a welfare reform bill at a time when the conservative Sununu was the Republican governor of New Hampshire.

In Arkansas, he learned to bridge the difficult gap between blacks and whites with the phrase "opportunity and responsibility." He appointed blacks to important positions throughout his government. According to the Rev. Hezekiah Stewart, who serves on the state board of corrections, Clinton sent a signal "to employers who had been skeptical about putting blacks in skilled jobs." As a result, job opportunities for blacks are significantly better in the state.

At the same time, Clinton has been able to initiate programs that appeal to conservatives: boot camps for youthful offenders and work requirements for welfare recipients. Instead of emphasizing a punitive nature, he describes the camps as centers to offer discipline and guidance and work requirements as a way to restore dignity.

"He is a redeemer," said Rev. Stewart. "He is constantly going in and looking for redeeming values." The minister is one of those who subscribes to the favorable analogy between Clinton and King as historic, unifying figures.

Taylor Branch, King's biographer and Clinton's friend, is not wholly convinced. "Tax cuts for the middle class and calls for better management don't have the ring of the prophet," Branch said.

Clinton, himself, makes no professions of mystical powers. He is proud to call himself a politician in a period when the word has become an epithet. And he has a simple definition of his character, which has been under attack all year.

"The real test of public character," Clinton said, "is whether you get up every day with conviction and you strive to act according to those convictions to enable the people whom you represent to live up to the fullest of their God-given potential."

33 Days That Defined a Candidate

(*Boston Globe Magazine*, July 12, 1992)

Clinton's "great escape" in the New Hampshire primary was high drama, and I was lucky to have been along for the ride. Months later, after recognizing the significance of that period in his campaign, I wanted to write a fuller account, feeling I knew so much "inside baseball" that hadn't fit my regular dispatches. I witnessed many of the episodes firsthand. (I once walked in on an intense strategy session between Clinton and his advisors in a men's room in the Manchester airport and had to say, "Excuse me, boys.")

Based on my own recollections and interviews with Bill and Hillary Clinton, members of his traveling team and other players in New Hampshire, I reconstructed the story for the *Globe*'s Sunday magazine on the eve of the Democratic convention. For the first time in my career, I used third-person narrative, writing as though it were a novel, with no direct attribution. It is the same device I used nearly twenty years later in my book, *The Fall of the House of Zeus*.

Bill Clinton's time was expiring in New Hampshire. Worn down by illness, his voice frayed by fatigue, his jogger's body swollen from the consumption of junk food, he seemed to be fighting a losing battle. A freezing rain cast a treacherous glaze on the highway as he was driven to Nashua less than sixty hours before the polls opened. Still, Clinton was encouraged when he arrived at the event and saw that an overflow crowd had come to hear him on the Saturday night before the primary. It was a good sign, he told his wife.

Hillary Clinton was not so sanguine. "How do we know," she said, "that they're not just coming to see the freak show?"

By that final weekend, the campaign had acquired the characteristics of a carnival, a frantic crusade, a portable Chautauqua. In little more than a month, it had taken Clinton on a journey from the cover of *Time* magazine to the tawdry scandal sheets sold at supermarket checkout stands, keelhauled him through a controversy that renewed the pain of Vietnam, and plunged him into a free fall in popularity.

It was one of the most extraordinary passages for a candidate in American political history, carried out on a Bruegelian landscape peopled with angry and skeptical voters. And even though Clinton had expected the accusations that bushwhacked him in New Hampshire and had developed plans to deal with them, no one fully anticipated the intensity of the storm.

Today, the Arkansas governor is on the threshold of the Democratic presidential nomination because he withstood the turbulence in New Hampshire, enduring where others had failed. In the last campaign, two of the party's most promising candidates, Gary Hart and Joe Biden, were forced out early, in the face of questions about their character.

Clinton has survived numerous tests en route to the Democratic convention in New York, fighting off formal opponents in a long season of primaries while fending off Washington oracles who whispered that a new Democratic candidate would emerge to save the party. But it was his performance in New Hampshire that gave him his commanding position in New York this week.

In the beginning, Clinton never considered New Hampshire critical to his interests. A credible finish in the Yankee state, he figured, was all he needed to return to the South poised to claim a cluster of primaries in the old Confederate states and march from there to the nomination.

That was before a series of crises converged on Clinton, like a forbidding confluence of planets that turned the primary into what one of his aides described as a "live-or-die situation." For thirty-three days this winter, Clinton's political career hung in the balance.

His problems defied the broad strategy he had developed in 1991, as well as the quick-fix gimmicks his advisers conceived in the heat of the moment. The New Hampshire primary became Bill Clinton's personal battle, and by the final days it was clear that his survival depended on his tenacity, his relentless optimism, and his inner reserves.

As early as last summer, as he reached his decision to run for president, Clinton was braced for adversity. In particular, he discussed his reputation as a philanderer, the subject of many rumors in political circles, with his closest friends and advisers. He laid out the dimensions of the problem and asked at one point, "Should this disqualify me?" He was assured that it was not an insurmountable obstacle.

His wife was included in these delicate consultations, and the Clintons finally decided to confront the issue together by publicly admitting to a history of "difficulties" in their marriage, problems that they said had been resolved. In private meetings with potential contributors, Clinton dealt with uncomfortable questions by quietly acknowledging he had been involved in extramarital affairs and emphasizing the present strength of his marriage. In an attempt to put down one persistent rumor that he had fathered a child with a well-known African American television personality, he blurted out at a closed-door meeting with Chicago Democrats: "Listen, I don't have a black baby."

The Clinton strategy was formally embodied in the governor's remarks to a group of Washington reporters last September. With Hillary at his side, Clinton said: "Like nearly everybody who has been together twenty years, our relationship has not been perfect or free of difficulties. But we feel good about where we are, and we believe in our obligation to each other." He indicated that he would not be drawn into specific discussions of alleged romances. The statement, he said, "ought to be enough" to answer the question of his fidelity to his marriage vows.

Several weeks later, his campaign was tested for the first time. A young aide, Steve Cohen, heard a Little Rock radio talk-show host discussing a story in *Penthouse* magazine in which a rock 'n' roll groupie claimed that Clinton had propositioned her. Cohen reported the news to Clinton's deputy campaign manager, George Stephanopoulos, who quickly collected affidavits from several of Clinton's associates who had witnessed the encounter. They swore that the woman had approached Clinton and been rebuffed.

The story enjoyed the mini-life of celebrity that Andy Warhol forecast for mankind—one mention on CNN *Headline News* the next day. Stephanopoulos immediately pounced on CNN, offered documentation to refute the woman's claim, and rebuked the producers for airing the story. The item was dropped.

That night, in Little Rock, a few members of Clinton's staff celebrated with pizzas, and Cohen was given the nickname Scoop. The Clinton campaign felt confident that the sex issue had been settled.

Another cloud still hovered in the background. It involved Clinton's draft record, a topic that had come up sporadically since he entered politics. But it had been dealt with as recently as his reelection campaign for governor in 1990, and there was no reason to believe that the issue would explode in the presidential campaign.

By the New Year, Clinton's future looked prosperous. Gov. Mario Cuomo of New York had decided not to enter the race, and Gov. Douglas Wilder of Virginia, who threatened to strip Clinton of vital black support, dropped out eight days into January.

Then, on January 16, a blemish appeared like the first, faint signs of a malignancy. It was a Thursday, the day of the week that became known as "garbage day" in the Clinton campaign, for it was on Thursdays that advance copies of *Star*, a national tabloid, were released.

Star's first broadside was a regurgitation of allegations that Clinton had used public funds to carry on affairs with five different women. The charges grew out of a lawsuit filed during the last gubernatorial race by a former state employee sacked for using his office phone to promote the Nicaraguan contras.

News agencies had investigated the allegations and failed to find any corroboration. The Clinton campaign was equipped with denials from the women named as Clinton's mistresses, including a nightclub singer named Gennifer Flowers. Nevertheless, the *Star* story seeped into daily tabloids the next day and precipitated the first mob scene of the political season. As soon as Clinton arrived in New Hampshire to attend a health-care conference at the Sheraton-Tara Hotel, a mock-Tudor fortress in Nashua, he was surrounded by reporters, photographers, and camera crews.

Maintaining a smile and an air of bemusement, Clinton followed a preordained plan. He described the story as old and false and ridiculed the source, dismissing *Star* as a newspaper "that says Martians walk on earth and cows have human heads." Although more than a score of reporters were on hand for the exchange with Clinton, editors at television networks and most newspapers made judgments not to use the story.

By mid-January, Clinton was leading his closest challenger, former Massachusetts Sen. Paul E. Tsongas, by twelve percentage points in *Boston Globe* polls in New Hampshire, and he was featured on the cover of *Time* magazine as "the Democrats' rising star."

Then Stephanopoulos got a tip that *Star* planned a new exposé involving Flowers. A few hours later, flying from Little Rock to Manchester on the next "garbage day," Clinton's small charter plane made a stop in Washington to pick up a consultant the governor had recently hired—James Carville, a shrewd and bombastic strategist who specializes in the tactics of confrontation.

Although the members of Clinton's entourage were apprehensive over the new development, Clinton was in a bluff mood when he arrived at a Manchester hotel, not recognizing the enormity of his problem until he reached his private suite. His staff had located a copy of *Star*, and a telephone facsimile of the article was waiting for him. He quickly read through the lurid account, with the headline "They Made Love All Over Her Apartment..."

Clinton had suspected for weeks that Flowers might become the source of allegations—she had called him once and told him she had been offered $50,000 to make public charges—but the story was stunning.

Emotions in the room ran from sinking sensations to a determination to fight back. Clinton's aides wondered, with false hope, if the mainstream press might again ignore the allegations. They knew that any counteroffensive would have to be undertaken in tandem with

Hillary Clinton. She was reached in Atlanta, where she was campaigning. After learning details of the allegations, she said she was ready to fly wherever necessary to make a joint appearance with her husband.

Meanwhile, Stephanopoulos obtained from Little Rock a copy of a year-old letter from Flowers's lawyer. It contained a threat to sue a radio station because a talk-show host "wrongfully and untruthfully alleged an affair between my client, Gennifer Flowers, and Bill Clinton." Stephanopoulos had copies of the letter reproduced for distribution to reporters.

Without knowing whether a frenzy awaited them, Clinton and his aides set off, an hour late, for a campaign appearance in Claremont. New Hampshire was enveloped in ice and fog and gloom. They wanted to fly but were forced to drive.

Clinton was burdened further by the knowledge that he had to return to Arkansas that night to handle last-minute appeals in connection with the execution of Rickey Ray Rector, condemned for killing a policeman. With events closing in around him, Clinton tried to keep his serenity. As the van carried him slowly over the icy roads, he read *Lincoln on Leadership*.

It was mid-afternoon by the time Clinton reached the American Brush Co. in Claremont, and news of Flowers's allegations had spread to a group of waiting reporters. He was cornered by questions as soon as he stepped into the foyer of the building. "It isn't true," he said, shaking his head sadly. "She's obviously taking money to change her story." Peppered by questions, he said flatly, "The affair did not happen."

Clinton worked his way past the pack of reporters and went on to deliver a speech inside the small factory without a sign that he was troubled. But he knew, instinctively, that he had erred by departing from his decision not to discuss specific rumors.

Clinton and his aides retreated to an upstairs office and spent the rest of the darkening afternoon on the telephone. Clinton talked with his wife, his aides, and others he trusted.

Stephanopoulos phoned Carville, who was in Manchester, to tell him that Clinton had been hit hard with questions on the Flowers case. "We can't be eaten up by this thing," Carville said, urging that Clinton "get in front of the story."

As they considered a forum to address the issue, they were contacted by Ted Koppel, who planned to use the sex allegations as his topic that evening on ABC's *Nightline*. Stephanopoulos also talked to an ABC executive about a Clinton appearance on *Primetime Live* that same night. There was a timing problem. Clinton was more than fifty miles from his chartered plane. A mixture of freezing rain and snow was falling. And the situation was complicated by the fact that arrangements had to be made for his wife to join him at ABC's studios in Washington in a few hours.

For a moment, decision-making was frozen. The network news shows carried no mention of the allegations other than a reference in a profile of Clinton on NBC. Downstairs, restive reporters, standing in line for one pay telephone, were having difficulty convincing their editors that the story was worthy of publication. Clinton felt that he might get another reprieve.

But WMUR-TV in Manchester, New Hampshire's major television station, carried a report from Claremont, showing Clinton pelted with questions, and the Associated Press soon moved a story. The furies were finally set in motion.

Sometime after 7:30 p.m., the van carrying Clinton began a meandering, erratic drive. He was hopelessly late for an event in Plymouth, at least two hours away in deteriorating conditions, but he headed in that direction anyway. Meanwhile, Clinton's aides kept up conversations with ABC. They explored the possibility of appearing the next day on *Good Morning America* and were discouraged to learn that the Clintons could get no more than six minutes on the air. A network executive tried to sell them on *20/20*, a Friday-night ABC program, but Clinton ruled out an appearance on the same night as the Rector execution in Arkansas. Reluctantly, Clinton gave up the attempt to go to Plymouth and abandoned plans to appear immediately on TV. He returned, instead, to Manchester and flew back to Little Rock, traveling much of the night to keep the grim duty of presiding over the execution of Rickey Ray Rector.

He also needed to regroup politically, because the next morning the Flowers story would be in every newspaper in the nation.

Clinton spent the day in seclusion, a practice he had followed on other execution days. It was a time for brooding. Paul Begala, one of his advisers, attempted to encourage him by sending a message: "Life breaks us all, but some of us emerge stronger in the broken places." The aphorism, Begala noted with some irony, was popularized by Max Cleland, the secretary of state of Georgia who had lost three limbs in Vietnam and was supporting Sen. Bob Kerrey for president.

Meanwhile, Clinton's campaign staff committed the governor to weekend appearances on CNN's *Newsmaker Saturday* as well as *This Week with David Brinkley* on ABC. Then Steve Kroft, a *60 Minutes* correspondent, called to offer a spot on the most popular news show on television, boasting an audience of millions that would be expanded because it would appear immediately after the Super Bowl. Stephanopoulos asked for a guarantee that the show would be promoted with unsensational language. In exchange, the Clintons agreed to give CBS an exclusive interview, and other appearances were canceled.

Clinton and his wife returned to New England for a rally in Manchester, New Hampshire, Saturday night, where a youthful crowd packed a downtown gymnasium, cheering the couple. After the event, in the comfort of the Ritz-Carlton hotel in Boston, the Clintons gathered with a few friends and advisers. Although the conversation drifted away from the political crisis, everyone in the room was preoccupied by the Clintons' date the next morning. *60 Minutes* would begin taping before noon.

James Carville, his nerves taut, woke the next morning weeping. Other Clinton aides were tense but tried to hide their emotions. The group assembled in the Clintons' suite for final preparations before the interview, which would take place in one of the hotel's stately rooms with a fireplace.

Mandy Grunwald, a media consultant, advised the Clintons that this would not be a normal political interview. Kroft, she said, had an entertainment orientation and was likely to ask questions that seemed disjointed. She predicted he would be persistent on the subject of adultery.

Hillary Clinton, who would later display the toughness of a courtroom lawyer during the interview, began to cry. She was distressed, she said, over the impact the show might have on their daughter, Chelsea, who was 11 at the time.

The candidate was outwardly dispassionate. He was prepared to acknowledge, implicitly, that he had been involved in affairs. But he was determined to do it his own way.

Once they were on the set, Don Hewitt, the producer of *60 Minutes*, urged Clinton to deal with the adultery question openly and to follow with an arching exposition of his political dreams. It could become a historic moment in American politics, Hewitt said. It could also be one hell of a TV show.

The taping went on for more than an hour. Kroft made about a dozen passes at the adultery question. Clinton stuck to his formula. He repeated his denial that he had been involved with Flowers. He admitted he had caused "pain in my marriage." And, near the end, he observed: "I think most Americans who are watching this tonight; they'll know what we're saying. They get it."

Watching the monitors in a control room, most of Clinton's aides were quietly weeping and thinking that he had survived the crucible. Before he left the Ritz-Carlton, Clinton had lunch with a journalist and defended his vagueness on the show. "If I say 'no,' you all will just go out and try to prove me wrong. And if I say 'yes,' that will mean there is no end to it. I'm not complaining, though; I signed on for the whole ride. If I made any mistake, it was talking about all this at all."

Less than fifteen minutes of the Clintons' interview aired that night. The campaign had no major quarrel with the editing, but one line was omitted that Clinton's aides wished had been used: In a philosophical moment, Clinton had said, "No one wants to be judged on the worst moment of his life."

For many of Clinton's supporters, the worst moment of the campaign occurred the next day. Gennifer Flowers's sponsors convened a press conference in Manhattan, and most of it was televised live by

CNN. She said she had loved Bill Clinton and insisted that he was "absolutely lying."

The spectacle led every network news show that evening, enjoying priority over a significant turn of events in Russia, the Middle East peace talks, and a Supreme Court decision. Clinton was campaigning in Louisiana and did not see Flowers's performance, but his aides watched in horror. Begala could not believe what he had seen. He thought: The networks just led with a failed lounge singer with a bad dye job holding a press conference at the Waldorf-Astoria to lie about us. He quickly came up with the "cash for trash" expression that Clinton would subsequently use to describe his accusers.

That night, Clinton's support fell dramatically, for the first time, in a poll conducted for the *Globe* in New Hampshire.

After an absence of several days, Clinton returned to New Hampshire on Wednesday, February 5, ill and feverish. During a speech at a Concord school, he constantly wiped perspiration from his face and drank two quarts of water. He had to cancel the rest of his schedule and went to bed at Day's Hotel, a modest lodging place in Manchester, which he had made his unofficial headquarters.

Clinton, however, was unable to rest. He learned that the *Wall Street Journal* was preparing to publish a story suggesting that in 1969 he had maneuvered his way out of the draft.

The key source was Col. Eugene Holmes, an ROTC officer at the University of Arkansas when Clinton enrolled in the program to get a deferment from his draft board. After Clinton broke the agreement, he was reclassified 1-A on October 30, 1969. For thirty-three days— exactly the same period he would dangle in New Hampshire more than two decades later—Clinton was exposed to the draft, but there was no call-up. On December 1, 1969, a draft lottery was held. Clinton's birthday drew a high number that spared him. The *Wall Street Journal* quoted Holmes: "Bill Clinton was able to manipulate things so that he didn't have to go in."

Clinton was staggered. He had always called Holmes his "first line of defense" when his draft record was raised in Arkansas campaigns, and he had often referred reporters to Holmes, who was retired. First,

Gennifer Flowers had changed her story, and now Holmes, Clinton's erstwhile defender, was accusing Clinton of manipulation.

Clinton's staff realized it was an explosive situation. They retrieved by fax from Little Rock papers from Clinton's draft file and simulated a press conference in his hotel room, interrogating him on details of the case.

But nothing prepared him for the scene Thursday morning. There was a sense of déjà vu in Nashua when he was again engulfed by a wave of reporters and photographers in the same lobby of the Sheraton-Tara Hotel where he had been besieged by questions about extramarital affairs. Cameras and lights were poked toward his face. Reporters encircled him. Questions struck like hail. He admitted being "bitterly opposed" to the war but denied that he had evaded it. He nearly lost his equilibrium in the violence of the exercise. In the midst of the turmoil, he lamented, "This is an unbelievable rewriting of history."

Stephanopoulos, who was becoming a specialist in damage control, produced copies of a story from the *Arkansas Democrat-Gazette* last October that dealt with the dispute over Clinton's lack of military service. In the article, Holmes, the former ROTC commander, said he had treated Clinton "just like I would have treated any other kid."

Although the draft story was front-page news on Friday, Clinton was not asked about the subject during questions from an audience at New Hampshire Technical College, in Stratham. Again, members of the campaign staff thought they had weathered the difficulty, heartened by a report from a private focus group conducted by their pollster, Stan Greenberg, who showed little hostility toward Clinton over the draft issue.

"I don't have anything more to say about it," Clinton told reporters as he left New Hampshire to spend a weekend at home. His departure from the state turned out to be one of the greatest tactical errors of the campaign. While Clinton took a break, the political environment in New Hampshire was roiling, and his local organizers implored the Little Rock headquarters to bring Clinton back for the time remaining. They feared he was losing command of the situation.

On Sunday night, February 9, Clinton met with key members of his staff at the governor's mansion in Little Rock to go over a battle plan. They were troubled by a new *Globe* poll that showed that Clinton and Tsongas were effectively tied.

There were suggestions that the campaign buy time for a television show in which Clinton would take spontaneous questions from viewers. There was talk of a fighting speech that would blame the Republicans for the perfidy that had hit the Clinton campaign. There were surrogates to deploy. And there were new television spots to consider, in which Clinton's chief TV consultant, Frank Greer, wanted to portray the governor "talking over the heads of the tabloid press."

Just before midnight, Greenberg telephoned with numbers from his latest survey in New Hampshire. An aide announced to the room: "There's big trouble in River City." Clinton had fallen from a peak of 37 percent support to 17 percent in a matter of days. It seemed that the bottom had dropped out of the campaign.

Begala was put to work on the draft of a short speech for Clinton, who rarely uses prepared texts. Others awakened Hershel Gober, the director of veterans' affairs for Arkansas, to tape a testimonial for Clinton that Greer would get on New Hampshire radio stations within hours.

Clinton went to bed late that night knowing that if he failed ignominiously in New Hampshire, his dream would die. He had eight days to save his campaign.

Clinton, his wife, and a few aides headed back to New Hampshire early Monday. On the way, Clinton marked up Begala's text, which raised the specter of a "Republican attack machine" orchestrating Clinton's misery.

He intended to deliver the speech as soon as he landed at a small airport near Nashua, and to declare that he would "fight like hell" for the last eight days. But his campaign could not get clearance for a political event at the airport.

One of the few journalists to meet the plane was Mark Halperin, an ABC producer who had covered Clinton all year. Halperin had a document to deliver, a copy of a letter, written by Clinton to Col. Holmes more than twenty-two years ago, describing his aversion to the draft.

Halperin gave the letter to Stephanopoulos, who had been wrestling with his own pessimism for days. The Clinton aide quickly scanned it. As soon as his eyes settled on the second paragraph, in which Clinton offered thanks "for saving me from the draft," Stephanopoulos had one thought: It's over.

The Clinton group squeezed into a tiny room at the airport to weigh the latest crisis. Clinton quickly read the letter and momentarily brightened. "This is mine," he told his wife. "I remember writing this letter." Imbued with a politician's ability to discover silver linings, Clinton said it proved his point that he had made himself "available for the draft." Others were not so sure. Stephanopoulos was despondent. Begala's legs trembled. But Carville, a Louisiana Catholic who had thought hours before that the campaign was in extremis, saw the possibility of redemption. He began shouting, which is his fashion. He described the letter in scatological terms, but he told Clinton it was "your friend."

The letter had come into ABC's hands over the weekend through an anonymous fax that the network eventually traced to Lt. Col. Clinton Jones, another former officer at the ROTC unit.

Jim Wooten, one of the network's chief political reporters, was handling the story, and Halperin asked Clinton to meet with him for an interview. After a desultory appearance in Nashua, where Clinton delivered his "fight like hell" message with little gusto, the candidate sat down with Wooten in a room at a Londonderry yogurt factory he had visited and insisted the letter vindicated his assertions.

Clinton assumed the story would break in a few hours on ABC's *World News Tonight.* But as night fell and Clinton waited in Manchester for a flight to New York, he heard from Wooten that the story was going to be delayed. The reporter was troubled by discrepancies between what Clinton Jones and Bill Clinton had said, and he wanted more time to sort it out.

For want of an office, Clinton took over the men's room at the airport. The governor perched on a lavatory, and his aides huddled around him, pondering what course to take next. Carville urged Clinton to release the letter immediately. Clinton was reluctant. He felt

Wooten had been fair with him, and he did not want to steal "Wooten's scoop."

He flew to New York and claimed at a $1,000-a-plate dinner that "reports of my demise are, as Mark Twain said, premature."

On the flight back to New Hampshire, Clinton and his wife appeared in good spirits. They played pinochle with a couple of reporters. He bantered about garbling the Twain quote, and he and Hillary reminisced about the antiwar movement, even though the reporters did not know about the existence of the letter. Clinton also talked about Southern politics, and he recalled the travails of another governor, Bill Allain of Mississippi, who was accused a few days before an election in 1983 of consorting with a gang of homosexual transvestites. Though Allain was elected, Clinton recalled, "He never recovered from that."

When they landed at Keene, it was after midnight. Clinton was hungry. The group found a Dunkin' Donuts shop that was open. He wolfed down a bowl of soup and two bagels with tuna salad. Then, before leaving, he engaged an astonished customer in a long discussion on health care. There was no sign that the letter was preying on his mind.

The next afternoon, Clinton was hit from another direction. Ted Koppel, whose *Nightline* program is independent from ABC's *World News Tonight* operation, contacted David Wilhelm, Clinton's campaign manager in Little Rock, and told him: "It is important that the governor and I talk."

Koppel also had a copy of the draft letter. Clinton's aides never made a public complaint, but privately they were troubled that leaks seemed to flow naturally toward ABC, a network where several executives had a strong Republican pedigree. It fed the campaign's paranoia over Republican plots.

The document that Koppel had received was at least a fourth-generation copy. A *World News Tonight* producer had obtained the letter from Jones in South Carolina and asked a hotel clerk to make copies. The intrigued clerk made himself a copy and faxed it to an acquaintance, a Washington businessman named James Tully, who travels in military-intelligence circles. Tully sent a copy to Clinton's political office in Washington, a move that mystified Clinton aides there, who knew nothing of the letter. He also sent a copy to former Air Force Maj. Gen. Richard Secord, a figure in the Iran-contra affair. Secord had it sent to *Nightline*.

Because of Secord's background, Koppel was concerned that he might be drawn into a "dirty tricks" operation. He told Wilhelm, vaguely, he was "under the impression that my source might have gotten it from someone in the Pentagon."

He was surprised to learn from Wilhelm that ABC had already interviewed Clinton on the subject. "Obviously, the right hand doesn't know what the left hand is doing," Koppel said.

Sensing that the letter represented a dramatic story, Koppel was anxious to get Clinton on *Nightline*, regardless of Wooten's prior interest. Koppel and Clinton's aides began discussing details. Stephanopoulos wanted to know where the letter had come from. "It beats the shit out of me," Koppel said. But he repeated his "impression" that it had come from the Pentagon.

Clinton's advisers felt that Koppel's answer reinforced their claim that their campaign was under attack by the Republican administration. It also played into Carville's demand for Clinton to go public with the letter.

On Wednesday, February 12, less than a week before the primary, Clinton triggered a day of high drama by calling Koppel at home. He said he hoped to release the letter and wanted to confirm that it had been leaked by the Pentagon. Koppel said again that it was his "impression." He warned Clinton that he was leaping to a conclusion.

Late that morning, Clinton called a press conference in a hangar of the Manchester airport, where a large American flag was hung as a backdrop. As his aides distributed copies of his letter, Clinton said: "Mr. Koppel confirmed to me that it is his understanding that ABC received a letter from two different sources, both of whom got it from the Pentagon. If this is true, the leak violates the Federal Privacy Act." Clinton said he would appear on *Nightline* that night to "discuss all of this."

The letter, a painful, eloquent, three-page epistle from a troubled time, coupled with Clinton's charge that "George Bush and the Republican Party will do anything it takes to win," burst upon the campaign like a thunderstorm.

Afterward, Clinton asked one of his state coordinators, Patricia McMahon, how she felt the event had gone. "I thought you did a very good job," she assured him. She said the letter was so moving it must have been leaked by a friend.

After hearing of Clinton's charge, Koppel's source contacted him again and described the circuitous route the letter had taken. In a late afternoon conversation with Clinton, Koppel told the candidate the letter had not come from the Pentagon.

Clinton knew the letter was creating a political earthquake, and now he realized that his contention that he was the victim of a Republican plot was discredited. A *Globe* poll completed that evening would show he had fallen eleven points behind Tsongas. As he boarded his sixteen-seat plane to fly to an event in Claremont, Clinton looked tired and stricken. As he moved to his seat, he greeted one of the passengers, Thomas Edsall of the *Washington Post*. Edsall and his wife had written a book Clinton admired, a book that described how Democratic Party policies, perceived as too soft on blacks, had driven away conservative whites.

Another reporter told Clinton he had recently written of him and Edsall in the same paragraph, suggesting the Clinton was better experienced than the other Democratic candidates to deal with the racial problems the Edsalls had written about.

"I was," Clinton said with resignation.

"What do you mean, 'I was'?" he was asked.

"Oh, hell I am," he said, putting the verb in the present tense. "It's just that I'm so busy fighting wars that are twenty-three years old . . ."

A large audience was waiting in Claremont, and another Arkansan was asked to give a long introduction, to enable Clinton to meet privately with some of his local supporters. David Matthews was a throwback to the old school of passionate Southern oratory, a former state representative who had responded to the negative reports from

New Hampshire by suspending his law practice in the little town of Rogers, Arkansas, and coming to the state to help his friend. This was his first real chance, and his light blue eyes burned like dry ice.

He started with a joke about the Baptist preacher whose description of Jesus Christ as "the only perfect man" was challenged by a man in the back pew: "Brother Jones, are you saying you're perfect?"

"Oh, no, I'm just standing up for my wife's first husband." Matthews went on to attack Gennifer Flowers's veracity, and he excoriated another supermarket tabloid for a headline that said: "Clinton Likes Four-Way Sex with Black Hookers."

"You probably haven't heard the one about him being buck naked in a tree at the University of Arkansas, protesting the war," Matthews shouted.

Dee Dee Myers, Clinton's press secretary, rolled her eyes and wondered: Where is he going? Actually, Matthews was moving skillfully from low comedy to graceful poignance. He said that Clinton was neither perfect nor a "two-headed monster," and he related the story of how the Arkansas governor had befriended a boy gravely ill with cancer, and how the boy had been inspired. Clinton was standing in the wings by now, listening. He covered his moist eyes with his oversized hands and bowed his head. He was struggling not to cry openly, but, somehow, he also seemed to be drawing a second wind.

During his Claremont speech Clinton fought off one heckler, then he flew to Dover for an Elks Club appearance that has by now taken on mythic proportions. Garry Trudeau, who was there, later had one of his *Doonesbury* characters describe the talk as "the most extraordinary political speech I've ever heard."

In the Dover address, Clinton described his political career as the "work of my life" and said his dreams represented the "vision thing" that Bush flippantly dismissed. "I hope you never raise a child without the vision thing," he told the crowd. "Life would be bleak and empty without the vision thing."

He reminded the New Hampshire audience that Bush had won a second chance in the state in 1988 after losing to Iowa caucuses and had subsequently spent "three hours here, mostly on his way to and from Kennebunkport, while you tripled your unemployment, welfare, and food-stamp rates."

It was a bravura performance. Surrounded by a few hundred spectators in an underlit and crowded room, the candidate was like a man on trial, making a closing argument for himself. "They say I'm on the ropes because other people have questioned my life, after years of public service," he bellowed, his hoarse voice rising. "I'll tell you something: I'm going to give you this election back, and if you'll give it to me, I won't be like George Bush. I'll never forget who gave me a second chance, and I'll be there for you till the last dog dies."

The day was still not finished. Clinton had returned to Manchester to appear on *Nightline*. Koppel, handling the interview from Washington, seemed oddly deferential, as though he felt responsible for the misunderstanding. Much of the half-hour program was consumed as Koppel read the entire letter while the screen showed Clinton, listening and nodding. The candidate was not only embracing the letter, he was spreading its word through newspaper advertisements reproducing the text. It was midnight when the show was over, and there was a glimmer of hope. It was a triumph, Clinton's aides told him, and they exchanged high-fives, like athletes.

For days, an exasperated Clinton had been complaining to his staff about his schedule in New Hampshire and demanding more grassroots events. "Just turn me loose," he said. On the Thursday before the primary, he began a breakneck schedule that took him back and forth across the densely populated areas in the southern part of the state. He bought a half-hour of TV time for two consecutive nights to submit to random questions from a statewide audience. He spoke at schools and addressed the legislature. He prowled suburban shopping malls near Salem and Nashua, and he walked the streets of seacoast towns.

During a visit to a home for the elderly in Nashua on the final Friday, Clinton watched Mary Annie Davis break into tears as she described how she and her husband could no longer afford prescription drugs. To comfort the sobbing woman, Clinton suddenly knelt on the floor and hugged her.

In the next room, Stephanopoulos was trying to discourage an editor of the *Nashua Telegraph* from publishing a story involving new allegations by a former campaign volunteer. The disgruntled source claimed he had overheard Clinton and Arkansas Lt. Gov. Jim Guy Tucker discussing a new job for Gennifer Flowers. Stephanopoulos insisted that the conversation dealt with a Clinton aide named Gloria. The newspaper decided to drop the matter for lack of supporting evidence.

After the Nashua event, a relieved Stephanopoulos was preparing to tell Clinton that the latest problem had been resolved when he realized the candidate was still so overcome with emotion that he could not speak. It was the only time Stephanopoulos saw the governor close to breaking. But the mood was upbeat as the Clinton team flew from Manchester to Keene that night. He had climbed back to within seven points of Tsongas in the *Globe* poll. On a portable television in the front of the plane, David Matthews was watching the news on WMUR-TV. He could make out, through static and snow, a scene of Clinton hugging the elderly woman earlier in the day. He yelled at the candidate, who was sitting in the rear of the sixteen-seat plane: "I don't know whether it's a good story or another sex scandal, but you led the news."

On Saturday, Clinton and his wife went to the Mall of New Hampshire, a labyrinth on the outskirts of Manchester that was teeming with weekend shoppers. It was supposed to be a half-hour stop, with the rest of the afternoon devoted to a preparation for the primary's final debate the following night. Clinton refused to leave. Standing in a McDonald's, he greeted knots of people who waited patiently to talk with him. It was not like a receiving line, with a word and a handshake, but an evangelical ceremony. He listened as much as he talked, and sometimes spent five to ten minutes with a couple of voters.

Hillary Clinton was standing a few feet away, detached for the moment from the clutter of cameras. A reporter suggested that while she might not like the comparison, the scene was reminiscent of Lyndon B. Johnson's irrepressible campaign for the presidency in 1964, when it seemed as if LBJ wanted to shake every hand in America. "I never saw Johnson," she said, "and I don't want to denigrate him. But my impression was that with Johnson it was all take. He took strength from his supporters, but he gave nothing back. If you look at Bill, you'll see that it's reciprocal. He gives as well as he takes."

A few minutes later, an incident took place as if on cue. A young man without a job, holding his small daughter in his arms, began to cry as he told Clinton of his anxiety that he might lose his home. The candidate reached out and held the man's arms until he regained his composure. After two and a half hours, Clinton's aides finally persuaded the candidate to leave the mall. As he was departing, a reporter asked facetiously if he also liked fund-raising, generally regarded as the most loathsome task for a politician. "Usually, I do," Clinton confessed. "But I like this best of all."

That night in Nashua, the people in the packed house who came to see Clinton seemed to have been drawn more by his magnetism than by the freakish aspects his wife had feared. The primary was approaching, and it was apparent that even if Clinton failed to win, he would finish, at worst, a respectable second, a result that would enable him to continue his campaign. Before a single vote was cast, he had won a grudging concession from his rivals that he was a candidate who would not wilt, and his supporters were attributing his survival to the power of his presence and the strength of his will.

Clinton would have to draw upon these resources again and again as he struggled toward the nomination in the primaries after New Hampshire. From the beginning, the candidate felt he could overcome any adversity if he could somehow reach the voters personally. He said it was important "to stand for something bigger than yourself."

And as he proclaimed himself the "Comeback Kid" at his primary-night rally in Merrimack, he added: "At least I proved one thing—I can take a punch."

Tracing a Web
of Accusations in Little Rock

(*Boston Globe*, December 26, 1993)

This was not how I would have chosen to celebrate Christmas, but
I had recently talked my editors into letting me live in New Orleans
and work from there as a national reporter. So when the assignment
came to go to Little Rock to put some perspective on the latest of what
Clinton's longtime aide Betsey Wright called his "bimbo eruptions," I
had to go. Thank God for the Capital Hotel, a comfortable inn where I
had spent many nights the year before. But even the Capital's elegance
seemed spoiled by the sordid story. For much of one afternoon,
Clinton's chief nemesis, Cliff Jackson, accompanied by the two troopers
armed with fresh allegations of Clinton's indiscretions, came to my
room to tell their tales, lounging on my bed and sofa while eating
sandwiches and drinking beer on my tab.

By Christmas Eve, I had completed my reporting and was prepared
to write. But when I went downstairs for breakfast, I found the lobby
crawling with tabloid reporters and crews from sensation-seeking
television shows. I retreated upstairs and ordered room service. Then
my phone rang. It was a reporter from one of London's scandal sheets.
In his clipped British accent, he told me he understood that I had the
names and addresses "of all the Clinton girls," and wondered if I might
share the list with him. I told our visitor from overseas that I had no list,
and even if I had one, I wouldn't give it to him. I knew Memphis, and
solitude, lay only two hours away. I called the Peabody, asked for a nice

room, and drove there to finish writing my story. When I woke there
the next morning, I calculated that it was the seventh Christmas in the
last ten that I had spent away from home.

LITTLE ROCK, Ark.—In the closing weeks of the 1992 presidential campaign, there were widespread rumors here that Arkansas state troopers assigned to Gov. Bill Clinton's security detail would be the source of a fresh story of his sexual escapades that might knock his candidacy off its feet.

When the story finally materialized last week, nearly a year into Clinton's presidency, it was the White House that was thrown off balance.

As the uproar threatened to spoil his Christmas week, Clinton denied accounts by the state troopers of how they arranged secret rendezvous for him. "They're outrageous and they're not so," the president said wearily in one interview Wednesday.

Clinton has battled allegations of sexual indiscretions for much of his political career. At one point last year, he implicitly acknowledged on national television that he had carried on affairs and declared that the marriage in which he had caused "pain" was now strong.

So the revival of suggestions that Clinton was a randy governor seemed to offer little new other than some titillating details, and it failed to trigger a public outcry against him. But tucked into the story were at least two larger questions:

Had Clinton promised some of the troopers federal jobs in exchange for their silence?

And had Clinton, a year after his pledge of marital fidelity, asked a trooper to smuggle a woman into the governor's mansion last January on the eve of his departure for the inauguration?

Although there appear to have been discussions with Clinton about jobs for the troopers, the president and Bruce Lindsey, who oversees personnel matters at the White House, have vehemently denied that any job was offered to keep the troopers quiet.

And there is no evidence, aside from the words of one trooper who remained anonymous, that the president-elect used the governor's mansion for a trysting place. The supervisor of the troopers as well as a Clinton aide who worked at the mansion during the period say it would have been almost impossible to breach Secret Service checkpoints.

The story, at this point, has dissolved into a mystery, a made-for-tabloid shower of sleaze that is pure Arkansas baroque. There is a welter of angry charges and countercharges, and there are no easy answers.

The central figures in the case, a pair of state troopers who publicly accused Clinton of using them to procure women for him, have had their motives and credibility challenged. And questions also linger about their handler, Little Rock lawyer Cliff Jackson, who has been bent on a mission to destroy Clinton for nearly three years.

Jackson was once Clinton's friend. A fellow Arkansan and a Fulbright scholar, he attended Oxford University at the same time Clinton was a Rhodes scholar. Jackson, who had connections to Republicans back home who controlled the state Selective Service offices, said the friendship withered when he felt he was used by Clinton to avoid the draft.

He was annoyed when Clinton reneged on an agreement to enroll in an ROTC program at the University of Arkansas Law School after escaping one round of the draft in 1969. "I can't help but suspect that his 'friendship' with me is Machiavellian," Jackson wrote in a letter to a friend the same year.

Shortly before Clinton became a candidate for president in 1991, Jackson helped found a group known by the acronym ARIAS—Alliance for the Rebirth of an American Spirit.

"It's a bunch of Republican rich folk that want to do Bill Clinton harm," said David Matthews, a former Arkansas legislator who is a close friend of the president.

According to Federal Election Commission records, ARIAS raised $35,000 and spent most of it in a campaign of radio and newspaper ads against Clinton during the New Hampshire primary. A Democratic Party official identified ARIAS's chief benefactor as James Keenan, an Arkansas industrialist who was also a heavy contributor to President Bush.

Jackson said that the Teamsters union was actually the largest single donor to his cause.

Although there is no indication that Jackson was involved in the leaks that nearly brought Clinton down in New Hampshire over the draft issues, he was the source for a story that caused Clinton problems during the New York primary. Jackson revealed that Clinton had actually received a draft notice in 1969—a fact the candidate had not mentioned in previous discussions of the draft.

"Cliff Jackson is like a bad penny," said Lindsey, a Little Rock lawyer before he went to the White House with Clinton. There are plots to sabotage Clinton "whenever we are doing well," Lindsey said. "When we were doing well in New Hampshire, this stuff came up. And now, when we're having a good year, they decide to use it again."

Ernie Dumas, a former reporter and editor with the *Arkansas Gazette*, a newspaper that went out of business in 1991, recalled that Jackson phoned him with partisan tips aimed at Clinton during the 1980s. "Cliff knew reporters and he talked to me frequently. But I didn't detect the visceral hatred that has since come out. He didn't seem as obsessed by Clinton then as he does now." Clinton's friends say they believe Jackson's animosity is the product of envy—while Clinton was emerging as a national leader, Jackson was merely a successful Little Rock trial lawyer, noted for winning a $17.5 million judgment against Texaco in a sex discrimination lawsuit.

The loquacious Jackson has generally operated openly against Clinton. In an interview on Friday, he said he had made "a mistake" last year when he contacted a private investigator in Little Rock who was collecting incriminating information on Clinton. Jackson reported that a friend had told him of a photograph of Clinton in bed with several women.

"It was a set-up," Jackson said. The detective taped his phone call and leaked the message to the *National Enquirer*, a tabloid that subsequently sought to buy the photo from Jackson. "It turned out that the photo didn't exist," Jackson said.

Until the latest controversy, it was his only attempt to harm Clinton with charges of sexual misconduct.

Jackson said that Sheffield Nelson, Clinton's Republican opponent in the 1990 governor's race, was the one who "pushed the woman thing" against Clinton last year. Jackson is often described by Clinton's friends as a "front" for Nelson, one of the leaders of the Arkansas Republican Party, but Jackson denied that he was close to Nelson.

For the past week, Jackson has been orchestrating the activities of the two troopers, and on Thursday he brought them to the Little Rock hotel room of a *Boston Globe* reporter for a long interview.

The troopers, Roger Perry and Larry Patterson, have the faces of men who have seen thousands of miles of hard road. Like Clinton and Jackson, they are men in their 40s. By their own accounts, they are divorced, paying child support, and struggling to get by on their $40,000 salaries. As Perry was confessing to having used a state telephone to call a girlfriend—a practice he accused Clinton of following—Jackson nodded to the trooper and cracked, "He's caused pain in his marriage."

They also acknowledged that they had lied in statements they gave investigators in 1990 after they wrecked a state police car during a night of drinking and honky-tonking.

That fact emerged at midweek after Roy Gene Sanders, a Little Rock attorney for an insurance company fighting Perry's claim for injuries, picked up the paper and recognized the troopers' names. "I had to bite my lip," Sanders said. "These were the same guys that lied like hell."

Sanders has depositions showing that Perry and Patterson fabricated a story to cover themselves after the wreck, then were forced to admit they had lied.

Both troopers are active in the Arkansas State Police Association, a lobbying organization that often clashed with Clinton over state policy. "We were promised things that he backed out on, things like salary and retirement legislation," said Perry, who was forced by his fellow troopers to resign last Tuesday as president of the organization as the tempest boiled.

However, the troopers said they were not motivated to attack Clinton because of his politics, but because of an accumulation of petty grievances.

They complained that Clinton used their services and then forgot them when he went to the White House. Perry said he had been forced to clean up "dog crap" when he was on Clinton's security detail. Patterson said he was told to take care of the family pet, Socks, even though he is allergic to cats.

After the Secret Service took over Clinton's security during the campaign, they complained they were relegated to sorting mail at the governor's mansion. "We got fifty to a hundred thousand pieces of mail a week, and 10,000 of them were for Socks," Perry said. After he told his supervisor, "I'm a state trooper, not a mailman," Perry said he was told he could transfer jobs.

Because they felt the governor's detail was prestigious, they said they endured the indignities.

Despite the comic nature of some of their complaints, Clinton's failure to follow through on their requests as he was leaving Arkansas seems to be at the heart of their anger.

"We lied and cheated and covered up for him for seven years," Perry said, charging that Clinton refused to authorize a job transfer within the state police department that Patterson sought and ignored Perry's appeal for a federal job.

Their former supervisor on the governor's security detail, Raymond L. (Buddy) Young, said in a telephone interview that Perry and Patterson were "disgruntled" with Clinton because "he didn't come out and slap them on the back after he was elected president. He didn't say 'What position do you want?' And they're mad."

Perry and Patterson said they once shared bonhomie with Clinton, swapping salacious stories with the governor when they drove him around the state. For Christmas presents, Clinton would give them bottles of whisky that had been given to the governor's mansion. Clinton rarely drinks.

"He wasn't a bad guy to be around," Patterson said. "He loved living on the edge, and one time he told me: 'Patterson, you love to live at the foot of the cross.'"

During the Gennifer Flowers imbroglio last year, Perry said, he exchanged repartee with Clinton over the charges of infidelity. "I told him: Governor, you would make Gary Hart look like a saint.' He just laughed."

After the election, Perry said, Clinton told him: "Roger, I've enjoyed working with you." He said he felt emboldened to ask if Clinton would consider appointing him to "something in law enforcement, a committee on dangerous drugs or something that had retired police officers on it. He told me: 'Just write me a little old letter and hand deliver it to me.' I wrote it in one paragraph and signed it and gave it to him. If he had offered me $300,000 to go to New York, there's no way I'd take it. Or Washington, D.C. If it was something in Memphis or Little Rock or Dallas, I would have considered it."

Perry said he never heard directly from Clinton again. "It would have been nice if I'd have had the opportunity to at least consider a move," he said. According to an affidavit issued last week by Danny Ferguson, another trooper who served as an anonymous source in the current stories about Clinton, Ferguson discussed Perry's old request for a job with Clinton when the president called in early September to explore rumors that the troopers were preparing a broadside against him.

"The president said he would try to track down Perry's request and asked Danny Ferguson to get in touch with Roger Perry to see what his memorandum said and to get back in touch with the president," the affidavit said. "No further discussion took place."

The Ferguson statement also said: "President Clinton never offered or indicated a willingness to offer any trooper a job in exchange for silence or help in shaping their stories."

The *Arkansas Democrat Gazette* reported Friday that Betsey Wright, Clinton's former chief of staff at the state capitol, prevailed upon Ferguson to issue the statement. "I did talk to him, and he was most willing to get that clarified," Wright told the newspaper.

Patterson, meanwhile, said he never wanted a federal job. He was seeking a transfer from the odd hours of the security detail to a regular forty-hour-a-week assignment for health reasons, he said, but Clinton never acted on his request.

The troopers said they avoided reporters exploring Clinton's rumored affairs after they were warned by their supervisor not to discuss the subject last year, but began considering a public move after he became president.

They approached Lynn Davis, a former director of the state police and a prominent Republican, for guidance. "Lynn tried to discourage us," Perry said. "The day he crossed the line was when he felt he was under surveillance by a state vehicle. He said it was chilling, and he told us: 'We need to do this.'"

Davis introduced the troopers to Jackson, who has been representing them without a fee.

Jackson said he first gave the story to the *Los Angeles Times* and the *American Spectator*, a conservative magazine, in August. The stories broke, like a one-two punch, a week ago.

Patterson said that, so far, the troopers had made "not one red cent" from their accusations, though they hope a publisher might be interested in a book of their stories from inside the governor's mansion. Flowers is believed to have made at least $150,000 from the tabloid press and television.

Clinton has lived with the threat of revelations against him for years. After he pulled back from a bid for the 1988 Democratic presidential nomination, there were rumors that Clinton feared the old *Gazette* "had stuff on his womanizing," according to Dumas, who worked for the newspaper. "None of it was true."

In 1990 a former state employee fired by Clinton filed suit against him, asserting the governor had used state funds to carry on affairs with at least five women, including Gennifer Flowers.

On the eve of the 1992 election, Guy Vander Jagt, a former Republican congressman from Michigan and head of the Republican Congressional Campaign Committee, publicly accused Clinton of having an affair with a reporter covering his campaign. Vander Jagt had no substantiation for his allegation, and it attracted little attention.

But the Flowers case was a lurid chapter in the 1992 campaign.

When he was sounding out potential contributors prior to his presidential run, Clinton was asked about rumors of marital infidelity. According to associates of Clinton, he privately admitted his involvement in affairs. Clinton was said to have insisted that he had stopped his extramarital activity and vowed that his marriage was strong.

After the Flowers case erupted, Clinton acknowledged that he had caused "pain in my marriage" during a dramatic appearance with his wife on *60 Minutes* in January 1992. He would go no further in his public statement. "I think most Americans who are watching this tonight; they'll know what we're saying. They get it," Clinton said.

Part V

Middle East Interlude

A Withered Wasteland

(*Boston Globe*, March 20, 1985)

The Israeli occupation in Lebanon, begun with its invasion of the country in 1982, lasted eighteen years. The Israeli army achieved its original purpose—to drive the PLO leadership from Beirut—but the decision to keep a military presence in hostile territory proved catastrophic. The occupation turned picturesque farmland along the Mediterranean into a war zone, encouraged the rise of a radical Islamic group, Hezbollah, and cost the lives of hundreds of civilians and soldiers in the region.

Often, I was able to call on the assistance of UN peacekeepers in order to get an inside view of the conflict, and I spent a lot of time in southern Lebanon between 1982 and my last visit in 1991.

Around the time I was writing this account, I arranged a meeting with a handful of Hezbollah fighters in the village of Marrakeh. They vowed resistance and proudly showed me a cache of weapons they planned to use against the Israelis. A couple of days later they were dead, killed by a bomb believed to have been placed in the annex of a mosque by Israeli saboteurs.

MAAROUB, Israeli-occupied Lebanon—The lush citrus orchards have been converted into fields of fire as the Israeli army reaps the bitter harvest of southern Lebanon.

Trees are bowed under the weight of their own fruit which now goes unpicked, and the ground is covered with rotting oranges and lemons that have already fallen. Farmers do not dare go into the fields, for any suspicious movement in the orchards—which serve as cover for snipers and roadside bombers—can draw fire from the Israelis.

The entire landscape of southern Lebanon is a picture of desolation today, a region in the thrall of a guerrilla war being fought by the local Shiite Moslem resistance and the counterterrorist tactics of the Israelis. Commerce in southern Lebanon, which is riddled with violence and isolated from the rest of the country by military roadblocks, has practically come to a halt. Villages have been abandoned, stores are shuttered, and there is little traffic on roads that once bustled with trucks loaded with produce and battered Mercedes.

Because of the threat of cars loaded with explosives and driven by suicidal Shiites, the Israeli army has imposed restrictions. Motorcycles are banned. Cars must carry at least two passengers or the driver risks being shot. The few cars on the road yield to Israeli troop convoys by pulling to the shoulder and stopping until the soldiers have passed. "That is one of the rules of survival in southern Lebanon," said a U.N. official stationed in the area.

An Israeli army officer who gave a *Globe* reporter permission to travel in the area this week insisted that he confine himself to U.N. vehicles. If the reporter attempted to move about in a Lebanese taxi without authorization—as he had done in the past to cover the conflict—he might draw "inadvertent fire," the officer warned.

But in the land where debris on the side of the road could be a bomb, where any moving vehicle could be on a suicide mission, even the marked U.N. truck belonging to the peacekeeping force was suspect. Nervous Israelis on foot patrols aimed their automatic rifles at the truck until it passed from sight.

There is fear in southern Lebanon, and it shows in the eyes of the soldiers of the army of the occupation.

Israeli forces struck Monday in Maaroub, a Shiite settlement in the hills seven miles east of the port city of Tyre.

Acting under a month-old policy known as Iron Fist to confiscate arms and round up suspected members of the Shiite resistance, the army surrounded the village just after dawn. It was a tame operation compared with some of the other Israeli raids. Thirty-four persons died at Zrariyeh, four miles north of here. No one was killed in Maaroub, although two Lebanese—identified as "terrorists" by the Israelis—were shot to death nearby that day. One house was bulldozed to the ground.

According to accounts from villagers and U.N. observers, the town was awakened by an Israeli truck equipped with a loudspeaker broadcasting orders, in Arabic, for all men to report to the local school. The women and children were told to stay inside their homes.

The Israelis used a small explosive charge to blow apart the door to the school, and shot locks on doors to open unoccupied homes as they conducted a house-to-house search.

By the time four American reporters and a photographer reached the village it was eerily quiet. About 150 Israeli soldiers were deployed around the village, but the only sounds were roosters and radio transmissions. Most of the male population—about 100 men—was being interrogated behind the walls of the school. Women peered warily out of the windows of their homes.

U.N. personnel, who had hurried to the scene, were perched on the tops of houses and in a minaret overlooking the schoolyard in order to watch the operation. The mandate of the U.N. Interim Force in Lebanon, or UNIFIL—which has served as a buffer between belligerents since 1978—calls for the protection of the civilian population in the embattled area.

The Israelis seized two new AK-47 assault rifles in one house, but centered their attention on a manhunt for Mohammed Shehadi, the director of the local school. A resident of Maaroub later said Shehadi is a leader of Amal, the chief arm of the Shiite resistance in southern Lebanon. "Of course, he is not here," he said.

Israeli soldiers, accompanied by Arabic-speaking agents of Shin Bet—an Israeli intelligence unit—questioned each of the village men individually, asking about weapons and the whereabouts of Mohammed Shehadi. The villagers were also led by a car where an informer, prepared to identify the suspect, was believed to be sitting.

Shehadi, who is in his 20s, could not be found, but the Israelis knew the house where his father lived. "We made as strong a protest as we can," said a U.N. observer, "but they are definitely going to blow up the house."

By late morning, the Israelis told the U.N. that the stone house where the Shehadi family lived was "the home of a terrorist" and had to be destroyed.

"All our protests are to no avail," the U.N. observer reported over radio to the UNIFIL headquarters.

A bulldozer was moved into town. As the family raced to rescue belongings from the house, the operator of the bulldozer mistakenly began attempts to push down a building next door. Told of his error, he moved on the Shehadi house. Within fifteen minutes it was reduced to a pile of rubble while the family watched from a house across the road.

Surrealism reached new heights when the Israelis pulled out of town. After a photographer indicated interest in a picture of the scene, about a dozen family members—including Shehadi's 57-year-old father and several women carrying children—gladly scrambled onto the ruins and assumed grief-stricken poses.

Fayad Dimashk, a 32-year-old schoolteacher, said that he and the rest of the men of the town were held more than six hours before being released. He said the Israelis told them they would be leaving southern Lebanon in ten weeks and hoped there would be no more fighting. He said they complained that the Lebanese "did not welcome them in a good manner."

During their search of his home, Dimashk said the Israelis stole two bottles of perfume. He said they broke into cupboards and looted other houses. In a further assertion—confirmed by the U.N. observers—Dimashk said an Israeli officer returned to the Mukhtar, the leader of the village, some money that soldiers had taken from the houses.

As the Israelis departed, Dimashk related, one officer gave the men of Maaroub a curious message. "He told us they hoped someday to come back and visit us with their families, and he said he hoped we would visit Israel." Did Dimashk have any interest in visiting Israel, whose border is less than twenty miles away? "I don't think so," he said.

In a two-sentence public report on the operation at Maaroub, the Israeli army concluded that "two terrorists who tried to flee the area were killed."

U.N. officials who found the bodies some distance from the village said they had apparently been shot by an Israeli patrol as they attempted to cross the Litani River. Two others who were thought to have been traveling in the same group were captured. One prisoner, blindfolded and his hands bound behind his back, was brought to Maaroub for interrogation.

Sources said that papers found on the bodies indicated they were connected with Hezbollah, the radical Shiite "Party of God," but there were no signs that they had been carrying weapons.

Maj. Lauri Ovaska, chief operations officer of a Finnish UNIFIL contingent, said that three bodies were found in the same area last week. The men had been shot repeatedly, and the face of one victim was mutilated by shots fired at close range. Because of Israeli road-blocks, many Lebanese try to return to their homes in the south by stealth. Instead of weapons, the three men killed last week were carrying plastic bags filled with tape cassettes and items for children, Ovaska said.

The Finns said there had been many incidents in the area lately. Homes have been hit with rifle fire and rocket-propelled grenades, though some of the strife is attributed to family feuds that have wracked Lebanon for decades.

On Saturday night, the wife of the sheik of the village of Khirbet Silm was wounded when their house was fired upon. The next night a rocket-propelled grenade hit the sheik's house again.

Israeli officials reiterated this week that their operations in southern Lebanon are designed to protect their own soldiers. They denied reports that they want to push hostile Shiites out of the area.

"Somebody," a U.N. official said of the attacks in Khirbet Silm, "intends to drive the sheik out."

The Last Vestiges of Civilization

(*Boston Globe*, December 15, 1985)

From the first time I saw the city, under siege by the Israeli army in
1982, Beirut seemed irrepressibly alluring, despite the danger. It was
the most Western of the Arab capitals, yet its people seemed trapped
in an endless war waged by many sides. The businesses of Beirut—still
functioning in the midst of violence—managed to offer some of the
best consumer goods in the Middle East. So I went there to take the
temperature of the civil war and to do a bit of Christmas shopping
for myself. I found the shortwave radio I had been seeking, but also
discovered another sad story.

BEIRUT—Life in Beirut—arguably the most civilized and, paradoxi-
cally, the most savage city in the Middle East—is finally turning into a
nightmare worthy of Kafka for many wealthy Lebanese who clung for
years to riches and comfort in the face of adversity.

The misery of the eleven-year-old civil war, which was usually concentrated in the impoverished southern suburbs and along the Green
Line that divides the city, has spread to Ras Beirut, the center of business and culture in the predominantly Moslem western sector.

In the days since two Moslem militias terrorized the neighborhood
in indiscriminate street fighting that killed at least sixty-eight persons
last month, people who had taken pride in maintaining a respectable
lifestyle seem traumatized and talk of leaving.

Their dilemma was underscored last week when two prominent
West Beirutis, both Christians, were kidnapped and held for three
days by Moslem fundamentalists before being released.

"It's a plot not just to eradicate Christians, it's to eliminate anyone who deals with civilization," said one of the hostages, Dr. Mounir Shamma'a, a Harvard-educated physician at American University Hospital. "Any intellectual group is at risk."

In an interview yesterday at his luxurious high-rise apartment overlooking the Mediterranean, Shamma'a said he was determined to stay in Beirut. "Out of conceit, I can say I'm the last person they should have kidnapped. I was born on this street. I'm a firm believer in co-religious habitation." But he long ago evacuated his family to London, and yesterday he acknowledged, "The rich bourgeoisie of Beirut are no longer in Beirut."

Joseph Salameh, who was kidnapped along with Shamma'a, was equally defiant. "Why do I stay?" he asked rhetorically in a separate interview. "Because I don't like to be pushed out." Salameh is a Greek Orthodox with leftist political views. He said, "I would live in Timbuktu before I'd live in East Beirut," where right-wing Maronite Catholics dominate.

Over lunch at his fashionable home in West Beirut, a wealthy Druze businessman who was educated in the United States said, "I think the pressure is psychological. It worries everyone with a Western culture. All my French friends have left. I think most people who can leave will leave."

He sent his daughter to safety during an evacuation of Swedes and says he only stays to tend to his family's considerable business interests "until they fold."

The terror is debilitating, he said. Moreover, he feels the economic end is approaching. "Maybe I'll move to Switzerland or London. Washington would be nice," he mused. "Maybe a sheep farm in New Zealand."

Even in affluent East Beirut, where residents gathered on high points to watch, like voyeurs, the Israeli bombardment of West Beirut in 1982, where bathers frolicked on the beaches while the other side of the city burned in the background, a bunker mentality is developing.

On Thursday, when it was possible to cross at one point along the Green Line, a visit to East Beirut found many stores barricaded with cement blocks.

THE LAST VESTIGES OF CIVILIZATION

When fighting closed the Green Line again this weekend, at least ten persons were killed in the shelling, and several of the casualties were in East Beirut, which was once inviolate.

The wealthy Beirutis, from both sides of the city, are fleeing—to nearby Cyprus, to Europe, to the United States—and the stench of burning garbage and decay associated with the wretched refugee camps and shantytowns hangs over Beirut like a miasma.

A West Beirut woman who operates a record store near the Green Line was almost hysterical the other day as she described her plight, cackling over her own jokes—black humor concerning Hezbollah, the Moslem "Party of God" that is believed responsible for the latest kidnappings. "Beirut is finished," she said, laughing in a desperate high pitch. "Not just our side, their side too."

At a lunch featuring sole meuniere and French wine at a hotel off Hamra Street, a longtime West Beirut resident—a Palestinian intellectual—told of how his partner had just left for the United States. "His nerves were gone. Every day, especially when there was firing, he would put his head on his desk. . . . Now I don't know how long I can continue myself."

Another Palestinian Christian—with an American wife, a British education, and a successful family-owned appliance store—invited a reporter, a friend from previous visits here, to his comfortable apartment for dinner Friday night. This family, too, is finally talking of leaving.

The catalyst was the fight last month between former allies—the Shiite militia Amal and guerrillas loyal to the Druze Progressive Socialist Party—that raged on the street below them for days.

"There were 16-year-old kids in jeans with rifles and RPGs. You couldn't tell whose side they were on. They were just shooting," said the Palestinian. RPGs are rocket-propelled grenades.

At the Hotel Commodore, which has long been a neutral sanctuary for foreign journalists in Ras Beirut, the Druze forces have forced the management to install its casino in the basement. The casino was an affront to Shiite Moslem fundamentalists, who smashed the hotel bar a year ago.

Now, neighborhood residents are waiting for the casino to be taken out with a bomb.

Bootleg cassettes are a major industry here. At a shop around the corner from the Commodore, one of the most popular albums is by Dire Straits, a British rock group, and the lyrics of its title track, "Brothers in Arms," are like a funeral chant for Beirut:

> Through these fields of destruction, baptisms of fire
> I've witnessed your suffering as the battle raged high
> and though it hurt me so bad in the fear and alarm
> you did not desert me, my brothers in arms . . .
> Let me bid you farewell, every man has to die
> But it's written in the starlight and every line in your palm
> We're fools to make war on our brothers in arms.

Land Without a Country

(*Boston Globe Magazine*, September 7, 1986)

Of all the hellholes I've visited around the world, the Gaza Strip may have been the worst. In the mid-1980s, I felt little was being written about the occupied territory seized by Israel in the 1967 war, so I spent a week there talking with the people of Gaza.

Looking back, I believe I captured the state of depression, but failed to detect an underlying mood of rebellion. A little more than a year after I wrote of Gaza, the region exploded with the first rocks thrown in the Intifadah, the first Palestinian revolt. It took years, but the uprising eventually led to Israel yielding control.

Gaza today is governed by Hamas, a radical Palestinian organization that broke with the old PLO and has engaged in frequent firefights with the Israelis. The Israeli occupation is over, but Gaza still exists as a maverick state.

Welcome.

The characters in Arabic, English, and obligatory Hebrew crawl in falsely bright colors, as sad as toys in a children's cancer ward, across an arch over the gateway to the city: "Welcome to Gaza."

Welcome to a twenty-five-mile stretch of almost unrelieved squalor, where raw sewage runs openly in the alleys of the Palestinian refugee camps and flows like a polluted tidal stream into the Mediterranean.

Welcome to a teeming territory that has served for nearly forty years as home for thousands of refugees who long ago lost hope.

Largely abandoned by their Arab brothers and ignored by the Western world, they are ruled by Israel's army of occupation and economically bled each day by measures imposed by the Israeli government.

Welcome to another of the great shames of twentieth-century civilization, this latest dwelling place of the "wretched of the earth," as the revolutionary writer Frantz Fanon once described another group of downtrodden Arabs living under colonization in North Africa. There is, however, no revolution brewing here; none of the palpable anger seething in the Palestinian West Bank cities of Hebron and Nablus. The people of Gaza have been beaten by circumstances into submission.

Welcome to Gaza, source of cheap labor, the "Soweto of the state of Israel," as it has been called. Since there are not nearly enough jobs for the local population, the highway to Tel Aviv is lined in the pre-dawn hours with thousands of men trying to find a ride to one of Israel's day-labor gathering spots in the hope they might get a job for as little as $5 a day. "I think we have reached the bottom," says Rashad Shawa, a local leader who has been twice deposed by the Israelis as mayor of Gaza for refusing to cooperate with the occupation. "We are enslaved by Israel. We have become the servants of Israel. All of the street sweepers of Israel are from Gaza. Our young people are forced to work in degrading jobs. . . . Even our breath is restricted. If we want to hold meetings, they are restricted. If we want to travel, we must get permission."

Welcome to the Gaza Strip, which exists in limbo. Unlike other Palestinians in their diaspora, including those in the West Bank, the people of Gaza are claimed by no country and wanted, it seems, by no one. They hold no passports. If they can obtain travel documents from Israel or neighboring Egypt, their nationality is listed simply as "undefined."

"We are stateless. We don't have an identity," says Mary Khass, the Gazan director of a preschool program for Palestinian children sponsored by the American Friends Service Committee, one of the few relief agencies at work here. Speaking with a cultured English accent, her voice rises in anger when she describes her experiences traveling outside Gaza. "On the plane, I'm equal until we land and I go to the immigration desk. Then I become a terrorist. I'm interrogated, searched. It's degrading and insulting. The world has no right to treat me like that."

Yet Gaza was being exploited before Mary Khass was born. The older generation has lived through the reign of four different foreign powers. At the turn of the century, Gaza was part of the Ottoman empire and Turkish law was applied. This gave way after World War I to the British mandate, a period that old-time Arab residents remember as repressive and tilted toward the eventual establishment of a Jewish state in the region.

The current crisis developed in 1948, when Arabs and Jews went to war over the land known by a name now consigned to history—Palestine. Thousands of Arabs living in the old Gaza district of Palestine, which once covered much of the area between Ashqelon, Beersheba, and the Sinai desert, fled their homes and their livelihood and poured into the narrow Gaza strip, which remained in the Arabs' control. With the creation of the state of Israel, Arab holdings in what was once southern Palestine were reduced by 90 percent. Palestinian refugee camps were erected, incongruously, along the sparkling shores of the Mediterranean. At first there were tent cities of the dispossessed. In time, the United Nations Relief and Works Agency—formed to deal with the problem—leased land from Arab landholders and built warrens of adobelike huts for shelter.

For nineteen years Gaza endured under an Egyptian administration. There was never prosperity, but the Gazans say these were glory days compared with what would come after Israel seized control of the strip after the Six-Day War in 1967. "When the Israelis came, it was not an occupation, but a system of extermination," Shawa says. "People were uprooted and crammed into a small area. Our land was reduced from 11 million dunams to 360,000 dunams (about 140 square miles). The Israeli confiscation of land is increasing every day. There are economic pressures, taxation—both indirect and direct. The pressure on the social life is increasing to force the people to quit."

Shawa's charges are supported in a new study, *The Gaza Strip Survey*, written by Sara M. Roy of Harvard University and published by a prominent Jerusalem-based research project headed by Meron Benvenisti, an Israeli. Over the first eighteen months of the Israeli occupation, between 60,000 and 100,000 people left Gaza, the study says. "This emigration resulted from a series of Israeli measures ranging from forcible exile to policies which encouraged residents to leave and prevented others, who happened to be outside of Gaza during the war, from returning."

In recent years, the move to create Jewish settlements in the region has intensified, and the Israeli government has taken over—through confiscation or eminent domain—nearly a third of the land left in Gaza. A bloc of settlements has claimed some of the most desirable beachfront property in the southern section of the strip. As one Gazan said with a sneer, "They say they are building the new Israeli Riviera."

Behind barricades and wire fences, protected by the Israeli military, the Jewish settlers are indeed establishing a beachhead in Gaza. At Neve Dekalim, one of the newest and most modern settlements, a synagogue in the shape of the Star of David rises in the sand dunes. The rows of neat, prefabricated homes stand in stark contrast to the decaying refugee camps. The settlement is developing the waterfront with a hotel and cabana-style cafes in hopes of luring Israeli tourists. Reuven Rosenblatt, the chairman of the board of Neve Dekalim, said it was no matter to the settlers that the government in Jerusalem does not officially consider Gaza part of "Eretz Israel," the biblical land of the Jews. "We believe it is Eretz Israel," he said. "If not we would not live here as Jews."

There have been no attacks on the settlement, where 180 Jewish families live, since it was erected three years ago, Rosenblatt said. They have coexisted with the Palestinians without incident, but he said the settlers were constantly aware that "we have a problem—every Jew has a problem with Arabs who want to kill him."

There has really been little resistance in Gaza since the Israeli army crushed a Palestinian guerrilla movement in 1971. "You cannot see murder in the eyes," says a spokesman for the Israeli command in Gaza. "Here you must remember the people got used to living under military governments for hundreds of years."

The army patrols the area in strength and maintains checkpoints and watchtowers throughout the strip. Gaza is governed by what the Israelis call a "civil administration," but it is a military operation. At one point in an interview with a colonel who serves as spokesman for the government, he referred to "soldiers in the civil administration." He stopped and reflected at his own Orwellian language, then shrugged and said, "Never mind."

Israeli foot patrols roam the streets of Gaza, and all Gazans must carry identification cards issued by the civil administration and are subject to arrest if they are stopped for questioning and found without the card.

In spite of these pressures, the Palestinian numbers are growing. There are now more than 500,000 residents of Gaza. According to the United Nations Relief and Works Agency, 427,000 of these are registered refugees, 236,000 actually live in eight refugee camps, and the rest are in resettlement projects or old cities such as Gaza, Khan Yunis, or Rafah.

The population density of Gaza is ten times greater than that of the West Bank, the larger, better-known of the Arab territories occupied by Israel. In fact, Gaza has become such an afterthought in political discussions that it is often generically included under the term West Bank—even though the West Bank Palestinians enjoy Jordanian citizenship and under vestiges of Jordanian law were once permitted municipal elections, in 1976. (Those West Bank mayors are all but gone now, maimed by Jewish terrorist bombs or deported or deposed by Israeli authorities. There have been no democratic elections since and none are contemplated.)

The situation in Gaza is simpler. There have been no elections. Shawa accepted Israeli appointment as mayor in 1971 after obtaining a petition of support from his Palestinian constituents and the blessings of the Palestine Liberation Organization. He was dismissed in

1973, reappointed in 1975, and finally deposed in 1982 for being too outspoken against the occupation.

Through the Israeli military command, the municipalities in Gaza are run by Israeli-appointed councils or an Israeli military officer. According to *The Gaza Strip Survey*: "There is no effective local government inside the Gaza strip today that is representative of and motivated by indigenous concerns."

In an effort to regain some Arab autonomy in the Gaza strip, Shawa recently approached Egyptian president Hosni Mubarak about the possibility of reaching an agreement with Israel wherein Egypt would again supervise the strip until the overall Palestinian problem could be resolved. Mubarak rejected the idea. His country effectively wrote off its claim on Gaza when it signed the Camp David Accords with Israel. Besides, Egypt has enough problems of its own without Gaza.

Before the accords, Egypt accepted as many as 1,500 Gazan students a year at its overcrowded universities. That opportunity has been shut off. At present, Egyptian universities take in no more than fifty Gazan students each year. Higher education in Gaza is confined to Islamic University, an institution where Moslem fundamentalists have a foothold. Secular Palestinians in Gaza have accused Shin Bet, the Israeli secret service, of subsidizing the efforts of the fundamentalists to disrupt the society under the "divide and conquer" theory.

Another effect of the Camp David Accords was to divide further the families of Gaza. When Egypt regained the Sinai in 1982, the border slashed through the heart of a refugee camp at Rafah. More than 5,000 Palestinians suddenly found themselves living behind Egyptian lines, separated by coils of barbed wire and patrol roads from their friends and relatives on the Israeli side. Every day, a heartbreaking scene takes place as the refugees, clinging to the wires, call out to one another across a 100-foot-wide military zone while Israeli and Egyptian soldiers enforce their separation.

There have been plans, bruited about for months, to move the refugees from Egyptian territory to the other side, but the relocation has been stalled by the bickering between Israel and Egypt over the sovereignty of Taba, another tiny piece of property on the eastern edge of the Sinai.

Gazans say they actually feel more affinity toward Jordan than Egypt, because Jordan is predominantly composed of Palestinians, and its culture—if not its proximity—is closer to Gaza. But there is no sign that King Hussein, locked in a struggle with PLO chairman Yasser Arafat, the leader of the Palestinians in exile, covets Gaza.

Asked recently if he were willing to extend Jordanian citizenship to the stateless people of Gaza, Hussein said, "It is a subject that needs to be studied." The Jordanian monarch said he has discussed Gaza's case with Mubarak but indicated that the Palestinian question could not be resolved through a "piecemeal" approach that tackled Gaza's problems first.

The situation in the Middle East has driven the people of Gaza to despair. "The majority of the Palestinians feel disappointed in the Arab countries," said one Gaza resident. "We feel they are using us just as badly as Israel. Israel may not want us either, but we are their market and their cheap labor."

The greatest anguish in Gaza lies in the refugee camps, the sprawling compounds of Jabaliya (population 51,000), Rafah (48,000), and Beach Camp (40,000), and five smaller camps along the strip.

At Beach Camp, the mother of ten children admits visitors into her home, where they are squeezed into two bedrooms and a kitchen area. Her teen-aged son lies on a mat on the floor, his face shielded from the morning light. Heat beats upon the camp in waves, and the stench of rotten vegetables and sewage is overpowering.

The mother says she has borne so many children because it was "Allah's will," but she says her husband is disabled and her family could not make it without the rations the United Nations Relief and Works Agency gives to the neediest: cooking oil, rice, used clothing. "We're completely dependent on rations," she says in Arabic. "If there are no rations, what are we to do?"

At least they have a roof over their heads. Families of men arrested for political activity or random sabotage against the Israeli occupation routinely have their homes bulldozed to the ground. In the cluster of makeshift shelters built of corrugated tin, pasteboard, and mud, there are gaps where homes have been demolished.

The army spokesman explains Israeli policy. "If there is blood in the story" of a Palestinian attack, then the homes of those arrested are automatically destroyed before any trial. "This has been the case since 1967." Sometimes, he says, the army is benevolent. Last year, soldiers went to demolish the home of a young man charged in an ambush of an Israeli taxi. "When the general saw so many children—there were seventeen at the house; two were blind—he decided only to destroy the room where the terrorist lived."

Recently, the army tore down several homes near the civil administration compound. They were destroyed, he says, because the homeowners had no license for the land.

Offshore at Gaza, the rotting hulk of a ship that ran aground years ago fits into the tableau at Beach Camp. Children pick through the sewage and wastewater for items that could be useful. Fishermen idle by their boats, beached on the glistening sand. It is a landscape of desperation.

Hatem Abu Ghazalah, the chairman of Gaza's Society for the Care of Handicapped Children, complained in a speech in Jerusalem in May that "development in the occupied territories has been held back and restricted to what will tie us to the Israeli economic machine." He charged that U.N. activities were "totally under the terms of the occupying authorities."

A similar charge is made by relief officials working in Gaza who serve as the outlet for U.S. aid projects. "What is America doing?" asked one Palestinian sarcastically. "That would be a nice joke if it were not so sad."

The state of Israel, with approximately four million residents, receives about $4 billion annually from the United States in military assistance, credits, and Agency for International Development (AID) grants. The annual AID package for Gaza is roughly $4 million. Israel has veto power over every AID project in the territory. "We want to control it," the army spokesman says.

An American diplomat involved in the process says the Israelis are now approving about 80 percent of the AID applications and characterizes as "very unfair" the assertion by some relief workers that much of the American money pumped into the territories is diverted for roads to improve the infrastructure for the Jewish settlements.

"They are farm-to-market roads built for the Gazans," he says. "We can't control who drives on them."

The diplomat concedes there is a striking disparity in the foreign aid to Israel and the allocation to Gaza. "It's not distributed fairly, that's correct," he says while pointing out that U.S. assistance to Gaza is greater than any other country gives.

A couple of years ago, U.S. Secretary of State George Shultz used an expression—repeated by American and Israeli officials—about improving the "quality of life" in the occupied territories. Shultz, however, represents an administration with a gift for euphemism—weapons of war are called "peacemakers," a friendly policy toward racism in South Africa is known as "constructive engagement," and children killed in air raids in Libya become "collateral damage."

A frustrated relief worker in Gaza, who says he repeatedly fights Israeli and American red tape to win approval for projects in the region, says, "It's a pretty selective view of 'quality of life.'"

In Bethlehem, a Bleak Christmas

(*Boston Globe*, December 23, 1988)

The Intifadah broke out a few weeks after I had moved from Jerusalem
back to Boston in late 1987. I was disappointed, as the old saying
goes, that "they started the revolution without me." But the *Globe*
sent me back to the Middle East on temporary duty to help cover the
upheaval, and I spent months operating out of my favorite hotel in the
world, the American Colony in Palestinian East Jerusalem. To depict the
scene on the West Bank, I believed a piece on Christmas in Bethlehem
represented a perfect metaphor.

BETHLEHEM, Israeli-occupied West Bank—There is a special Christmas irony in the little town of Bethlehem this year. The Jewish command of Israel's army of occupation is trying to persuade Christian officials and merchants to observe the holiday by putting up decorations.

In spite of the Israeli efforts, Bethlehem's businessmen are following the municipality's decision to hold a muted Christmas. There will be traditional church services here tomorrow night, but no decorations and no expected air of celebration.

The gloom in Bethlehem, a Palestinian town a few miles south of Jerusalem that is the Biblical birthplace of Jesus Christ, is expected to cut the number of pilgrims drastically and to add to the depression of the tourist industry in Israel, as well as in the Israeli-occupied West Bank.

Many of the hotels in Jerusalem are practically deserted. Normally at this time of year, they are full of pilgrims.

"The political atmosphere is so difficult and discouraging that our Christian people don't want to celebrate Christmas," the mayor of Bethlehem, Elias Freij, said in an interview yesterday.

"We don't want to put decorations on a Christmas tree or buy gifts for our children. It is an act to tell the whole world that we are people who live under duress and persecution. There is no incentive to decorate the town."

Israeli officials are trying to put the best light on the situation.

"There are false rumors that Christmas celebrations are canceled, but that is not true," said Mordechai Ben-Ari, a spokesman for the Israeli Ministry of Tourism. "No secular authority—neither our ministry nor the municipality—can cancel a religious holiday."

Freij, who is a Christian, said he had discussions with Israeli authorities after the municipality announced it would not erect Christmas lights this year.

"If I yield to pressure, I would not be mayor for seventeen years," he said, adding that his decision to abandon the decorations was popular with his constituents.

Freij also said he had no intention of being host to Israeli officials for the annual celebration as he has done in the past. Two years ago, both Prime Minister Yitzhak Shamir and Shimon Peres, the leader of Israel's Labor Party, attended Freij's Christmas Eve reception as a gesture of good will between the Israelis and the Palestinians.

Before the Palestinian uprising—the intifadah—against Israeli rule began a little more than a year ago, Bethlehem was the scene of an elaborate Christmas Eve ceremony, climaxed by an internationally televised midnight Mass at the Church of the Nativity. The church is said to have been built over the manger where Mary gave birth to Jesus.

Palestinian shopkeepers, who are predominantly Christian, said they were summoned to the Israeli military governor's office this week and encouraged to decorate their stores.

"I don't see anything going on," said a local merchant, gesturing at Manger Square, a melange of empty souvenir shops and cafes where City Hall is set across the plaza from the Church of the Nativity.

The shopkeeper, who did not want to give his name, said that ordinarily his store would be decorated with Christmas garlands and colored windows. But this year, there are no signs that the Christmas season is at hand.

There were virtually no tourists in Bethlehem yesterday. Like every other location in the West Bank, stores in the town have been closed for four days in the past week to observe a general strike called by the underground leadership of the intifadah. On "normal" days, the stores are only open from 9 a.m. to noon, in keeping with the instructions of the intifadah communiques.

"We are open and we are closed," the merchant said. "Some days, we don't make a one-shekel sale."

Other merchants, open and gregarious in the days before the intifadah began, were sullen and reluctant to talk yesterday.

There was little activity around Manger Square: a few Palestinian shoppers, Israeli army foot patrols stopping young men to check their identification cards, other Israeli soldiers trying to cobble together a stage near the Church of the Nativity for five international choirs coming to sing on Christmas Eve.

Near the Israeli police station, located on the square, a star left over from last year was hanging from a bedraggled fir tree, but the sockets on the star had few bulbs. Nearby, an Israeli workman on a ladder was trying to screw colored bulbs into another star on a post near the church.

Ben-Ari said the Ministry of Tourism, rather than the municipality, had provided Bethlehem with Christmas lights in the past. "Out of respect for the request of the host city," he said, there will be no major display.

However, Freij said that Bethlehem had been paying for the lights and that Palestinian electricians had been installing them for the past four years. Until this year, they were turned on a couple of days before Dec. 25 and kept lighted through the Greek Orthodox celebration in early January, he said.

The pilgrims who come to Bethlehem this year, Freij said, "are most welcome. We welcome all people of good will."

IN BETHLEHEM, A BLEAK CHRISTMAS

Bethlehem is suffering because of its support of the intifadah, he said. The economic hardship "is ten times more difficult" than last Christmas, at the beginning of the uprising.

"We have eighty-four restaurants closed. About 2,000 craftsmen who work with olive wood and mother-of-pearl, mostly" are "out of work. Unemployment is 50 percent," Freij said.

"Even if we are in a bad situation," the mayor said, "we wish all people of good will a very happy Christmas. We appeal to all the world to help the Palestinians and the Israelis reach a peace settlement where both people can live in peace as good neighbors, free neighbors, equal neighbors, who can join hands to improve the quality of life for everybody in the Holy Land. This is my Christmas wish."

Gaza Homesteading a Tough Sell

(*Boston Globe*, January 10, 1989)

Occasionally there were comic stories to come out of the Middle East, and an attempt by government-subsidized Israeli entrepreneurs to develop an attractive seaside Jewish community in the midst of the seething Gaza Strip was one of them. My friend, the late Israeli writer Amos Elon, invited me to accompany him on an expedition to look at the home sites. We posed as potential "investors," got a promotional tour, then laughed all the way back to Jerusalem.

NEVE DEKALIM, Israeli-occupied Gaza Strip—The advertisements hold out all of the false promise of a distant piece of property in the backwaters of Florida.

"Enjoy the good life," Israeli newspaper ads say. "Live in a young, effervescent community."

Television commercials, sponsored by the Israeli government, show happy children's faces in a beach atmosphere. The pictures are known in the TV trade as "tight shots," focusing closely on the subject without revealing the surroundings.

The promotions are part of this month's campaign to "Populate the Katif," an area the Israelis call the "coast of the Negev."

In fact, the Katif lies in the heart of the Gaza Strip, surrounded by 650,000 impoverished and angry Palestinians, and beckoning Jewish settlers to the region during the intifadah is a little like trying to lure pioneers to the American West at the height of the Indian wars.

Instead of a stagecoach with a shotgun rider, a promotional bus tour sets out twice a week from Ashkelon, an Israeli city on the Mediterranean, to show "entrepreneurs and investors" the Katif. The bus is guarded by a young man wearing a kippa, a religious skullcap, and carrying an automatic rifle. For additional protection, some of the prospective settlers take their own pistols.

Meron Benvenisti, a prominent Israeli analyst of affairs in the occupied territories, dismisses as "ridiculous" the "Populate the Katif" campaign. "They have chutzpah to show it as if it is Hawaii, 500 yards from the most congested part of the world," he said.

Most of the passengers on a promotional tour last week appeared to be young Israeli newlyweds. Their clothing indicated a working-class background. The young men wore religious skullcaps and held hands with their wives. They showed none of the nationalist fervor of Gush Emunim, the settlers movement.

The young Israelis simply seemed to be in search of an inexpensive home on the sea, and that was the sales pitch employed by the promoters, who extolled the Mediterranean while ignoring the indigenous Palestinians.

The "Populate the Katif" campaign is a joint venture underwritten by the government's Ministry of Labor and Social Affairs, the World Zionist Council, and the Gaza Strip District Council, a settlers' organization.

Critics of the program say it is an attempt by the Israeli government to mollify the settlers, who have been demanding greater protection and services.

According to the sponsors, homes with low interest rates are available in the Katif for as little as 85,000 shekels ($47,000). The project is heavily subsidized by the government. Coupled with the low cost of land and labor, housing is 40 percent less than in neighboring Ashkelon, one official estimated.

Israeli cynics say it is a desperate giveaway to try to establish a Jewish presence in Gaza. One Israeli source suggested that some people might be willing to invest a small amount in the region in the hope of getting back an enormous compensation from the government if Israel withdraws from the territory.

Settlers in the Sinai, south of here, were rewarded with handsome sums when Israel returned the land to Egypt in 1982. Settlers in Gaza acknowledge they have no assurance from the government that Gaza will never be yielded back to Arab hands.

The current campaign concentrates on the theme of the "good life," encouraging young Israelis to join less than 3,000 Jews who are already living in a collection of settlements along the Mediterranean in Gaza.

As the bus traveled to the Katif, it avoided the main roads and population centers of Gaza, passing only benign Bedouin encampments with camels and tents and random Palestinian farm boys hauling goods to market on donkeys.

The tour guide told the group that the government was "building a new road to enable people to go to the Katif without passing through Gaza City." He promised that a new power station in Ashkelon would give "top priority" to settlers for jobs. There would be a new marina built for those who wanted to approach the Katif by boat, he said, and another new road from Beersheba, an Israeli city in the Negev desert.

"Our aim," said the guide, "is to turn the Katif into a resort beach for the entire region."

With their rust-colored terra cotta roofs and glistening white walls, the houses of the settlements look as though they belong in a tropical paradise, not in a hostile environment.

Near the southern tip of the Katif, where the wooden framework was set up for construction projects, the guide said the homes would have windows that looked only to the west, to the sea. The vista to the southeast is less picturesque—the teeming Palestinian city and refugee camps of Rafah on the Egyptian border.

When the guide showed off another settlement near Gaza City, the group was oblivious to the fact that eleven Palestinians had been shot and wounded that day by the Israeli army a few miles away during disturbances at Beach Camp, a squalid refugee encampment.

Aside from the critical demographical problems for Israelis, the Katif is actually a beautiful beachfront that stretches several miles between Gaza City and the Egyptian border. Before the intifadah erupted in Gaza in December 1987, visionaries predicted that the area would become the "Israeli Riviera."

A seaside hotel was erected a couple of years ago, along with a thatch-roofed cabana cafe and a cluster of bungalows. It is all closed now.

Menachem Deutsch, an official with the Gaza Strip District Council, blamed the operation's failure last year on the Israeli Ministry of Tourism. The government "did not give the money that was promised on time," he said. "The hotel's problems were coincidental with the intifadah. Both caused negative reactions. Maybe the intifadah influenced the problems, but last summer in the middle of the intifadah, the hotel was full."

There is still hope. Michael Dekel, a ranking Likud official in the new government, met with the Gaza settlers last week. He promised an increased commitment and claimed that 400 families had expressed interest in moving to the Katif.

Benvenisti said that fifty families would be more realistic. "Some people will go there. The impact of the intifadah is less startling today. It has become a way of life," he said.

But near the end of last week's trip, after lectures on the potential of growing tomatoes year-round, the hospitable climate, and even the prospect that Arabs might someday disappear from Gaza, the tour guide asked the group if they would like to see more or return to Ashkelon.

"Ashkelon!" they shouted. "Ashkelon!"

Part VI

Writers

Israel's Faulkner

(*Boston Globe*, January 9, 1987)

During my years in Jerusalem, I found that Faulkner held an honored
place in some Israeli circles. Once, when I interviewed Prime Minister
Shimon Peres, he volunteered the information that he read Faulkner.
So when I discovered A. B. Yehoshua's novels and saw a Faulkner
reference, I asked a mutual friend to arrange a meeting with him at his
home in Haifa, up the Mediterranean coast from Tel Aviv.

HAIFA, Israel—He is 50, of strong Sephardic stock, his mother Moroccan, his father's family running five generations deep into this tortured land, so he writes passionately of the divisions in Israel and prophesies the day when a Palestinian nation will lie in peace beside the Jewish state, a dream that is shared by only the good and the innocent.

A. B. Yehoshua is Israel's Faulkner, obsessed by the conflict in his homeland. Like William Faulkner, his novels are tapestries woven with narratives and streams of consciousness from various characters; scenes and dialogue are often repeated, with subtle changes from different perspectives. He has created heroic figures as well as Snopesian connivers; his tales are haunted by sad, misunderstood children and victims demented by madness.

His brilliant novel, *A Late Divorce*, actually begins with a citation from *The Sound and the Fury*.

In contrast to his dark and brooding books, Yehoshua is effervescent—an animated conversationalist and an optimist. In an interview in his office at the University of Haifa, where he writes and teaches literature, Yehoshua was quick to pay homage to Faulkner.

"I have taken from Faulkner the technique of divided voices because the reality in Israel is so diverse. There are so many points of view at the same moment," he said. The style is used in *A Late Divorce* as well as his first novel, *The Lover*. Both books have been translated into English and can be found in U.S. bookstores.

> What happened on Saturday three years ago? I hadn't even
> remembered that there was such a day. It vanished without
> a trace, without even leaving behind its own phantom pain.
> Saturday? Somehow I lost it—I, who tended each one of those
> days like a priestess at the altar; who stubbornly salvaged them,
> forever frozen in clarity, from the passage of time; who zealously
> assembled and preserved their story person by person and day
> by day down to its last detail, color, smell, fragment of conversa-
> tion, article of clothing, shift of mood and of weather . . . (*A Late
> Divorce*)

Yehoshua indicated he is using a more traditional approach in a new work that is being published in Hebrew this month. In *Molcho*, which will not be available in English for another year, the central character is a 50-year-old widower. As he tries to build a new life for himself, he leaves troubled Jerusalem to visit the divided city of Berlin.

With the same frankness that characterizes his views as a social critic, Yehoshua says he actually approves of partitioned cities and longs for the day when the Palestinians will be given back control of their half of his hometown, Jerusalem.

Yehoshua's books are filled with lamentations for Jerusalem, where the most hallowed Jewish site is the Western Wall, the remains of a temple torn down by the Romans nearly 2,000 years ago.

> A hybrid of town and wasteland. Jerusalem at its saddest, for-
> ever destroyed. However much it is built, Jerusalem will always

be marked by the memory of its destruction. (*A Poet's Continuing Silence*)

Visitors to Jerusalem fail to recognize the problems that lurk behind the facade of holy attractions, he says. "Jerusalem is becoming dangerous. The religious aspect is increasing; so is the conflict between Arabs and Jews. The city is heavy with symbols. Jerusalem is an unsolved problem. A lost case. Nobody gives any concession and they'll fight and kill to their deaths."

The author, who grew up in an affluent Jerusalem neighborhood, has chosen to live in the port city of Haifa. "The balances are good here," he says. "There are good relations between Arabs and Jews, Ashkenazi and Sephardi, religious and secular. There is never a stone thrown here." Jerusalem, on the other hand, "is becoming totalitarian."

Yehoshua is a man with outspoken convictions. He was once involved with a maverick leftist party, but says he has joined the mainstream Labor Party in an effort to push its leadership to the left. Although he originally endorsed the coalition government, he now says the compatibility between Labor and the right-wing Likud bloc is "destroying democracy" in Israel.

Yehoshua, whose voice is respected because of his literary work, is an exponent of a proposal to return the captured territories to the Arabs—the West Bank and Gaza Strip, as well as East Jerusalem. He would like to see a demilitarized Palestinian state created, and if it were endangered by hostile Arab states such as Iraq or Syria, he sees Israel as the protector of the Palestinians.

The Israeli occupation, he says, is self-defeating. To yield the territories, Israel "might have to give up some stones, some houses, but it would gain values, tranquility, and ideals."

He would like for the United States—"which already has its hands here" with its enormous foreign aid program—to use moral suasion to push Israel to give up the occupied Arab territories. "I want America to come here with a big stick." He described former President Jimmy Carter, who is vilified in some Israeli circles because he forced Israel to pull back from its first invasion of Lebanon in 1978 and encouraged the peace treaty with Egypt, as "a true lover of Israel."

By increasing U.S. assistance to Israel, President Reagan is generally viewed as a major ally of Israel. But Yehoshua faults Reagan for failing to put diplomatic pressure on Israel.

> Knowing where to draw the line, that's what matters, and whoever doesn't want to know had better stay in the village and laugh alone in the fields or sit in the orchard and curse the Jews as long as he likes. Those of us who are with them all day have to be careful. No, they don't hate us. Anyone who thinks they hate us is completely wrong. We're beyond hatred, for them we're like shadows. Take, fetch, hold, clean, lift, sweep, unload, move. That's the way they think of us . . . (Na'im in *The Lover*)

The Lover is primarily the story of a search by a garage owner for his wife's lover, who disappeared during the Yom Kippur War. It contains vivid scenes of fighting in the Sinai, which Yehoshua drew from his own experience as an Israeli paratrooper during the Sinai campaign in the 1950s.

There is an important subplot in *The Lover* that involves the garage owner's daughter and a 14-year-old Arab boy, Na'im. Yehoshua seems to have been successful in putting himself into the mind of the young Arab, just as Faulkner, a white Mississippian, was able to portray blacks in the segregated South. "It wasn't difficult to do at the time I did it," Yehoshua says. "Na'im came to my head like a trumpet, singing in very loud and clear music. He was a poor Arab, not too hostile, who wanted to advance in society and was unable to do so. When I created him in 1973, I didn't have the guilt feeling toward the Arabs like today because of Lebanon and the West Bank. I feel too contradictory toward the Arabs today—guilt because of what we're doing to them and anger that they're not coming to us for negotiations."

He says he feels he is no longer able to convey the Arab mentality in his writings, but is still hopeful that someday the Palestinian question will be settled, that there will be an open border between Israel and the new Palestine.

After all, he says, Middle East miracles have occurred before.

The Book of Lamentations

(*Boston Globe Magazine*, November 29, 1987)

I got to know David Grossman when I lived in Jerusalem. His courage
and work as a young journalist was impressive. Israel, like Mississippi,
has an inordinate number of writers and David was emerging as a new
literary voice. As I prepared to move back to the States, his provocative
book, *The Yellow Wind*, was scheduled to be published in the U.S.,
so I took advantage of the timing to do a magazine piece. Over the
past quarter-century I believe David's triumphs as a novelist and a
thoughtful social critic have vindicated my early judgments.

For several years, David Grossman, born a sabra, native son of Israel,
avoided the Arab quarters of Jerusalem as well as the West Bank. "I
wanted to spare myself," he says, because he spoke their language flu-
ently and knew what they muttered about him and other Jews. "Even
the people in the stores, who act obedient and subordinate, had nasty
remarks," not realizing that he understood them. More important, he
appreciated their anger, and he could not bear the inequity of the relationship between Israelis and Palestinians, the conquerors and the
vanquished.

This past spring, with the approach of the twentieth anniversary
of Israel's triumph in the Six-Day War and the beginning of the occupation of the Arab territories, Grossman was persuaded to return.
As the author of the only Israeli novel based on the occupation, *The
Smile of the Lamb,* as one who has anguished over the subject, Grossman was asked to spend several weeks traveling and talking in the

West Bank and to report what he found for a popular, leftist weekly magazine, *Koteret Rashit*.

The result was a stunning article in which the discordant voices of embittered, hopeless Palestinians and zealous Jewish settlers were turned into a chorus of lamentation. The special issue of *Koteret Rashit*, which was devoted entirely to Grossman's piece, sold out overnight. Grossman went back to the West Bank to collect more dialogue and expanded his story to book length. *The Yellow Time* was rushed into print in Hebrew and became one of the fastest-selling books in the history of Israel. And also one of the most controversial.

The theme, which is as clear and striking as the summer sky over Jerusalem, is that the occupation is sinister and, in the end, mutually destructive to Israel and the Palestinians.

Unlike such latter-day Jeremiahs as Yehoshafat Harkabi and Meron Benvenisti, two outspoken Israeli scholars who have warned that the country stands to lose its soul if it insists on keeping the occupied territories, Grossman is quiet and shy. He would rather let his book and its mosaic of voices speak for itself. However, he agreed to an interview, conducted over breakfast in the courtyard of the American Colony Hotel in the Arab section of East Jerusalem, a landmark favored by foreign journalists. As a measure of the hatred and suspicion that exists between the two sides, right-wing Israelis call the hotel "the PLO headquarters." Palestinian waiters in starched white jackets poured coffee and hovered quietly in the background, like ghosts. As Grossman says, "We live with the Arabs. They serve us, and yet we pass without seeing each other."

Writing the book was a catharsis for Grossman, and as he talked— in English—the words began to rush in the same manner that enabled him to report and write a Middle East masterpiece in seven weeks. He produced the original magazine piece, from the beginning interview to the finished manuscript, in five weeks. "Writing it was like an explosion. I didn't sleep," he says. Then he returned to the territories, seeking out Palestinians who live in anonymity, to gather material for four additional chapters, which swelled the final text to 75,000 words. That phase took only two weeks. "It was terrible to go back. I realized how desperate the West Bank was when I put my feelings into words. The process was so intense, so strong, and there was nobody to share it. I had decided not to talk to anyone for advice. I felt I was detached from Israel as a nation. I felt to be in exile."

Grossman had just begun a new novel when he interrupted his schedule for the West Bank project. Now he finds it difficult to resume the novel. He says he is still consumed by what he calls his journey through that part of "the land of Ishmael" that is under Israeli control.

He completed the piece for *Koteret Rashit* the week before Israel's Independence Day in early May, a time when many Israelis celebrate by dancing the hora in the streets. Others spend the holiday evening more reflectively at small parties in homes where songs evoking the Zionist-Socialist movement that founded the nation are sung. Grossman's circle of friends tends to be liberal, allied with the Labor Party tradition or newer, left-wing groups such as Peace Now and the Citizens Rights Movement. Nevertheless, this year it was different for him at the Independence Day gathering. "I wanted to sing; usually I like it. I sat with people I knew, but suddenly I felt detached. I felt that these were not my songs anymore, and I was lost."

He blinked against the morning sun. Grossman is only 33, red-haired, and usually looks impish, but as he recalled the moment, his face was pained. "I realized the thing I used to call my world was a lost battle. These Independence Day phrases are false, these things we're taught in school. The slogans are not true anymore."

Grossman's roots are deeper in the country than many Israelis'. His parents were both pioneers. His mother is a sabra whose family moved to the land from Poland, long before Jews fled the Holocaust. His father arrived as a child in 1936 when economic deprivation forced his family to leave a town in Galicia that is now part of the Soviet Union. Grossman's wife is a sabra. So, obviously, are their two children. He is committed to Israel and has no desire to leave his country. But he is shattered by his experience in the West Bank.

In his book, Grossman writes, "Like so many others, I began to think of that kidney-shaped expanse of land, the West Bank, as an organ transplanted into my body against my wishes." He calls the occupation "a continuing and stubborn test for both sides trapped in it."

In a society already bitterly divided over the morality of the occupation, the book reinforced the thinking of those who believe Israel must give back most, if not all, of the land. Its greatest impact, according to Nahum Barnea, the editor of *Koteret Rashit*, was felt by Israelis who had attempted to ignore the situation; the book made them confront the question. Predictably, Grossman was assailed from the right. One leader of the settlers' movement went so far as to suggest he should have his head examined.

Grossman is well-known in Israel. He is the author of popular children's books, and critics have hailed another novel, *See Under: Love*, as a classic. He is also the host of a morning show on Kol Israel, the national radio system. Because it is state-owned, he is precluded from partisan political activity, but he has not hidden his leftist views. When he recently interviewed Prime Minister Yitzhak Shamir on the air and asked him about "the price of the occupation," the author says Shamir's "eyebrows jumped up, and he said, 'It is no occupation. We have the right to be there.'" Shamir claimed that the term "occupation" was a "journalistic invention."

When *The Yellow Time* was adapted for the stage, the play attracted large audiences at a Tel Aviv theater this past summer. In an effort to stifle attention, the Israeli army forbade soldiers to attend. The government at first said that no one under 18 would be permitted to see the show, but later dropped the restriction after the decision was ridiculed in the Israeli press.

Even mainstream politicians such as Foreign Minister Shimon Peres, the head of the Labor Party, complained that the book did not take into account that Israel came to rule the land after a war triggered by an Arab mobilization that threatened Israel's existence.

"It's no longer important who started the war," Grossman says, calling Peres's argument "childish." What is important, the author says, is for the Israeli government to recognize that the occupation is self-defeating and to reach a resolution.

The title of his book in Hebrew is apocalyptic, and almost every paragraph is written with passion. "The name of a book should be like perfume, it should give an aroma," he says. He wanted *The Yellow Time* to give "the impression of light in the desert, something very heavy that lies on the soul. In Hebrew, yellow is not the color of fear, but hatred." Yellow, he points out, is the color adopted by Rabbi Meir Kahane's radical Kach movement, which aims to throw all Arabs out of Israel and the West Bank. In a passage of his book, written after the magazine article appeared, Grossman tells of one of his Arab interlocutors, Abu Harb, and how the title for his work came about:

> He asked me if I had heard about the yellow wind that would soon come, maybe even in his lifetime: the wind would come from the gate of hell . . . a hot and terrible east wind which comes once in a few generations, sets the world afire, and people seek shelter from its heat in the caves and caverns, but even there it finds those it seeks, those who have performed cruel and unjust deeds, and there, in the cracks in the boulders, it exterminates them, one by one. After that day, Abu Harb says, the land will be covered with bodies. The rocks will be white from the heat, and the mountains will crumble into a powder which will cover the land like yellow cotton.

In the English translation, the title has been changed to *The Yellow Wind*. *The New Yorker* is planning to excerpt selections from the book. Farrar, Straus & Giroux will publish the book in the United States in April. Jonathan Galassi, the executive editor of the New York publishing house, says he was attracted to *The Yellow Wind* because "it's such a vivid exposition of a problem. It makes you care about something that perhaps you had not cared about before." Galassi says he cannot calculate the effect it will ultimately have on the American Jewish community, but he expects "it will be hotly debated in Jewish circles because it's a moral call to arms."

British and French publishing houses have also bought rights to the book, and it is expected to be sold elsewhere in Europe. But Grossman is especially curious about its reception in the United States, which wields so much influence in Israel.

"I once thought we needed somebody from the outside to shake us," he says. "That we were caught in a nightmare and we needed somebody to wake us up. But why am I hesitant in my expectations about public opinion in the United States? Because I still think it is necessary for Israel to go through this process ourselves and pay the price until we come back to our senses."

As long as the occupation is part of government policy, the vast majority of the American Jewish community is not likely to be critical. Unless they have relatives living in West Bank settlements, a visit to Israel by American Jews is usually confined to the holy places in Jerusalem, the scenic Galilee, the Tel Aviv beachfront, and the rich, strictly kosher hotels—such as the King David and the Jerusalem Plaza—in the capital. These Americans rarely see the other side, just as they fail to recognize that a substantial segment of the Israeli population is troubled by the occupation.

Public opinion polls indicate that almost half of the Israeli citizens would be willing to withdraw their army from most of the West Bank if security for the Jewish state could be assured. Grossman is representative of thousands of Israelis who have marched in the streets, calling upon the government to return territory. Labor Party policy formally supports "territorial compromise," in which Arab population centers and much of the land would be exchanged for a peace agreement with the Arabs.

These Israelis know what lurks just across the old Green Line, the border that once physically separated Arabs from Jews in the Holy Land. The barricades may have been knocked down after the 1967 war, but the division remains as palpable as if the stone blockades and ugly barbed wire were still there.

Israel quickly annexed the restive Arab quarter of Jerusalem, but its attempts to impose military rule on the rest of the West Bank, to colonize the Arab territory with Jewish settlements, has bred violence over the years: Arab attacks on Israeli vehicles in the West Bank beget retaliatory raids by Israeli soldiers which beget bombs planted in downtown Jerusalem which beget curfews and wholesale arrests of Arabs. Innocents on both sides suffer.

"Here in Jerusalem, we are exposed to the problem every day," says Grossman of the divided city. "In Tel Aviv, it's different. It's easier to forget. But here, six or seven years ago, there was even a bomb in my yard."

This is why Grossman's message takes on importance—an Israeli is telling the story instead of aggrieved Arabs, bloodless academic observers, or goyishe foreign correspondents. "I was exposed to sharp and brutal realities. For the first time, I realized that in front of me there is no void; there are people. From now on, the Israeli people can't find shelter by saying they don't know what's going on."

The language of Grossman's book, translated into English by Haim Watzman, is as lyrical as poetry, but it is permeated with fury.

He talks with a man identified only as "A.N.," who spent ten years in prison after being convicted by the Israelis of belonging to the Popular Front for the Liberation of Palestine, a faction of the PLO. The PLO is outlawed, yet virtually all Palestinians living in the West Bank recognize the organization as their government-in-exile. During a conversation that takes place in the West Bank city of Nablus, "A.N." tells Grossman:

> "Of course I hate you. Maybe at the beginning I didn't hate and only feared. Afterwards, I began to hate. . . . Before I went to jail I didn't even know I was a Palestinian. There they taught me who I am. Now I have opinions. Don't believe the ones who tell you that the Palestinians don't really hate you. Understand: the average Palestinian is not the fascist and hating type, but you and the life under your occupation push him into hatred. Look at me, for example. You took ten years of my life from me."

Just south of Jerusalem, Grossman discovered the same sentiments in a kindergarten at the Dehaishe refugee camp, among the fourth generation of dispossessed Palestinians. He recounts the following colloquy between a small child and two teachers:

> "Who do you want to shoot?" the teachers ask, smiling, like two mothers taking pride in a smart child.
> "Jews."
> Their lips make out the answer with him.
> "Now tell him why," they encourage the little one.
> "Because the Jews took my uncle," he says, "at night they came in and stole him from the bed, so now I sleep with my mother all the time."

Grossman asks the teachers: "Is this the answer, to bring up another generation and another in hatred? To teach them that this hatred justifies the refusal to work towards a solution? Couldn't you try, maybe, another way?"

> "There is no other way," they answer, both of them, each in her own way, in a whisper or with self-assurance, but the same words.
> I stand and listen and try to be neutral. To understand. Not to judge. And also not to be like an American or French correspondent, completely severed from the whole complex of events, and quick to pass judgment. But I also stand here as a reserve soldier in the Israeli army, and as a human being, rising up against this education in blind hatred, and against such tremendous energy being expended in the preservation of malice, instead of being spent in an effort to get out of this barrenness, this ugliness in which this kindergarten lies, these little children who are so good at hating me.

As effectively as Grossman documents the hatred, he explores the cause of it in vignette after vignette. In a chapter titled "Catch 44," Grossman tells of a ludicrous trial before an Israeli military judge.

The defendant is a Palestinian student accused of having contact with an "enemy organization." Actually, it was the young man's father who applied to Al Fatah, the main faction of the PLO, for financial assistance to send his son to school overseas. So Jafar Haj Hassan obtained a scholarship to attend a German university and study German. When he changed his major, the PLO revoked the scholarship on the grounds that he could only study courses beneficial to the organization. Hassan stayed in Germany anyway, had no further connection with the PLO, married a German woman, and finally came home after several years. A week after he arrived back in the West Bank he was arrested. He was held in prison for 44 days before the trial began.

According to Grossman's account, the evidence showed that Jafar Haj Hassan was not guilty. But the judge was confronted with the questions: "Can a military court of an occupying power admit that the military government of the occupation made a mistake? And, if so, how will that influence its authority, esteem, and power in the eyes of the inhabitants?" The judge decided to sentence the defendant to 44 days in prison—the time he had already served—after finding him guilty of another violation with which he was never charged and that he had never committed.

Israeli authorities use the word "terrorist" loosely. To them, the PLO is a "terrorist" organization. PLO sympathizers are "terrorists." Newscasters on state radio and TV are instructed to refer to any resistance groups as "terrorist cells." One Palestinian woman tells the author how her husband was arrested merely on the suspicion that he took part in "terrorist acts." Immediately after his arrest, before any trial, Israeli soldiers destroyed their house:

> It was a new house, just completed. The family was not
> given enough time to remove all its belongings. When it was
> destroyed, it collapsed on 10 sacks of sugar and 10 sacks of
> flour that had been bought at great cost, and had been stored
> in the house for the housewarming celebration. The husband
> was released right afterwards without any charges having been
> brought against him.

From his own experience in the Israeli military, Grossman tells how raids are routinely carried out in the West Bank refugee camps in search of suspects or weapons:

> The violent entry into rooms where several people sleep, crowded, in unaired stench, three or four together under scratchy wool blankets, wearing their work clothes still in their sleep, as if ready at any moment to get up and go wherever they are told. They wake in confusion, squinting from the flashlight, children wail, sometimes a couple is making love, soldiers surround the house, some of them—shoes full of mud after tramping through the paths of the camp—walking over the sleep-warm blankets, some pounding on the tin roof above.

Grossman details the deceit that is practiced in the occupied territories: the Palestinians with connections to the Israeli army who serve as middlemen—known as "wastonaires"—to arrange permits for a price, including a $9,000 charge to reunify families separated by the occupation; the Palestinian secret agents who betray their own people for personal gain.

When influential Palestinians refuse to cooperate with the occupation, the Israelis sometimes resort to a tactic that falsely brands them as collaborators, thus damning them in the eyes of their fellow villagers. In one chapter, Grossman gives a fictionalized account of an anecdote that he cannot describe in complete detail because of government censorship. He uses the name of Gidi for an officer of Shin Bet, the Israeli internal secret service. He tells how Gidi, who is in charge of intelligence in a West Bank village, dealt with a problem:

> Only once, about two years ago, he had to make small use of the "starling" procedure on one of the village teachers, who had suddenly turned into a young and disgruntled "crow," darkly shrieking. Gidi warned him a few times, surprised him with an exact quote of things he had said to his pupils during a Koran lesson and explained to him reasonably what those things

would lead to. The man refused to take the hint. He had a bitter soul and was full of hate, and blasted Gidi with strident words, so strange to the spirit of the tacit and unwritten agreement Gidi had with the village. Gidi really had no choice but to use the "starling" procedure. It was almost fun to see in actual use a simple and subtle exercise from the course. Officers, friends of Gidi's who had borrowed senior officers' insignia, would arrive in luxurious military cars, not the usual trucks, and would invite themselves to lunch at the house of the "crow." At the end of the meal they would ask him to show them out, and outside the house, in front of everyone, they would slap him on the back and shower him with smiles and winks. The village was soon muttering and giggling. It had been necessary to direct the matter wisely and with great sensitivity. Not to awaken a real uproar against the teacher, but only to ostracize him. Within two weeks the pupils in the crow's class were boycotting his lessons, and a month later he took his wife and four children and moved to another village. Eviatar, Gidi's colleague there, reported that the man was quiet. He became a canary.

Then there are the settlers, fired by a sense of nationalism or a religious commitment to establish a Jewish presence in the land they are convinced is part of the biblical land of Israel. Grossman does not deal with those who are political ciphers, living in West Bank bedroom suburbs subsidized by the government. Instead, he accentuates the voices of the zealots, the leaders and the followers of Gush Emunim, the Bloc of the Faithful, who insist the Jews have more right to the land than the Arabs.

The author spends a Sabbath at a settlement, attempting a dialogue with his fellow Jews, asking them to try to put themselves, mentally, into the place of the Palestinians. He fails, and the session turns, against his will, into a debate. One settler tells him not to pity the Arabs too much. "Haven't you seen their mansions along the road to Ramallah?" the settler asks, referring to the comfortable, two-story stone houses outside Jerusalem with their miniature Eiffel Tower television antennas owned by well-to-do Palestinians. Another woman insists, "We haven't taken one meter of land from Arabs," a statement that flies in the face of repeated Israeli confiscation of land in the West Bank.

Grossman despairs of conducting rational conversations with the group and concludes that "the people of Gush Emunim have distanced themselves greatly from the center of the Israeli consensus."

During his travels, Grossman was witness to the drama carried out in late spring after a Molotov cocktail, pitched into the auto of a passing family of settlers, resulted in the death of a young woman, Ofra Moses, and her small son, and inflamed the region. Jewish vigilantes stormed through the nearby Arab town of Kalkilya, sundering orange orchards—to avenge symbolically the cutting down of a Jewish family—smashing windows and burning fields.

Afterward, they rallied at Alfei Menashe, the settlement where Ofra Moses lived. Grossman's account of the meeting is as chilling as the cold hatred he found among the Palestinians:

> The secretariat of Gush Emunim and the heads of the Jewish settlements in the West Bank and Gaza Strip meet in the gymnasium of the school in Alfei Menashe. They are all here, those whose names you see in the newspapers, and many of their friends. They damn the army, the chief of staff, the minister of defense, and the entire government with fire and brimstone. They sit around tables in the gym, between ladders and vaulting horses, their faces red with fury, fingering their pistols. . . . Hooliganism echoes in everything the leaders of Gush Emunim say. A smooth, sharp hooliganism, but hooliganism none the less. With television cameras in the auditorium, every speaker makes sure to give lip service to "the need to work within the law," but they pronounce the words like someone spitting a rotten piece of apple from his mouth.

Rabbi Moshe Levinger, a founder of the settlers' movement, calls Yitzhak Rabin, the defense minister, a murderer, "his hands spilled with blood" for not taking more strenuous action to contain the Palestinians in the territories. Levinger warns that another Jewish underground—similar to the one broken up by Israeli authorities after a series of bomb attacks on Arab West Bank mayors and the attempt to dynamite the Dome of the Rock in Jerusalem, Islam's third-holiest shrine—will arise. He also calls for the death penalty. "Beside the preacher of death," Grossman reports, sat Daniella Weiss, another Gush Emunim leader, who "nods and her eyes sparkle, two rings of red raised on her cheeks, but it seems to me it is not the spring that is bringing out this bloom."

Also in attendance is Elyakim Haetzni, a self-appointed attorney general for the West Bank. Haetzni is constantly bringing charges against Palestinians. Five years ago, in the midst of Israel's invasion of Lebanon, he succeeded in getting Grossman suspended for two weeks from his radio job after Grossman made a disparaging comment about Ariel Sharon, the defense minister who engineered the disastrous adventure in Lebanon. The reader who knows this background senses that Grossman is settling an old score as he describes how Haetzni "stands and froths" before the assembly:

> His voice is so high that the echoes bouncing off the walls of the gymnasium crash into each other, and it is very hard to hear what he is saying. It is almost certainly fascinating—it seems that he has prepared a list of steps the authorities must take against PLO activists in the territories, and, maybe, against anyone who has ambitions which clash with Haetzni's. I make out the words "expulsion . . . closure . . . imprisonment . . . death penalty . . . destruction" and for a short, mad moment I see Haetzni prancing happily through a West Bank completely emptied of people.

According to Grossman, most of the residents of Alfei Menashe "wanted nothing to do with this political convention, exploiting their sorrow for its own purposes," and most of them refused to attend the event.

The description of the end of Ofra Moses's funeral, after the provocateurs and television crews had left, evokes the loss of the young Jewish mother whose son would later die from his wounds, but Grossman's words also serve as an elegy for everyone in the West Bank:

> The sun was covered by a slight cloud, shimmering through it, as if covered by a handkerchief. Ofra Moses' close friends and relatives quietly approached the grave. Now they were alone, without politicians and functionaries and merchants of tragedy. The close friends gathered into a tight group, embracing and solid in their pain around the small, long mound of earth, and tightened their circle more and more . . .

Wrestling with Israel's Paradox

(*Boston Globe*, November 30, 1987)

While living in Jerusalem, I became acquainted with several of the country's leading literary figures and admired their work. Yet I never met Amos Oz, perhaps the best-known of the modern Israeli novelists. For his son's health Oz's family lived outside the centers of Tel Aviv or Jerusalem, in a distant town in the Negev Desert. Serendipitously, I returned to Boston at the same time Oz joined the Boston University faculty for a semester, and the *Globe* asked me to do a piece on him.

When Amos Oz talks about his native land of Israel, the paradoxes of that troubled yet vibrant state become a theme of the conversation, reminiscent of his book of essays where he warns readers in the preface that there is no such thing as a "typical cross-section" of Israel.

Oz, who is serving as a writer-in-residence at Boston University this semester, knows the danger of making generalizations about Israel. The tiny country is so full of conflicts and passions that it defies easy description. As a result, Oz is both a critic and a champion of Israel.

Although the message from many of those Oz interviewed for *In the Land of Israel*—the collection of essays that was published in the U.S. in 1983—sounded despairing about the prospects of peace and the future of the country, the author said the work had the opposite effect on him. "I was encouraged, for it testifies to the basic morality and openness in Israel." As a prominent leftist and writer, Oz said he was able to talk to right-wing extremists who condemned his views in one breath and offered him hospitality in the next.

The real message, he said, is to have patience with Israel.

"We have a kind of civil war going on," he said in an interview the other evening at his apartment near Kenmore Square. "It is very uncivil. But so far, we are only giving each other ulcers and heart attacks instead of actually shooting."

A real civil war may come, he said, that may be fought between religious and secular forces. "I think the question of state and church, or the Israeli version—state and synagogue—will not be sorted out in my lifetime. Bear in mind, other nations sorted out their religious problems in bloody civil wars," he said, mentioning France, England, and Germany. No Israeli lives have been lost in the turmoil unleashed by the ultraorthodox who want to impose a virtual theocracy on the Jewish state, but Oz said it would be "unrealistic to expect" Israel to escape a holy war.

In the meantime, he said, Israel should be appreciated for its strengths—just as its weaknesses should be better understood.

"The country is a flawed democracy, but it is the case of the half-empty glass or the half-full one. Of all the countries formed after World War II, only two or three are democracies. Israel is still in a decent league. It may rate fairly low, but despite all of its conflict, tremendous diversity, problems with religion, it has still managed to stay in a decent league," he said. "I don't think Israel is going down the drain."

Oz, who is 48, has been one of the dominant literary figures in Israel for more than two decades. Although *In the Land of Israel* gained recent notoriety in the U.S., he is actually better known for his fiction.

In one of his earliest novels, *Elsewhere, Perhaps*, Oz offered another caveat at the beginning. The mythical town in the Galilee where the story is set is not "a reflection in miniature," Oz wrote, but was created "to reflect a faraway kingdom by a sea, perhaps elsewhere." Nevertheless, the bittersweet novel is very evocative of Israel, dealing with liberal sexual mores as well as claustrophobic conditions of life on a kibbutz.

Other of Oz's books that have been translated into English—*The Hill of Evil Counsel*, which is a trilogy of novellas, *My Michael*, and

Unto Death, which contains a pair of novellas—are all suffused with a melancholy air.

Even though the works are set in Israel, Oz attributed the sadness to "a universal truth" instead of the situation inside his country where, he said, the people are "paying the price of fulfilled dreams." Like any dream that becomes reality, he said, "it's not quite the same." He writes in Hebrew, but his command of the English language is outstanding, and he was especially eloquent on the subject. Israel was built around the concept of Zionist socialism, the stuff of dreams. "Compared to the magnificent dream," Oz said, "Israel is a miserable failure," still mired in conflict.

Over the years, the country has been torn by three major disputes: the struggle between Arabs and Jews over the land, the battle between the religious and secular Jews, and the clash of cultures between the Western-oriented Ashkenazi Jews and the newer Jewish immigrants, the Sephardim, who fled to the state from other Middle East countries.

Many Israelis have had their spirits broken by the long, costly occupation of the Arab territories, by the blood that is still being spilled among the rival sons of Abraham. The constant friction, compounded by economic troubles, makes it a hard place to live. There has been a disturbing exodus from Israel in recent years by the disillusioned, and Oz said, "I think Israel has a slim chance of being attractive as long as the conflict goes on."

Nevertheless, he believes the outside world has not recognized that Israel is solving one of its greatest problems. "I think the single most important phenomenon on the Israeli scene—that has been ignored by the press—is the emergence of the Sephardic middle class," Oz said. Once dismissed by the Ashkenazi establishment as ignorant, intolerant, and bellicose, the Sephardim are now practically indistinguishable from the rest of Israel. They constitute a majority of the population and—to the extent they can be collectively characterized—hold essentially moderate views.

Oz noted with irony that "the most nationalistic, the religious extremists, the ultraorthodox" are not only Ashkenazim, but often immigrants from America, such the leaders of Gush Emunim, the settlers' movement, and Rabbi Meir Kahane and his followers in the racist, anti-Arab Kach party.

Even though he has been associated for years with the Peace Now movement, a powerful, nonpartisan group that seeks a resolution with the Arabs, Oz blamed "left-wing, dovish hysteria" for fostering an image that Israel's present problems are caused by hawkish, right-wing Sephardim. These leftist intellectuals, Oz said, "are frustrated, they've lost their perspective on reality because they assume the nation is not listening to them."

Oz also seemed amused by the attitude of the American Jewish community toward Israel, an attitude that is paternal and, he believes, sometimes misguided. When he was asked how much influence American Jews—who have helped keep Israel alive with private donations and political pressure—should have on Israeli policy, Oz smiled and said, "My conviction is that everyone is entitled to have an opinion, which does not mean we have to abide by it. There's hardly a chance for Jews, or non-Jews, to run Israel through remote control."

Did he feel, as many Israelis, that all Jews should make Israel their home? "Let me say that I would like for Israel to be a tempting option for every Jew. I think the Israeli drama is fairly exciting, and any Jew steering clear of this action is wasting life. But I am not in the business of promoting a guilty feeling. I am more in the seductive school." If Americans want to dictate Israeli policy, he said, then "let them mount the stage and steal the show" by moving to Israel.

Oz was born in Jerusalem, a city of terrible beauty and religious fanaticism. "I would never want to live there again, because of personal reasons," he said. His family belongs to a kibbutz, but are now making their home in Arad, on the edge of the Negev Desert overlooking the Dead Sea, where the climate is propitious for their young, asthmatic son. In his search to find a healthy place, Oz also spent a year teaching at Colorado College in Colorado Springs, Colorado, a couple of years ago.

At Boston University, he is teaching a graduate course in creative writing, and plans to return to Israel in December.

Oz said he had no trouble writing outside Israel. "In some sense, it gives me a better perspective. Here, watching the River Charles, gives me a better picture."

His latest novel, *Black Box*, which was published in Israel last January, will come out in English next May. And a new collection of essays, *The Slope of Lebanon*, has just been published in Israel.

The essays are drawn from his pieces in *Davar*, a leftist Israeli daily newspaper, as well as *Yediot Aharonot*, a mass circulation daily that he uses, he said, "to reach the other half." His essays, he said, are outlets for his "rage."

"As it happens," Oz said, "when I have a disagreement with myself, hearing two or more voices, then I write a story." Israel, he said, "is a very exciting place for a storyteller."

The Doctor Is In

(*Boston Globe Magazine*, January 7, 1988)

The *Globe Magazine* featured this story as a parody of a *Rolling Stone* article, and I tried to craft it in the style of a writer with an enormous cult following.

I had known Hunter since the 1972 presidential campaign, when we were thrown together in planes, trains, buses, and hotel bars covering George McGovern. Hunter missed one of our wildest rides that year on the "zoo plane" (where television technicians and obscure newspaper scribes were relegated) when mischief erupted on a night flight to California. A woman named Luci Goldberg, posing as a reporter for a women's news agency, got in the cockpit and peeled the pants off the pilot. I gave Hunter an account of the trip, and he incorporated it into his book, *Fear and Loathing on the Campaign Trail '72.* We didn't know it at the time, but Goldberg was a spy for the Nixon campaign and resurfaced a quarter-century later as an operative in the plot to trap Bill Clinton in the Lewinski affair.

Hunter was outrageously funny, with an explosive personality, but he had a brooding side, too. After he killed himself in 2005, I looked up this old piece and confirmed my recollection that he had talked of suicide near the end of one long, all-night conversation at his cabin near Aspen where he would eventually take his life.

Fear and Loathing at Woody Creek . . . Notes from a Strange Time . . . A New "Generation of Swine" . . . Gonzo Man Joins Jingo Paper . . .

I'm older now, but still running against the wind.—Bob Seger, "Against the Wind"

So many of the icons of our generation are in ruins, victims of time and Reagan's cultural revolution. "Just say no" are the new catch-words, and the Red Queen and White Rabbit have been replaced by King Condom. John Lennon is seven years dead, and Timothy Leary might as well be. Jerry Rubin promotes capitalism. Janis and Jimi, Duane Allman and Jim Morrison are gone. Otis Redding and Mama Cass, gone. All gone. James Brown's screams have lost their pitch. Lynyrd Skynyrd's "Free Bird" crashed in a swamp. Richard Brautigan snuffed himself. The landscape is littered with burned-out cases, children of the 1950s who spent themselves over the next two decades like Roman candles.

But there is a survivor, unrepentant and unforgiving, lurking in a log cabin high in the Colorado Rockies. Hunter S. Thompson just reached the landmark age of 50, and after a midlife lull when it was feared he was finished, the outlaw prince of gonzo journalism is writing again with the fury of a shark in a feeding frenzy. As one of the last two-fisted drinkers, Thompson defies the legacy of Dylan Thomas, who died before 40 of what the coroner called "insult to the brain." Despite years of physical abuse—best characterized by an orgy of drugs and alcohol at a law-enforcement convention he chronicled in *Fear and Loathing in Las Vegas* in the early 1970s—Thompson, amazingly, still looks healthy enough to challenge a professional athlete.

Searching through my beer-sodden notes after several days in his company on the fringes of Aspen in December, I find one of his quotes: "It only feels like one long year since I was 22. I never grew up." Exactly. After a half-century, Hunter Thompson is a macho Peter Pan.

His political writing, which appears in a syndicated weekly column in the *San Francisco Examiner*, has regained the intensity of his work in *Rolling Stone* magazine nearly twenty years ago, when he was heaping scorn on Richard M. Nixon, Hubert H. Humphrey, and other officials. His chief target these days is the right-wing gang in the Republican Party. If Thompson can get his act together—and his book editor was threatening to abort the project while I was in Aspen unless he met a deadline—a collection of his recent columns will be published this year by Summit Books under the title *Generation of Swine.*

Just as he described Humphrey in 1972 as "a treacherous, gutless old ward-heeler who should be put in a goddamn bottle and sent out with the Japanese Current," Thompson is now relentlessly keelhauling another vice president, George Bush. Of Bush, Thompson wrote in a recent column: "He has the instincts of a dung beetle. No living politician can match his talent for soiling himself in public. Bush will seek out filth wherever it lives—going without sleep for days at a time if necessary—and when he finds a new heap he will fall down and wallow crazily in it, making snorting sounds out of his nose and rolling over on his back and kicking his legs up in the air like a wild hog coming to water."

Why am I repeating these things? It is all madness, these irresponsible descriptions and apocryphal stories: gonzo journalism run amok. Yet underneath the lurid gibberish it is possible to sniff out, like truffles, kernels of wisdom and truth. Thompson describes gonzo journalism—his term for his work—as "a style of reporting based on William Faulkner's idea that the best fiction is far more true than any kind of journalism."

He sprung on the world this novel approach to political journalism during the 1972 presidential campaign, as he followed Edmund S. Muskie's breakdown in the primaries, a collapse accompanied by the candidate's public tears in New Hampshire and private fits of rage. In his reports to *Rolling Stone*, which resulted in the book *Fear and Loathing on the Campaign Trail '72*, Thompson speculated that Muskie's reactions were caused by injections of the jungle drug Ibogaine, which left his "brain almost paralyzed by hallucinations at the time; he looked out at that crowd and saw gila monsters instead of people. . . ."

This year, Thompson has a new mandate to skewer the latest generation of politicians, and his pulpit, of all places, is that flagship of the Hearst empire, the *San Francisco Examiner*, a newspaper he once described as "particularly influential among those who fear King

George III might still be alive in Argentina." Under the leadership of William Randolph Hearst III, the paper has hired Thompson and, among others, another '60s renegade, Warren Hinckle, in an effort to jazz up its traditionally conservative image.

The arrangement permits Thompson to write from his own lair, a cabin at Woody Creek, about ten miles outside Aspen. "I'm a hillbilly," he says, "a lazy bastard." Late one night, while Thompson and I were talking in the cluttered kitchen of his home—the erstwhile "National Affairs Desk" of *Rolling Stone*—Will Hearst telephoned to inquire about the whereabouts of an overdue column. Thompson put me on the line and disappeared. An awkward conversation ensued. I observed that the *Examiner* seemed a strange outlet for Hunter Thompson. Hearst replied that publishing Thompson was in the "libertarian" tradition of a newspaper chain that once carried iconoclasts such as Mark Twain and Ambrose Bierce. "It is slow getting copy out of him," Will Hearst admitted. Thompson had still not reappeared. "Tell him we demand his copy tonight," Hearst said. "He has got to call back in two hours."

Under pressure, and using an old-fashioned typewriter, Thompson cobbled together two thoughts he had already put down on tattered paper. As the supply of Molson dwindled in an auxiliary beer refrigerator outside the kitchen where he writes, Hunter Thompson met another deadline.

The Doctor Is In . . .Brainrapers and Greedheads . . . Reagan on the Gibbet . . . The Secret Service Is Watching . . .

Whether he is writing the exact truth—or has raised it a few
notches to make a point about hypocrisy and greed in modern
America—is not the point. The point is that he is writing well,
and with humor, an acid-head Mencken reincarnated. . . .
—William Zinsser, *On Writing Well*

In person, Thompson is as wild and undisciplined, entertaining and irreverent, as his writing. If he sleeps, it is like a vampire—by day. An avowed speed freak, he can go for several days without rest. The night does not belong to Michelob; it belongs to Hunter Stockton Thompson. Dr. Thompson, if you will. He insists upon the title, saying that he is a doctor of "philosophy, chemotherapy, and divinity."

He is from Louisville, Kentucky, but vague about his educational background, mumbling something about attending Columbia University and other institutions of higher learning. In a piece on "The Nonstudent Left" he wrote for the *Nation* in 1965, Thompson said, "In 1958, I drifted north from Kentucky and became a nonstudent at Columbia. I signed up for two courses and am still getting bills for the tuition." No matter. How many prophets do you know with a college education?

For a while, he toiled as a straight journalist. As a young man, he applied for a job on the *San Juan Star* in Puerto Rico, but the managing editor, a fellow named William Kennedy, turned him down. (All is forgiven. Thompson hopes Kennedy, who became a prize-winning novelist in Albany, New York, will write an introduction for *Generation of Swine*.) Thompson's first job in journalism was at *Time* magazine. He was a copy boy. He later wrote for a daily newspaper in Middletown, New York, but was fired after attacking a vending machine with a hammer. He finally gained employment at a respectable weekly newspaper, the *National Observer*, but it went out of business. At the time, he was reporting the news conventionally. All that would change.

Living in California's Big Sur country, he wrote a book, *Hell's Angels*, which culminated with his own stomping by the motorcycle gang. But the real catharsis would come in Chicago, just as it did for so many of his contemporaries. In an essay about the episode that turned an age of idealists into cynics, Thompson wrote:

> Probably it was Chicago—that brainraping week in August
> of '68. I went to the Democratic convention as a journalist, and
> returned a raving beast. For me, that week in Chicago was far
> worse than the worst bad acid trip I'd even heard rumors about.
> It permanently altered my brain chemistry, and my first new

idea—when I finally calmed down—was an absolute conviction there was no possibility for any personal truce, for me, in a nation that could hatch and be proud of a malignant monster like Chicago.

He moved to Aspen and helped lead an insurgent political movement against "a mean bunch of rednecks" who ruled the county. The "Freak Power" ticket had its headquarters in the bar of the Hotel Jerome, a gathering spot at the time for "freaks, heads, fun-hogs, and weird night-people of every description." Thompson ran for sheriff in 1970, mocking the law-and-order crowd by shaving his head and wearing sinister sunglasses in campaign posters. His platform called for ripping the streets with jackhammers and planting sod in place of asphalt, renaming Aspen "Fat City" in order to "prevent greedheads, landrapers, and other human jackals from capitalizing" on the town's name, and installing a "bastinado platform and a set of stocks" on the courthouse lawn to punish drug dealers who cheated customers.

He lost, but the political complexion of Aspen was changed irrevocably. Today the little town, with a population of 8,000 people and an altitude of 8,000 feet, is both precious and radicalized. It serves as the winter home of Jack Nicholson, Goldie Hawn, and other celebrities as well as hundreds of sybaritic visitors. Aspen's streets are lined with chic boutiques and bars with names like the Red Onion.

The town has become so trendy that Thompson rarely goes beyond the Woody Creek Tavern, a rustic watering spot located a couple of switchbacks down the mountain from Owl Farm, where he lives. Cigarette smoke hangs low in the tavern, where cowboys and construction workers wear ragged sheepskin jackets, denims, and frayed ten-gallon hats. The food is cheap but sustaining, and the jukebox does not carry Barry Manilow. Jill, the cook, points out that it may be the only bar in the world without a mirror. The clientele at the Woody Creek Tavern is not narcissistic.

One night we met there for dinner, and Thompson burst through the door carrying a hideous, rubber facsimile of a sickly grinning Ronald Reagan he had bought at an airport. The cowboys cheered, but one table was occupied by stylishly dressed apres-skiers who had apparently decided to visit this "quaint little place" for dinner. The tourists watched in horror as Thompson puffed the Reagan device to life-size. He cursed loudly after discovering it was not the sort of steel-based toy he could use as a punching bag. A cry of "String him up!" arose from the bar.

Thompson and Gaylord Guenin, the major-domo of Woody Creek Tavern, disappeared into the attic and returned with a coil of rope. As he worked on a goblet of Chivas Regal and a Molson on the side, Thompson constructed a hangman's noose, fitted it over the rubberized neck, and left the ersatz president dangling in effigy from a rafter. "I always thought he was an elderly dingbat," he declared, "a silly old fool."

The Secret Service would not have been amused. The agency's travails with Thompson date back to the time in Florida in 1972 when he loaned his press credentials during a Muskie whistle-stop trip to "The Boohoo," a bartender-desperado named Peter Sheridan who would eventually kill himself in a motorcycle wreck. While Muskie, then an august senator and the leading candidate for the Democratic nomination, attempted to deliver a speech from the caboose at the Miami train station, "The Boohoo" used his place in the press area to claw at Muskie's pants, demanding more gin.

This past year, Thompson says, the Secret Service has investigated his vicious comments about George Bush, whom Thompson claims is "doomed." As the Iran-contra affair unfolded, Thompson wrote that the "hallways in the White House basement were slick with human scum. Even the Gipper was bleeding and George Bush was walking around like a man with both wrists slit and trying to ignore the blood." Blaming Bush for the contra connection, Thompson continued his screed: "Before this thing is over, George will know agonies far worse than simple gout, or leech fever, or even the heartbreak of psoriasis. There is already talk among his neighbors up there in Kennebunkport about strapping him onto one of those old-timey dunking stools and letting the local boys have a go at him."

In a subsequent column, he depicted a scene in which Bush learns he is linked to Lt. Col. Oliver North, a man Thompson described as "the Charles Manson figure in this hideous scandal that crawls like a plague of maggots. . . ." At a White House meeting, Thompson reported, "George went stiff, then dropped to his knees like a wino and wept openly in front of his staff people. . . . The shrewd and treacherous vice president was no longer clean."

Thompson prides himself on his own "outlaw" status. Last year, golfing with his friend Ed Bradley of *60 Minutes*, he was charged with firing a shotgun on the Aspen municipal course. My sources say he fired two "warning shots" near a man on a lawn-mower tractor who was disrupting their game. Thompson showed me how he stuffs the shotgun, like a 3-wood, into his golf bag for "protection." He insisted he simply shot it once into the air for fun. Bradley testified he heard a mysterious shot, but saw nothing. Thompson was fined $100.

There is a pickle jar on the shelf of the Woody Creek Tavern devoted to the "Hunter S. Thompson Defense Fund." A sign on the jar says, "Help Save This Pathetic Victim of Police Brutality. FREE THE DOCTOR." Contributions have included small change, dollar bills, condoms, a piece of beef jerky, and some hamster droppings.

Flight to the Unknown . . . The Phoenix Also Rises . . .
Remembrance of Things Past . . . Revenge in Orlando . . .

O lost, and by the wind grieved, ghost, come back again.—
Thomas Wolfe, *Look Homeward, Angel*

The inspiration to track down Thompson came after a Boston cab-driver, who admired his reporting, asked me whatever happened to the wizard of gonzo journalism. After falling out with Jann Wenner, the editor and publisher of *Rolling Stone*, Thompson seemed to have disappeared from the scene. But I knew he was now writing a column for the *Examiner*, and after placing calls to his answering service, his editor, and the Woody Creek Tavern, I got a collect call late one night from "Dr. Thompson."

We agreed to meet in Aspen in early December. He urged me not to fly Continental Airlines, which had just suffered a crash in the snow at Denver that cost a number of lives. In that week's column, Thompson savaged Continental for earning "what is beginning to look like the ugliest reputation in the American business community since the Edsel, thalidomide, or the economic wisdom of Herbert Hoover." So I took United. En route to Denver, rereading *The Great Shark Hunt*, an anthology of Thompson's work, I came across this paragraph from 1970: "Flying United, to me, is like crossing the Andes in a prison bus. There is no question in my mind that somebody like Pat Nixon personally approves every United stewardess. Nowhere in the Western world is there anything to equal the collection of self-righteous shrews who staff the 'friendly skies' of United."

By the time I got to Aspen, the author had vanished. At the Woody Creek Tavern there were reports of a "sighting" in Phoenix. The next day, Thompson called the Hotel Jerome to assure me he was on his way home after dealing with an "emergency." He related a strange tale of how his travels had been diverted to Phoenix in order for him to see Maria—who may or may not be his wife. After returning to Colorado, he showed me her photograph. She is young and lovely and, according to Thompson, the daughter of a wealthy Pakistani who is not amused by their relationship. The father, he swears, put out a contract on his life. "When we met, he asked me, 'Just what kind of doctor are you?' He didn't have the vaguest idea who I was. Now he knows. It gets me in a lot of trouble." Thompson's voice trailed off, "If my daughter ran off with a freak when she was 22 . . ."

I first encountered Hunter Thompson during the McGovern campaign in 1972. We met one night covering the Ohio primary. J. Edgar Hoover had just died, and we celebrated the end of his despotic rule of the FBI through a long night's journey into morning, while corrupt politicians delayed the count of the primary vote in an attempt to steal the election for Humphrey.

I was witness to Thompson's aberrant behavior later that year as a trainload of journalists followed George McGovern through the San Joaquin Valley during the California primary. A European camera crew had been particularly obnoxious, pushing and shoving us to obtain a better angle. Thompson produced a hunting knife and threatened to cut the cord that bound the soundman to the cameraman—indeed, to relieve them of certain vital organs if they did not desist. They fled in terror.

Four years later, we were having dinner at the Sheraton Wayfarer near Manchester as the New Hampshire primary approached. The management had informed Thompson there was no room for him at the inn. He was seething because he felt he had helped immortalize the hotel in his book about the last campaign. He took matters into his own hands, literally. Grabbing a fork, he marched to the desk and vowed to gouge out the eardrum of the night clerk. A room was found for him.

Thompson was partially responsible for the rise of Jimmy Carter that year, "turning on" the readers of *Rolling Stone* to this obscure governor of Georgia. He lavishly praised a Law Day speech Carter had delivered in 1974, a performance Thompson ranked with Gen. Douglas MacArthur's "old soldiers never die" address to Congress as a Great American Speech. Carter was grateful, and over the course of the early 1976 campaign, Thompson felt he had a special franchise with the candidate. He expected an interview with Carter as they flew from Orlando to Chicago on the morning after Carter's triumph in the Florida primary, but Carter stiffed him. The future Democratic nominee said he was too tired and wanted to sleep. Muttering and glowering upon arrival at O'Hare Airport, Thompson caught the next plane back to Orlando to besiege the hotel room where Hamilton Jordan—Carter's campaign manager—was still sleeping. When Jordan refused to respond to Thompson's screeching, the national affairs correspondent for *Rolling Stone* soaked the base of Jordan's door with lighter fluid and set it ablaze.

Over the course of his career, Thompson has pillaged many hotels. One correspondent who attended the cataclysmic events in Vietnam in 1975 remembers that the sound of Thompson crashing down the steps of Saigon's Continental Hotel was louder than the artillery of the approaching North Vietnamese Army.

The Duke of Doonesbury . . . Bimbos and Bombshells . . . Giving Odds in an Odd Time . . . The Doctor of Philosophy . . .

By sundown on Friday the banshee had screamed for more stiffs than the morgues could hold, and the jails were filling up like cheap hotels in Calcutta.
—Hunter S. Thompson, *San Francisco Examiner*

Thompson has been cultivating an outlandish persona for years—the drunken, raving dope fiend who narrated *Fear and Loathing in Las Vegas*. The book first appeared in *Rolling Stone* and was allegedly written by "Raoul Duke," a pseudonym that Thompson says he picked "off the wall." Raoul Duke is still listed as "Contributing Editor (Sports)" on the *Rolling Stone* masthead. Thompson, for that matter, has the title of "Health & Fitness Editor" for a publication named *Bathroom Journal.*

Duke, of course, was transmogrified by Garry Trudeau into a durable cartoon-strip character in *Doonesbury*. Trudeau's Duke resembles Thompson: the balding head, the sunglasses, the cigarette holder, the reckless talk of drug deals and scams. Oddly enough, Thompson and Trudeau, the two high priests of American satire who both harass Bush unmercifully, have never met. It is just as well.

After Duke first appeared in the cartoon more than a decade ago, Thompson sent Trudeau several menacing letters in which the subject of the artist's dismemberment was raised. At the time, Thompson's marriage to his first wife, Sandy, was crumbling, and he resented the inclusion of her name in the comic strip. Thompson says he no longer looks at *Doonesbury*, where Duke has degenerated to zombie status.

Even today, Thompson will not discuss his divorce. He gestured as if to slit my throat, brandishing a steak knife from the Woody Creek Tavern, if I brought it up. But he is proud of a product of that union, his 22-year-old son, Juan, a student at the University of Colorado.

There may not be a sober side to Hunter Thompson, but there is a generous one. It turns out that one of his running mates is Semmes

Luckett, who was my college roommate in 1960. Like half of the residents of Aspen, it seems, Luckett got turned in to the Feds by an informer a few years ago. He copped a plea for moving massive shipments of what he calls "herbs," did some time in a halfway house, and is now in the midst of a five-year probation period. Things have not always been easy for him, but when he was down-and-out, he says, Thompson sent him a large, unsolicited check.

While I was in Aspen, another of Thompson's friends was badly hurt in a car wreck. He immediately began making arrangements to take care of the victim's 16-year-old son.

And for all of the nihilistic language he uses, Thompson cares about the American political process. When he accepts speaking engagements on campuses, he says, "I preach to the college students that politics is the art to control your environment. . . . In a democracy, you've got to believe you can make a difference."

His problem is that he distrusts most of the politicians involved. We didn't know it the last night we talked politics, but Gary Hart would be back in the race the next day. Even though Hart was supposedly gone at that moment, he was not forgotten. In fact, he was the butt of much derision, even though Thompson and Hart are old Colorado friends. (I remember Thompson arriving at a low moment during the Hart effort in 1984 with heavy-duty cables to "jump-start" the campaign.) There is a bogus letter signed "Gary," written on U.S. Senate stationery, that adorns one wall of the Woody Creek Tavern. Written in a style suspiciously similar to Thompson's prose, the letter refers to the Donna Rice affair and concludes, "Thank God I got rid of her before she got her rotten little teeth into me."

Thompson says that as a reporter, he would never stake out a candidate's home "unless he was suspected of selling cocaine to little children. There we might draw the line. We all know these candidates are womanizers. Sex never hurt anybody. In the meantime we lose track of what matters. The press becomes obsessed with the *National Enquirer* syndrome. There are more ominous things happening in politics than a bimbo from Miami. They've been around all the time."

Thompson predicts Sen. Edward M. Kennedy will get into the race and hopes he will win the presidency this year, though he adds, "I like Gary Hart better than Kennedy." Thompson is not bothered by what tarnishes both men. "So Kennedy ran off a bridge. Hell, Bush killed 243 Marines and another 69 at the embassy," he says in reference to the administration's policy in Lebanon.

Handicapping the presidential field, Thompson sounds like a police sergeant reading out a rap sheet on each candidate:

Gov. Michael Dukakis. "His wife spent twenty-six years as a speed freak. She is more interesting than her husband. She makes Rosalynn Carter look like a charwoman. She should be running."

Sen. Albert Gore. "I have no interest in Gore, and I'd be surprised if anybody else does."

Rep. Richard Gephardt. "He won't be around by Super Tuesday."

Former governor Bruce Babbitt. "Are you kidding? Really?"

Sen. Paul Simon. "I like Simon. I think he's honest in a simple way. But you don't run for president as a simpleton. Look at him. He couldn't win an election for sheriff in most places."

Rev. Jesse Jackson. "My inclination is to vote for Jesse. I like Jesse. He makes politics what it should be." Then, and stressing that he means the words to be complimentary, like a soul brother, he calls Jackson "a wild nigger."

Gorbachev, he says, "could win in Iowa."

No Republicans need apply:

Bush he dismisses as an obsequious geek. "Electing him would be the continuation of Nixon." In one diatribe in the *Examiner*, Thompson wrote that Bush's "face has become swollen and he is said to be plagued by a growth of dead fatty tissue on his back, which is gathering in a lump in the area between his shoulder blades and prevents him from walking normally."

Sen. Robert Dole. "Against Bush, I'd make him 3-to-1. Electing Dole would be like electing Jim Wright [the Speaker of the House]. It's the Peter Principle at work."

Former governor Pierre S. du Pont. "A dilettante."

Al Haig. "I enjoy Haig. He's crazy as a loon. I like him like I like Pat Buchanan." In one column, Thompson wrote of "Cruel Crazy Patrick and Big Al, the Wild Boys, roaming around Washington like a pair of Foam Frogs in heat, laying 3,000 eggs every night and cranking up a genuinely mean ticket—Haig & Buchanan, Buchanan & Haig. What does it matter? 'We will kill the ones who eat us, and eat the ones we kill. . . .'"

Rep. Jack Kemp. "An airhead stuck with that 'trickle-down' crap."

Rev. Pat Robertson. "He's in it to sell his revival tapes."

Thompson confesses, "My great fear is that it'll go by default to Bush. If Bush wins, we all might as well give up on this country until the year 3000."

Thompson has no apologies for his treatment of Bush, or for his verbal manhandling of Humphrey. Nearly ten years after Humphrey died of cancer, Thompson was excoriating another old New Deal Democrat in a recent column in which he said, "Even Hubert Humphrey was shamed, all alone in his unquiet grave down in the depths of the River Styx." Humphrey, he says, "cost us control of the country for ten years." Thompson's only regret is that once he wrote that Humphrey should have been castrated, then later learned that Humphrey had a handicapped grandchild. "I felt bad about that."

It was five below zero outside Thompson's cabin, and the dawn sky was gray as slate. The cabdriver from Mellow Yellow Taxi Co., who had been waiting outside for me, came inside to warm up and pop a Molson for himself.

We were talking about books and, flushed with drink, mortality. Thompson has completed a novel he calls *The Night Manager*, which he hopes will be published someday. Thompson has had no fiction published, although critics might say that the body of his work should be considered fiction. He particularly admires Joseph Conrad. "He's a gloomy bastard."

I reminded Thompson of his own introduction to *The Great Shark Hunt*, a despondent author's note written on another winter night ten years before when he was contemplating suicide: "I have already lived and finished the life I planned to live and everything from now on will be A New Life, a different thing. . . ."

Thompson replied that he had been unnecessarily morbid at the time; the words were a cryptic reference to his marriage that was failing. He may have been troubled about being 40 years old then, but he insisted he doesn't mind being 50 today. There are new politicians to gore, new pomposities to puncture. He is back in command of his career. There is another presidential campaign to cover, and there is no one who can spare the candidates from the wrath of Hunter Thompson.

Getting to the Heart of Robert Stone

(*Boston Globe*, April 16, 1998)

From the time I read *Dog Soldiers* in 1974, I've considered Robert Stone
one of America's finest novelists. Years later, when the *Globe* drew on
my Jerusalem background to assign me to do a piece on Stone and
his new book, *Damascus Gate*, I leapt at the opportunity. It took me to
funky Key West, where Stone proved to be good company with plenty
of intelligent, introspective comments.

KEY WEST, Fla.—A sense of menace and doom hangs over Robert
Stone's fiction like a pall, yet it is often fused with a religious element,
a Conradian search for redemption in the ruins of broken lives.

After using such troubled and exotic locales as Saigon, Central
America, New Orleans, and the high seas as locations for his earlier books, Stone has chosen Jerusalem, that holiest of holy places, as
the setting for his sixth novel, *Damascus Gate*, to be published next
month by Houghton Mifflin.

It is a story of religious fanaticism, political skullduggery, betrayal,
and death, built around a plot to blow up the sacred Moslem shrines
on Temple Mount in the beating heart of the Old City of Jerusalem.

"I have a lot of nerve setting a novel in a country I know so relatively little about," Stone said in an interview at his winter home here.
"But my characters are my usual characters, my exiles, my drifters.
They're Americans for the most part, and it's a world I know well. It
moves from city to city. I feel I know the city of Jerusalem, and I know
the world I'm writing about."

Stone has lived in many places. He and his wife are selling their longtime home in Westport, Conn., and plan to move to Manhattan, but he will keep an apartment in New Haven, where he teaches at Yale, as well as their comfortable house in Key West.

He was not daunted by the idea of Jerusalem as a locale because he has always operated as a skeptic at work in the fields of the Lord, relying on literature as a transcendent power. He says he "turned to art as a kind of religion."

During conversations over a two-day period, Stone discussed his own loss of faith and his belief in his work, and he sounded, not surprisingly, like a character from one of his novels, a refugee from the Beat Generation struggling to cope in a strange new world.

Raised a Catholic, he gave up on its rituals as a young man. "My life had a lot of holes in it. My mother was schizophrenic, so she was institutionalized and I was institutionalized" in an orphanage, he said. "I didn't have a father to turn to. I never knew what a father meant until I had my own kids, so the closest thing to a father was God, you know. When I did leave religion, I left with a great sense of liberation, but it took a great many years for me to realize that half my head was missing."

He paused, as if groping for purchase on a precipice.

"Over the years, I realized that something really great to me, psychologically, was gone, and I have a lot of resentments and feelings of anger and longings. It's been replaced in various ways by work. I continue to believe in the sacredness of insight. I try to turn that to my work. I believe a lot of the satisfactions that literature provides are the same satisfactions that religion provides. Serious literature makes the world less lonely. It makes people's experiences seem less singular, makes them feel less abandoned. They recognize themselves in certain stories, and the less lonely you feel in a lonely and dangerous place, the better off you are."

Stone is 60, with a tapered gray beard. At first, his eyes seemed world-weary—he was one of Ken Kesey's Merry Pranksters and a freelance journalist in Vietnam—but they became recharged with energy when he related how he was drawn to Jerusalem from the moment he first saw the sun striking the city's pale pink stone. Stone and his wife arrived there on an early morning in 1986, riding out of the Sinai desert, where he had been writing a travel piece. He recognized Jerusalem as a place where not only heaven meets earth, but where centuries of mystic tradition collide with the approach of a new millennium.

"I've always been turned on by the prospect of a new city," Stone said. "For me, cities have a kind of meaning, a context. They're a unit I like to deal with. I like to make them a character: Saigon in *Dog Soldiers*, New Orleans in *Hall of Mirrors*." For this book, the city came first, before the characters or the plot.

His scenes are evocative: the twisting corridors of the Arab souk, the little bar in Fink's on the Jewish side of the city, the smell of strong spices, and the air of incipient violence.

Over the five years he worked on the book, Stone visited Israel and the occupied territories several times during the height of the Palestinian uprising, the intifada. At one point, he and his wife, Janice, were caught up in a riot while riding with a U.N. official in the Gaza Strip.

"When we got to Khan Yunis," Stone said, "there was a lot of smoke, tear gas, these women ululating and banging on the car. We drove another block and we saw these kids carrying the body of a boy, propped up like a crucifix. He was 12 or 13, shot in the head with a rubber bullet, obviously at close range."

Then they encountered a Danish soldier, assigned to a U.N. detail, single-handedly confronting the Israeli army unit that shot the boy. Stone turned the incident into a harrowing episode in his book.

Stone's fictional world is often visited by violence and peopled by rogue agents, corrupt officials, dope dealers, and misfits. In *Damascus Gate*, Protestant fundamentalist hucksters—first encountered in *Hall of Mirrors*—form an unholy alliance with Jewish zealots and Israeli intelligence operatives.

Though Stone said the novel is "tough on the Palestinians for their foibles," he expects the greatest criticism will come "from people who don't want to see Israel treated as anything other than a very superior and special place which has no justified enemies."

Damascus Gate is a radical departure from Leon Uris's novels, *Exodus* and *The Haj*, which idealized the Israelis, "completely demonized the Arabs," and pandered to an audience that believed Israel was "innocent of any kind of wrongdoing," Stone said.

"I am in favor of Israel. I think Israel has the right to take steps to ensure its survival," he said. But he is critical of Israeli policy, just as he has been of the United States. "I never believed communism should win the Cold War," Stone said, "but that didn't make me like what was happening in Vietnam or in Central America."

He said influential *Washington Post* literary critic Jonathan Yardley was long ago convinced Stone was "an anti-American commie."

Stone became a major force in American literature by defying convention, and his novels are admired by most critics and have attracted a loyal following of readers. *Dog Soldiers* won the 1974 National Book Award, and *Hall of Mirrors* received a Faulkner Foundation Award. Despite the honors, Stone's sales are regularly eclipsed by, for instance, Robert Ludlum's thrillers. In a tongue-in-cheek tribute, Stone named an aberrant terrorist in his new novel "Willie Ludlum." In fact, many of Stone's characters suffer from a religious obsession known as "Jerusalem Syndrome," which sounds like the title of a Ludlum book.

Stone's novels, ambitious and complex, have all been optioned by Hollywood, but only two have been made into movies. *Dog Soldiers* became *Who'll Stop the Rain*. It worked, Stone said, "because the acting was so damned good."

Hall of Mirrors, made into *WUSA* with Paul Newman, "was flat-out terrible," Stone said. "I make my living by trying to avoid cliches, to put as many miles between us and the nearest cliche I can," Stone said. But the director, Stuart Rosenberg, "would get his telescope out and by Christ he'd spot a cliche on the horizon and make straight for it."

With a story steeped in psychological and theological intrigue, *Damascus Gate* is not Hollywood-friendly. Death, as always, is a presence, though Stone said: "I'm not playing for the ugliness of it." It is a characteristic of his novels that "individuals get caught in hopeless situations."

In *A Flag for Sunrise*, as a nun is tortured for her revolutionary sympathies by agents of the Guardia in a mythical Central American country, Stone writes: "He had hurt her head somehow and closed off light. She knew it would not get better and that she would never come back." As her life ebbs, her last words to her tormentors are: "Behold the handmaid of the Lord."

In *Outerbridge Reach*, a disgraced sailor in a round-the-world boating race throws himself overboard. Stone writes simply: "Then the ocean smothered him."

In *Damascus Gate*, a female character is hanged by thugs. Stone writes: "So with her breath all the thoughts of her devotion were expunged while the angry men stood watching her in the beam of their light and she wondered if she would ever ever die and then a deeper darkness, in its mercy, came."

Stone's been compared to Joseph Conrad and acknowledges his debt. "Conrad is my greatest teacher," he said. "Without Conrad you can't have Graham Greene, you can't have V. S. Naipaul. There's some question whether you can have Hemingway. I'm absolutely influenced by his rendering of what obsesses people and how they deal with their own sense of inadequacy. He was a very hard man, philosophically, but it's a hard world and I think he pretty much got it right."

Part VII
Characters

"Mahatma Gandhi Is Not the Mayor's Style"

(*Boston Globe*, November 4, 1974)

I returned to Mississippi to do this piece on Charles Evers after
his indictment in 1974, when his career seemed to take a sharp,
downward turn. Although I had known Evers in the 1960s, I was not
able to track him down for an interview. Still, I managed to talk with
many others, and my long piece first appeared in the *News-Journal*
papers of Wilmington, Delaware, where I was working at the time. The
Boston Globe also published the story, a couple of months before they
hired me.

Evers extricated himself from criminal charges after a mistrial was
declared in 1975. He went on to become a conservative Republican
legislator and a talk-show host well into the twenty-first century.

FAYETTE, Miss.—Suddenly, the kudzu that clings to the trees and
covers the ground along the road from Jackson gives way to civilization.

On the left, a housing project is being carved from a knoll on the
forty-acre farm of Charles Evers.

It will become the Martin Luther King Memorial Apartments, Inc.
The developer is Charles Evers.

Just down the road a bit is a red brick complex, the Evers Restaurant and Motel and the Evers Fountain Lounge.

On a hillside overlooking the entry to Fayette stands the Medgar

Evers Community Center, an imposing gray brick structure housing a variety of anti-poverty programs. The Medgar Evers Mobile Health Clinic, donated by the Medgar Evers Fund, Inc., is parked outside. At the foot of the hill is a playground and a swimming pool, the Robert F. Kennedy Memorial Park.

Charles Evers arranged for it all.

The road bends into the little town and its speed limit of 35 mph is strictly enforced by policemen hired by Mayor Charles Evers.

Evers's seat of political power is City Hall, newer and brighter than the tattered old Jefferson County Courthouse across the street where the last vestiges of white man's government hold out, aging and embittered.

As the highway runs its course through the row of stores in Fayette it dips into a hollow. Tucked to the right is an ugly blood-red brick building behind a solid wall. A Dr. Pepper sign says it is the Medgar Evers Shopping Center.

But most of the building is vacant. A grocery and a washateria are shut down. The only space in use is taken up by a liquor store and the apartment of Charles Evers.

Charles Evers: civil rights firebrand of the Sixties, capitalist, a man in trouble.

A Federal grand jury indicted Evers in August on three counts of income tax evasion. He was charged with understating his taxable income by $159,336 during 1968–70 and therefore evading $52,594 in taxes.

With characteristic combativeness Evers quickly asserted his innocence and claimed that "someone" was trying "to destroy me."

At a press conference following his indictment, Evers disputed the figures and waved copies of his tax returns. But he would not permit reporters to inspect the returns on the grounds that "you don't understand this stuff." When asked to read figures from his returns, Evers refused, saying he didn't have his glasses. He doesn't wear glasses.

He acknowledged that "there could be some mistakes" in his returns and said he had offered to pay the difference. Instead, he said, an Internal Revenue Service officer told him "We want you."

"I can categorically deny that he was ever told this," said Glenn Dale Harrison, who headed the investigation. "There is no basis in fact for his charges that the IRS is trying to harass him.

"The case originated in the same manner as the majority of our cases," Harrison said, "either through referral from our audit division, our collection division, or from information received from public or private sources."

After the investigation began in 1972, Evers filed amended returns for the years in question. Yet they still failed to agree with figures reached by Federal investigators.

Evers's adjusted returns showed a gross income of more than a half million dollars and a net profit of $48,000 for the three-year period.

If they did nothing else, Evers's own figures confirmed what he has never denied. Charles Evers likes to make and spend a lot of money.

Money has been the touchstone of Evers's career. He once talked of "green power" to counter the "black power" chant of Stokely Carmichael, whom he disliked.

At the civil rights rallies of the Sixties, Evers would tell the audience: "You can't do anything with an empty black fist, but you can with one crammed with green dollars."

He led black boycotts of white merchants in Natchez and Port Gibson and Fayette, in the southwest Mississippi kingdom of the Ku Klux Klan. And after he became established in business himself, he would exhort his followers to trade with him.

"I want all of you, if you want me to be your leader, to keep me in business," he would say. "Don't give your money to the people who hate you."

Evers's emphasis on economics troubled many of his allies in the civil rights movement. The ideologues who ran the Delta Ministry distrusted him and broke off relations with him. The national leadership of the NAACP was prepared to oust him as Mississippi field secretary at one time. Even Evers's loyalists had their moments of doubt, but came to see his tactics as means to an end.

"I guess it bothers a lot of people," said Charles Ramberg, a 30-year-old white lawyer who came south as a latter-day civil rights volunteer in 1969 and ended up working for Evers. "It bothered me at first. But when you see how necessary economic freedom is in Mississippi—even if his style is abrasive—so what?"

"The only way to have true civil rights is to have money," says Charles Young of Meridian, a compatriot of Evers in the NAACP and one of the state's leading black entrepreneurs.

As Ramberg observed, "Mahatma Gandhi is not the mayor's style."

In fact, Evers comes closer to Flem Snopes, the avaricious redneck businessman who struggled up from poverty in the Faulkner trilogy.

The 52-year-old Evers is part prizefighter, messiah, hustler, and snake oil salesman. His is a complex personality forged by the hardships of growing up black in Mississippi during the Depression.

"I ain't nobody's saint," he says at the outset of his confessional autobiography, *Evers*. He relates tales of petty thievery as a child, of operating brothels in the Philippines as a soldier during World War II, of pimping and running numbers in Chicago.

He boasts of getting three girls pregnant while a college student. His recent divorce settlement shows that he and his wife of twenty-three years have a daughter, 25, and another adopted daughter, also 25.

Yet some of his friends believe he laid it on a little thick in the book; that he romanticized his connection with the mob in Chicago and inflated his role as prostitution king in the Philippines.

The autobiography appalled many of Evers's sympathizers when it was published in 1971.

"You should have seen the original version," said Patricia Derian, Democratic national committeewoman from Mississippi. After receiving galley proofs, she said she persuaded Evers and the publisher to delete some of the rawer passages.

Nevertheless, the white liberals who worked in Evers's gubernatorial campaign that year felt that the book was ill-conceived.

"We weren't able to understand that he was dealing with a different culture," Ramberg recalled. "He'd say, 'The people will understand.' Redemption is so strong in a church-related culture that it was an asset. But it certainly was not a useful ploy to attract white votes which we were ostensibly going after."

Although the book dramatizes Evers's exploits in crime and civil rights, his obsession with making money is also evident on almost every page.

"I never gambled. I never drank. I never smoked. That kind of vice is too expensive, it's too destructive to the body, and I just didn't feel like I needed it. But I've done about everything a man could do to make money," Evers said.

He declared that "you don't get business mixed up with civil rights." But he has not heeded his own advice.

After his brother, Medgar Evers, was assassinated in 1963, he returned to Mississippi to take his place in the civil rights movement and he brought his penchant for making money with him.

Fayette is the kind of town that Yankee journalists like to describe as sleepy. It is set in the Mississippi backwoods, a few miles off the Natchez Trace, on Highway 61—the route that generations of blacks have used to flee the state for the North. Two-thirds of the 1,800 residents of Fayette are black. Yet the whites controlled the commerce, worshipped in the big churches, lived on paved streets, segregated the schools and dominated the town. Until 1969.

Like a cagey gambler, Charles Evers picked his spot. Though he was reared in central Mississippi, he attended Alcorn A&M near Fayette, and was familiar with the area and its potential. It was as bereft of black business as it was of black leadership. He moved to fill the vacuum.

With the passage of the Voting Rights Act of 1965, he began to register black voters. He acquired property with almost the same alacrity. A piece of land here, an adjacent plot there, purchased usually in the name of his wife and daughters and paid for often in cash.

He maintained an attractive home for his family in Jackson, ninety miles away, but established residency in Fayette. He opened a liquor store and a grocery and a café and paid his employees minimum wage.

At the same time he was becoming more moderate as a civil rights spokesman. His anger over his brother's murder and oppression in Mississippi was at first directed at all whites. By 1968 he was a leader of an insurgent biracial delegation seated at the Democratic National Convention, where he refused to attend a black caucus because it excluded whites.

The next year, Evers was elected mayor of Fayette and swept in a slate of black aldermen to take over completely the town government.

He complained on national television that the previous administration had spent up all of the town's budget out of spite. He was rewarded with upwards of $100,000 that arrived in the mail in cash and checks from people throughout the country.

The money was put in a special account called the "emergency fund" and was used by Evers to set up a spoils system unlike any ever seen in Fayette.

He hired dozens of employees and paid them from the fund. "The mayor regards each job as his bailiwick," said Ramberg, the mayor's assistant who was paid $800 a month from the fund before becoming a legal services lawyer in Brandon.

Evers didn't mind intimidating his employees when it came time to cast their votes. On election days he would tell them, "All you people who have jobs and do wrong ain't going to have them anymore."

In a small town, a few votes are important.

"Since we've been in office we've got one hundred people under city jurisdiction," says Alderman James Gales. "Previously, we had only five."

Richard M. (Bo) Truly Jr., a lawyer from an old Fayette family, cites as an example Evers's move to shut down a black-operated juke joint on the grounds it was a nuisance. Actually, Truly said, it was competition for Evers's enterprises.

Last month Truly, in a taxpayers' suit, won a $1,134 judgment against Evers and other town officials. They had spent town money on the defense of a former policeman and bodyguard for Evers who was indicted for assault and battery in another county. The lawyer who received the payment is also representing Evers in a suit over the mayor's refusal to pay off an $11,640 mortgage.

Evers's associates are either vague or not knowledgeable when asked about the town's finances. "I was never privy to finances," said one. "The mayor plays that close to his chest."

Evers works with a town budget of $100,000 raised from taxes plus thousands of dollars from the Federal government and private sources. Some of the money supports his travels around the country as he promotes Fayette, himself, and tries to lure new money and industry for the town.

He has been both adroit and clumsy in his handling of the money. His political connections in Washington ensured favorable treatment for Fayette's applications for Federal aid, and his magnetism attracted donations from foundations.

But he sometimes spent it foolishly.

One of Evers's first ventures as mayor was to hire an inept road contractor, a white man, to repair a couple of streets. The project cost about $30,000 and was awarded without bids. The contractor, one man said, "didn't know any more about streets than I do. They started cracking right away."

When the same contractor paved the land around Evers's motel complex eyebrows were raised in Fayette, though the mayor said he paid for the work personally.

Around the same time Evers set up a Delaware tax-exempt organization, the Medgar Evers Fund, which has become a virtual branch of government in Fayette.

Drawing support from foundations and direct mail solicitations, the fund has pumped more than $1 million into Fayette during the Evers administration. It puts up the local share on Federal grants and provides garbage trucks, ambulances, and medical equipment for the town.

Gilbert Jonas, who runs the fund out of New York, said that Evers— who serves as president of the organization—had "never received any salary or remuneration from the fund" other than "a few thousand a year" for travel expenses.

However, the fund is involved in a housing project in Fayette where Evers this year sold land to the project for twice as much as he paid for it in 1969.

Moreover, the Federal government is guaranteeing a $1.2 million mortgage for the construction of the project. No bid was required and the job went to a black contractor who was a friend of Evers.

If there are to be sweetheart arrangements, Evers wants them on his own terms.

Earlier this year he "blew the whistle" on corruption within the Economic Development Administration (EDA), according to a government official. Evers's complaint was justified, the source said, because it is impossible to swing EDA approval for a contract unless certain engineers are involved.

The source, an EDA official himself, said the investigation was covered up. Instead of cleaning up its own house, the EDA is now refusing to cooperate with Evers on Federal projects for Fayette, the source said. He speculated that the Federal agency "stimulated" the income tax investigation of the mayor.

Feelings about Charles Evers are mixed in Fayette, like they'd be for most mayors in most towns.

"You take a look at Hitler, Nixon, and him and you'll see they're all the same," says one white resident who did not want to be identified. Most whites don't want to discuss him, but some grudgingly admit he's helped the town.

Gov. Bill Waller, who defeated Evers in 1971, says, "He's made a contribution. . . . There's no enmity in the state toward him. He's accepted as part of our political fabric."

Gales, the black alderman who has lived all of his 54 years in Fayette, said the town "is heaven compared to twenty years ago."

The town board has had its differences with Evers, such as the time they blocked his effort to loan one of the town's two fire trucks to another town that had just elected its own black mayor. But they generally get along with Evers.

Efforts to reach Evers for fresh comment over the past several weeks have been unsuccessful.

The sharpest criticism about Evers is directed at his business operations.

"Some people who have never been in a restaurant may go to his place and eat a $4 steak and think they've been overcharged," said Lillie Lee, a young city hall secretary who remembers the days when she paid six cents to sit in the balcony of Fayette's now-defunct movie house.

"You've got a problem of blacks understanding blacks in business," Miss Lee said. "They're used to the white businessman. The first thing that comes to their mind is that some blacks can't do business. Some people have a hang up and dislike him [Evers] because he's an aggressive businessman."

Evers's flashiest operation is the Fountain Lounge, a sprawling new roadhouse which seats 1,400, features big-name soul bands, and rivals a big-city nightclub for its garish opulence. The cover charge is $4 a person on dance nights. A half-pint of liquor with set-ups is $3.50. Beer is fifty cents a bottle.

It opened a year ago after a fire destroyed a smaller lounge owned by Evers. He said at the time that it was uninsured and placed the loss at $40,000, but the Fountain Lounge was rebuilt quickly.

Evers's lifestyle is as brassy as the lounge. His apartment is furnished, said one friend, "like a Turkish whorehouse." A big safe is conspicuous in the apartment.

Evers has four offices in town: at the city hall, at the community center, at his apartment, and at the lounge. The last is his favorite. It is deep in carpeting and its paneled walls are covered with photographs of Evers campaigning with Bobby Kennedy in the last days of his life in California.

There are picture of other victims: his brother Medgar; Martin Luther King Jr.; John F. Kennedy. Profiles in martyrdom.

Charles Evers carried a gun when bushwhacking and bombings were a constant threat to civil rights activities. After he was elected mayor, he imposed gun control in Fayette, and as time ebbs from those years of violence fear has diminished.

He perceives his income tax investigation as a new threat, though, a threat to black independence. And the old guard in the civil rights movement is closing ranks behind him and picking up the theme of persecution.

"I'm not saying Charles is not guilty," says Aaron Henry, president of the NAACP in Mississippi. "It's just that other people have been advised of tax delinquency and have been given years to pay, such as Joe Louis and Richard Nixon."

"Charles Evers Appreciation Days" are being organized throughout the state. The first was held in Meridian last month and drew several hundred people to a church during a rainstorm. A couple of hundred dollars were raised, just like in the old days when the hat was passed at civil rights rallies to raise bail money for demonstrators.

Evers prefers that the government deal with him as a cause célèbre rather than a crook.

Despite the latest wave of publicity over his indictment, some observers feel that Evers is a fading figure.

W. F. Minor, the veteran Mississippi correspondent for the New Orleans *Times-Picayune*, wrote recently that Evers was losing respect in the civil rights movement. The column was denounced by the Evers camp as gratuitous. But Minor contends that Evers's power base is being undercut by his own erratic behavior and the rise of the black bourgeoisie.

"He's dependent upon the masses," Minor says. "As more and more blacks become middle-class, they're going to look to him as a leader less and less."

Evers's political performance has been bizarre. He was elected to the coveted position of national committeeman when civil rights forces won recognition from the national Democratic Party in 1968. But he has attended only two national committee meetings since then. He has missed half of the Fayette town meetings this year; he has campaigned for a Republican, Nelson Rockefeller; he made a politically perverse endorsement of a racist candidate for governor, then urged his constituents to disregard their hard-won right to vote and stay home in one election; he embraced Gov. George Wallace as fit for vice president; and he recently made sympathetic noises for Richard Nixon. His pro-Nixon sentiment was expressed, friends say, "to try to ease the heat" from his own income tax investigation.

"He's the last of America's semi-literate political leaders," says his friend and fellow Democratic committee member Patt Derian, speaking of Evers as if he had already passed from the scene. "But he was a hero when we needed one."

Another journalist compared Evers to a benign Mafia boss. "He's got a totally different moral code. So he cuts a few corners here and there. So what? He takes care of his people."

Among Evers's problems is that he does indeed live by a code and in a culture that are distinct from those of the white opinion-makers and officials who judge him.

He grew up in a rural black society that was the precursor of the new moralism; where common-law marriages and "illegitimate" children were customary long before it became fashionable; where young men depended upon cunning instead of inheritance to make good.

"Very few whites really understand blacks," said Marjorie Baroni, a matronly white woman from Natchez who is devoted to the Evers cause in Fayette and has worked as his secretary since his election. "I've learned a lot about this culture and society since then," she said, "and I've found that we've made some ghastly judgments."

The greatest misjudgment that is made about Charles Evers, however, is the tendency of many of his sympathizers to canonize him.

He is the first to say that he is not the kind of man who will suffer in a Birmingham jail or starve himself to protest injustice or turn the other cheek.

He is, instead, the spiritual descendant of George Washington Plunkitt, the turn-of-the-century Tammany ward boss who declared, "I seen my opportunities and I took 'em."

Secret History

(*George* magazine, June 1997)

Trent Lott didn't like this story. After it was published, I ran into him in
the Grove before an Ole Miss football game. (We had been in school
at the same time.) He complained. I responded that the piece had
lacked "his voice" and that I had tried to get it, going so far as to fly to
Washington for an interview I had arranged through his staff only to
have him "stiff me." Later in the Grove, I saw Lott's close friend, the
late Allen Pepper—who became a Federal judge. Pepper told me he
enjoyed the piece and thought their Sigma Nu fraternity should "use it
in rush."

Several years later, Trent and I attended a dinner at the chancellor's
house on campus and wound up bantering with each other over his
book, *Herding Cats*, which had recently come out. I invited him to join a
panel discussion about political writing at the next Oxford Conference
for the Book. He appeared and more than held his own in a good-
humored exchange with a couple of other liberal writers. I thought it
was one of the best panels I've been on.

In the beginning, there were the Sigma Nus, and Trent Lott was created in their image. The Snakes, as the Sigma Nus called themselves,
were the gung ho fraternity at the University of Mississippi, strivers
and achievers united by ambition. While the sons of wealthy planters and physicians gravitated toward the elitist houses—the stately,
columned mansions of the Phi Delts and Kappa Alphas that anchored
Fraternity Row—the young men just starting to climb society's ladder

found a foothold with the Sigma Nus, who lived in a starkly modernistic structure on a backstreet behind Fraternity Row. The 1960 Ole Miss yearbook observed that the Snakes liked to pick themes for their activities, such as their annual "Redneck Party (equivalent to a come-as-you-are party)." Undeterred by the condescension of the other fraternities, the Sigma Nus welcomed the boys who worked their way through school, and they pledged promising freshmen from obscure rural towns.

Trent Lott was a natural fit. The son of a shipyard worker, he had more moxie than money, and he exuded the freshly scrubbed charisma of the televangelists already monopolizing Sunday mornings on black-and-white television screens across the South. He had a winning smile and firm handshake and the bearing of a salesman who could be trusted. More than a generation later, after Lott had moved on to the highest ranks of Congress, then Republican national chairman Haley Barbour, another Ole Miss man, would describe Lott as "the ultimate Sigma Nu."

Lott's rise also signifies the realization of the Southern Strategy conceived for President Nixon nearly three decades ago, when Southern Democrats were recoiling from their party's civil rights platforms and beginning flirtations with the GOP. Since the decline of House Speaker Newt Gingrich, Lott reigns as a paradigm of the new Republican party. The Eastern establishment has been routed by Southerners who broke from the Democratic party like some renegade strain of amoeba and took over the body politic of the GOP. The party of Lincoln has become the party of Lott.

The 55-year-old Lott started his ascension back at the University of Mississippi, where a young man's path to political glory depended on obtaining a law degree and making connections. Lott would later travel to Washington to work on the Hill and run for Congress. But for all Lott's many alliances and compromises along the way, his oldest friends believe his embrace of the Sigma Nus is his most significant political bond. The fraternity introduced him to a class struggle, a clash between old power and fresh aspirations, and he built a career along this fault line until he himself embodied the establishment.

Lott's office did not respond to repeated requests for an interview for this article. His friends say he seldom talks about his early life, and in an interview last winter with the *New York Times Magazine* concerning his role as Republican leader, Lott acknowledged, "I just don't like to get into personal things." When he has talked about his past, he has claimed the shipyard town of Pascagoula, where his family moved before Lott entered junior high, as his home. Rarely has he mentioned that his childhood was spent in the shadows of Duck Hill, in neighboring Carroll County, a patch of worn-out Mississippi farmland heartbreaking in its meanness.

Though moonshine flourished more readily than cotton in the county's hills and bottoms, Lott's father challenged the land for a living. Chester Lott was a sharecropper—a job ordinarily held by poor blacks—and a drinking man. Lott's mother, Iona, was a sober, churchgoing woman who taught elementary school. "My mother was . . . very blunt, a disciplinarian, a great lady," Lott told the *Times*. "My dad was a little bit of a happy-go-lucky fellow and he liked to have a good time . . . Had a drinking problem. He had problems with it all his life. And that sort of problem does affect you . . . It makes you maybe grow up a little early."

In the early '50s, Lott's parents picked up stakes and moved to Pascagoula, where his father found a job as a pipe fitter at Ingalls Shipbuilding, the lifeblood of the Gulf Coast town of 10,000. After World War II, Mississippi's congressional delegation funneled dozens of Cold War contracts to the shipyards, providing a steady living for the workers there. The Lotts lived in one of the "navy houses" off Ingalls Avenue, where most of the small two-bedroom homes were occupied by the families of shipyard workers.

At Pascagoula High School, Lott was a model student. "He was very friendly, neat, and organized," says John Corlew, a Pascagoula native who followed Lott to Ole Miss and into the Sigma Nus. Lott's classmates called him "Mr. Pascagoula High," president of the student council, homecoming king, most popular, senior favorite, neatest, and most polite. He was runner-up as the most handsome but was selected as the most likely to succeed.

When Lott enrolled in 1959, the University of Mississippi—known as Ole Miss since the days of slavery—was rich with symbols of the Civil War. The only school in the state considered to be a university, it was an all-white institution. In 1861, most of the all-male student body had gone off to fight the Yankees. A hundred years later, one of the old red-brick buildings on campus was still known as the Dead House, for it was there that the bodies of rebel soldiers were brought from the battle at Shiloh. A best-selling statuette at the campus store featured Colonel Rebel, a caricature of a Confederate gentleman muttering "Forget, Hell!" Halftimes at football games were highlighted by the unfurling of a giant Confederate battle flag—said to be the world's largest—that covered most of the playing field. Much of the student body was preoccupied with championship football teams, beauty contests—the school produced Miss Americas in consecutive years— and methods to circumvent prohibition, which still prevailed in the Baptist country of north Mississippi.

But while many of the sons of the landed gentry were squandering their college years before going home to lose the family farm or soak their lives in Jack Daniel's, the Sigma Nus hustled to get ahead. They always competed vigorously at the annual Stunt Night, a contest of songs and skits between fraternities that packed the campus auditorium. They didn't particularly excel in athletics, but no one exceeded their enthusiasm; the brothers brought dates to all the intramural games to root for the Sigma Nus. During Lott's freshman year, Roy "Rah Rah" Williams, a Sigma Nu from Pascagoula, commandeered a crop duster to fly to Baton Rouge and bomb the Louisiana State University campus with leaflets bearing the message GO TO HELL, LSU. "Trent was a great leader inside the fraternity," says Corlew. "He encouraged a lot of student activity, getting people to serve in student government, on the newspaper."

"Trent had a fantastic recall of names," says Ernie Lane, another Sigma Nu contemporary. "He ran for and held just about every office in Sigma Nu. He was neat. Didn't wear sloppy blue jeans like some of us. Didn't take part in the late-night poker games. He was always trying not to make enemies." Lott, who enforces a strict dress code in his Washington office, was compulsively orderly. He dressed in slacks and starched shirts, and there was never a hair out of place on his head. In his room at the Snake House, he kept his pencils in a line and stacked his papers neatly on his desk. He shared the room with Allen Pepper, known as "the Rabbi" for his serious demeanor. They went to bed at respectable hours, and on Sunday mornings, while many of the brothers nursed hangovers, Lott and Pepper would attend services at Oxford's First Baptist Church. "He was neat, Hot dog! He was very neat," says Pepper of his old friend. "Of course, it's awful hard to be messy when you've got one pair of shoes."

Lott and Pepper were also part of a Sigma Nu foursome called the Chancellors, patterned after the wholesome quartets of the day, the Four Lads and the Four Freshmen. They sang fraternity ballads and old barbershop standards such as "Heart of My Heart." One member of the group, Guy Hovis, went on to sing on *The Lawrence Welk Show* for more than a decade before returning to Mississippi, where he now runs Lott's Jackson office. "We'd sing for all kinds of campus activities," says Hovis. "If a guy got pinned, we'd go to the sorority house and sing for the girls." In 1961 Lott was one of four males and four females elected cheerleaders in campuswide voting. On Saturdays, they would garb themselves in white sweaters emblazoned with a big M, swirl Confederate battle flags, and exhort the rowdy student masses with the Rebels' school cheer: "Hotty Toddy, Gosh almighty, who the hell are we? Hey! Flim flam, bim bam, Ole Miss, by damn!"

Cheerleading was serious stuff at Ole Miss. In a 1969 article entitled "Up From Sis-boom-bah," the *Mississippi Freelance*, a monthly tabloid, listed "many of the men on top of Mississippi's power heap" who had once been cheerleaders in the state: several prominent legislators, the venerable Senator John C. Stennis, the young newspaper publisher Hodding Carter III, and "Trent Lott of Pascagoula." The article failed to spot the potential of another former Ole Miss cheerleader, Thad Cochran, who was quietly practicing law in Jackson at the time and would become Lott's colleague, and nemesis.

As his senior year approached, Lott parlayed the recognition he'd gotten as a cheerleader and as president of the interfraternity council into a campaign for president of the student body. His opponent was Dick Wilson, a well-connected Kappa Alpha from Jackson. Wilson had the backing of the establishment fraternities as well as his sister's prestigious sorority, the Chi Omegas, home of the two Miss Americas. Lott was left to troll the backwater frat houses and the dormitories—the base for half the student body, the "independents" who either spurned the Greek system or could not afford it. To mock the lettered names of the fraternities, the unaligned students liked to call themselves GDIs: God-damned independents.

"We always felt we wouldn't get a lot of support from Fraternity Row," recalls Corlew, "so we knocked on the doors in the dorms." In the end, Lott fell short by sixty votes. It would be the only formal election Lott ever lost, and he took it as a rebuke from the sons of privilege. Wilson, now a retired lawyer, believes he won because he was a more established candidate. "I had served as vice president of the student body, and I had ties to a lot of fraternities and sororities."

But Lott faulted himself for not doing enough to woo the outsiders. One bloc of independents sided with Wilson because they felt he would provide more thoughtful leadership in the gathering integration crisis, according to Gerald Blessey, a leading campus independent. Faced with a choice between two fraternity candidates, many other independents simply didn't bother to vote. Blessey recalls that Lott was distraught about the outcome. "He came up to me and asked, 'What went wrong? Why didn't I get that vote?'"

"That's still a scar," says another of Lott's longtime acquaintances. "He's convinced he didn't pay enough attention to the rednecks or to Vet Village," where married students lived. "He didn't organize the independents. And he never forgot it. From then on, his campaigns were like [Alabama governor] George Wallace's. He worked the Evangelicals, the right-to-lifers, the Pentecostals. Those groups are his groups now."

If Lott needed further incentive to gravitate toward disaffected white voters, the government handed him an issue in the fall of 1962, when the U.S. Fifth Circuit Court of Appeals ordered Ole Miss to admit James Meredith, its first black student. Governor Ross Barnett stoked opposition to the court order, and when Meredith arrived on campus on September 30, violence erupted. Thousands of paratroopers, U.S. marshals, and federalized national guardsmen finally put down the insurrection after two people were killed and scores injured. Lott played no role in the riot, but those who knew him then recall that privately he inveighed against the federal government and President Kennedy, who Lott felt had unfairly made an example of Ole Miss. "My recollection," says one Mississippi lawyer, "is that he was still very defiant about the admission of Meredith" several years after the event.

Another seminal event took place at Ole Miss while Lott was studying law there. In 1966, a progressive faction of law students invited Robert F. Kennedy to speak on campus. The move was denounced by a conservative element that was "very adamant on race," according to one classmate of Lott's. Lott was associated with the conservatives, though no one remembers if he was specifically involved in the squabble. Kennedy, who had been attorney general when Ole Miss was forced to integrate, agreed to come to the school, but he had one stipulation: that there be a question-and-answer session after his speech.

"It didn't take a rocket scientist to figure out what he wanted to be asked," recalls Frank Thackston, a Greenville attorney who was then a law student. For some time, Mississippians had been intrigued by reports that even as Governor Barnett had rallied the rednecks with cries of "Never!" to the integration order, he had privately proposed compromises with the Kennedy brothers. After Kennedy's speech, Thackston asked him if the rumors were true. The New York senator proceeded to regale the audience with a long account of Barnett's bizarre proposals, which included the suggestion that the gun-toting federal marshals force the governor to accept Meredith.

For some of Lott's classmates, Kennedy's appearance was a liberating break with Mississippi's conservative leadership. Lott, however, was busy making connections with that very same old guard through a job as liaison between the law school and its alumni association, a position that enabled him to begin building a network of contacts among lawyers—a key element in the courthouse cliques that ran local politics around the state.

In December 1964, Lott had made another important connection. He married Patricia Thompson, the daughter of a popular dentist in Pascagoula and a member of a prominent sorority at Ole Miss. Trent and Tricia, as the couple are known, first met in the high school band, where she played the flute and he the tuba. The early years of their marriage were shadowed by the Vietnam War. Like most Mississippians reared in a military tradition, Lott supported the war.

But as American involvement grew and the monthly draft call expanded, he maneuvered to escape military service—with the help of a local draft board protective of a golden boy. Selective-service records indicate that Lott applied for and got four student deferments to avoid the draft while at Ole Miss. He was given a 2-S classification "because of activity in study" in 1963 and again in 1964. He was 1-A, "available for military service," for six months in 1965 but then obtained another 2-S exemption that was renewed in 1966. On April 12, 1967, shortly before he graduated from law school and a year before his first child was born, Lott requested and was given an unusual 3-A classification "by reason of extreme hardship to dependents" that freed him forever from the threat of the draft.

After school, Lott went home to Pascagoula to practice law and politics. He quickly became an active volunteer in the gubernatorial campaign of John Bell Williams, a contest that proved to be the last carnival of open racism in Mississippi politics. Williams was a congressman who had been stripped of his seniority by national Democrats for supporting Barry Goldwater in 1964.

Proclaiming himself a defender of Mississippi against the tyranny of the national party, he came home to run for governor. It was a common practice for Mississippi lawyers to use their influence among clients and friends to promote candidates, and Lott threw his weight behind Williams. Williams's positions were far to the right of the two Democratic moderates in the race. In the five years after the first Mississippi school was integrated, blacks were pressing for equal rights in the state. So Williams punctuated his campaign speeches with the promise that "when I am you governor, we are not going to have gangs of marauding hoodlums parading up and down our streets and destroying our property. I know how to nip in the bud that kind of thing."

His election, which the Associated Press described as "a smashing conservative victory that left Negro voting hopes wrecked," gave Lott a good friend in a high place. Within a year, the young lawyer used his local connections to reach out to another member of Mississippi's congressional delegation, William M. Colmer, a Pascagoula Democrat and chair of the House Rules Committee. Colmer was a proud segregationist with a habit of throwing roadblocks at civil rights legislation. He opposed public housing, welfare, and civil rights legislation, and lamented that Martin Luther King Jr.'s assassination resulted in a stronger open-housing bill.

Colmer brought Lott to Washington as his administrative assistant in 1968, and the relationship blossomed. After Lott's dad was killed in a car wreck in 1969, Colmer and Lott became like father and son. Studying the arcane rules and the legislative tactics of the House, Lott was also an apprentice congressman. His mentor was known to have a vindictive streak, quick to strike at anyone who challenged him. Lott picked that up from him too.

One story is illustrative. Lott and his wife were still new to Washington when they were invited to a dinner party at the home of fellow Mississippians. The hostess, Bettye Jolly, worked for G. V. "Sonny" Montgomery, a new Mississippi congressman. But the host, E. Grady Jolly, had a job that roused Lott's suspicions: He worked at the Department of Justice. Even though Jolly was not involved in civil rights actions, Lott still viewed him as an agent of the department that regularly hauled Mississippi officials into court. Moreover, Jolly had been a Phi Delta Theta at Ole Miss, and "Trent resented the Phi Delts because they represented the Delta planter class," according to one of the Mississippians on hand. Back in 1958, Jolly had knocked the Sigma Nu candidate out of a runoff for student body president, so "Trent had inherited this anti-Phi Delt attitude," says another Mississippian familiar with the dinner. Jolly's acerbic wit did not allay the tension.

Over the coq au vin, it became apparent that the host concluded "that Trent was quite shallow," the Mississippian says. "He started poking fun at him. Grady called Colmer a troglodyte and things like that, and it really embarrassed Trent."

Jolly would eventually return to Mississippi, becoming a successful attorney. In 1978, he managed Thad Cochran's winning campaign to become the state's first Republican to win a U.S. Senate seat since Reconstruction. Three years later, Cochran asked President Reagan to nominate Jolly to the U.S. Fifth Circuit Court of Appeals. Lott, a congressman with no official standing in the case, waged a guerilla war against Jolly at the White House, depicting the nominee too liberal. Jolly was eventually confirmed, but Lott delayed the nomination for a full year.

In 1972, the 82-year-old Colmer decided to retire and gave Lott his blessing to succeed him. But Lott's announcement that he would run as a Republican shocked even his closest friends. Practically every politician in the state was a Democrat, albeit well to the right of the national party. But Lott proclaimed he was "tired of the Muskies and the Kennedys and the Humphreys . . . I will fight against the ever-increasing efforts of the so-called liberals to concentrate more power in the government in Washington." He made a smart calculation. Nixon won his greatest majority that fall in Lott's Fifth Congressional District, taking 87 percent of the vote, and Lott won with 55 percent.

At the same time, Cochran, who had managed Democrats for Nixon in Mississippi in 1968, had also switched parties and was elected congressman from the Jackson district. Lott and Cochran established a GOP beachhead in the Mississippi congressional delegation. But their relationship soon deteriorated into a feud that was still simmering as recently as last summer, when the two competed against each other for the right to replace Bob Dole as Senate majority leader. "It all goes back to Ole Miss," says a Republican consultant, explaining that Cochran, a Pi Kappa Alpha, was chosen student body vice president in another election in which the Sigma Nus lost. "Everything was always easy for Thad. Trent had to strive more."

Their rivalry had split the state party. Cochran, an easygoing moderate, has the backing of the planters and the better-educated, country-club set. Lott is said to be uncomfortable attending the obligatory functions of the Delta Council, a powerful organization of big farming interests. Instead, Lott is a favorite of both the old Citizens Councils crowd, the bitter-end opponents of integration, and the newly rich who have made fortunes in oil and gas.

The relationship grew worse still in 1978, when Senator James O. Eastland announced his retirement, opening a Senate seat from Mississippi for the first time in more than thirty years. According to Mike Retzer, chairman of the state GOP, Cochran immediately told party officials that he was weary of running for re-election every two years; he would fight for the party nomination for a six-year Senate term, and if he lost, he'd simply return to Jackson and practice law. Lott reluctantly decided not to challenge Cochran. "Trent loved Washington and didn't want to risk losing his seat," Retzer says. In the House, meanwhile, Lott's partisan style had won him friends, especially among the younger members of the GOP caucus. After only eight years in the House, he was elected to minority whip, his party's number-two rank.

Flush with his new authority, Lott moved against Mississippi's old bête noire: the Department of Justice. He began papering DOJ with angry letters that scolded the federal government for inspecting Mississippi jails and upholding regulations. He challenged the legality of DOJ decisions and the credentials of department officials. Inside the Justice building on Constitution Avenue, weary officials started calling Lott their "pen pal."

One letter, however, backfired. Late in 1981, Lott objected to a policy denying tax-exempt status to private schools practicing racial discrimination. The policy penalized some of the party's loyal supporters, Lott wrote Reagan, calling upon the president to intervene. In the margin of Lott's letter, Reagan wrote, "I think we should." A few days later, the Justice Department sided with all-white Bob Jones University in a federal court motion designed to allow segregated schools to qualify for tax breaks. The action triggered a public uproar and forced an embarrassed Reagan to back down. Lott, who had written the letter on behalf of a church school in Mississippi—one of the "seg academies" that had sprouted across the state to circumvent the desegregation of public schools—conceded that he too had mishandled the affair: "I regret what I did," he said. After two decades of opposing civil rights measures, Lott now called segregation "a ghost of the past that we'd like to put behind us."

Not, apparently, entirely. At about the same time, Lott joined Jefferson Davis Camp 635 of the Sons of Confederate Veterans, a historical organization. In 1984 he addressed the group's convention, declaring that "the spirit of [Confederate president] Jefferson Davis lives in the 1984 Republican platform." In a subsequent interview with *Southern Partisan*, a magazine that serves as a voice for the devotees of the Lost Cause, Lott explained that the "fundamental principles" of the Confederate president "apply to the Republican party . . . The 1984 Republican platform, all the ideas we supported there—from tax policy to foreign policy, from individual rights to neighborhood security—are things that Jefferson Davis and his people believed in."

In Washington, however, such provocative language started to fade from Lott's vocabulary. With a growing number of black voters in his home state, Lott emulated other old-line politicians such as George Wallace and South Carolina's Senator Strom Thurmond by dropping racial innuendo and courting the black vote. Gerald Blessey, the Ole Miss GDI who became a Democratic mayor of Biloxi and challenged Lott in a 1976 House race, now speaks admiringly of Lott's constituent work and says Lott "recognized the challenging times."

"When Trent started out, he was very partisan," says one longtime Republican Hill aide. "He generated strong feelings among other members—and most of them were negative. There was a lot of retribution involved, a determination to get even. But he's changed that. He's no longer shrill and biting, and he made the transition from the House to the Senate real easy."

Lott waited until Mississippi legend John Stennis retired before he ran for the Senate in 1988, trouncing his Democratic opponent. As soon as he arrived there, he began building new coalitions. Three years ago, Lott counted the votes and concluded that he had the support to become GOP whip, the second-ranking Republican. Despite earlier promises not to, he ran against Alan K. Simpson of Wyoming and won by a single vote. When the GOP gained control of the Senate, Lott was suddenly the chamber's second most powerful Republican.

Last year, while Bob Dole, still serving as the majority leader, was busy running for the presidential nomination and Gingrich was creating ill will with his petulant partisanship, the Clinton administration seized on Lott as a figure of stability. "We like dealing with Lott," says a White House aide. "We disagree philosophically, but you know what the deal is with him. He's a charming man, and he's a deal maker."

When Dole decided to give up the majority leader's job last summer, Lott was poised to take over. The race to succeed Dole became another contest between Lott and Cochran, and Lott won decisively, 44 to 8. Sen. Fred Thompson of Tennessee says it was an easy choice. "He has the characteristics we need—the focus, the discipline, and the ability to articulate our message on TV. He's also a tough tactician, always thinking, always planning." And Thompson suggests, it is not unreasonable to think that Lott will aim higher yet. "He's going to be a hard dog to keep on the porch."

A week after last November's elections, when the Republicans strengthened their hold on Senate, Trent and Tricia Lott went back to the Ole Miss homecoming to celebrate. On a smoky autumn Saturday afternoon, they strolled hand in hand through the Grove, the tree-studded greensward where thousands of Ole Miss followers laid out bountiful supplies of food and drink for the all-day festival. Thad Cochran and Haley Barbour were there too, but with their own families and friends. The Lotts were seeking out Sigma Nus. The night before, they had attended a Sigma Nu reunion. All four members of the Chancellors were there, and they sang together again. They had enjoyed it so much that they did it again Saturday night at Kiamie's, an off-campus hangout.

"Oh man, we had an incredible time," says Roy Williams, Lott's old friend. "Trent and Pepper and Hovis and Gaylen Roberts performed just like the old days. We've been friends for forty years and we'll be friends forever. The Sigma Nus have great affection for one another." Williams pauses for a moment, then adds, "That, I think, is the essence of Trent Lott."

The Lott piece was accompanied by this sidebar:

Mother's Little Helper

Over the years, Trent Lott had not hesitated to wield his clout on behalf of friends and financial supporters. But his closest brush with trouble came during a fight about a 1983 contract to provide security at the NASA John C. Stennis Space Center on the Mississippi Gulf Coast.

Lott backed Isadore O. Hyde, an entrepreneur whose firm lost the bidding for the multimillion-dollar job. Lott pushed for an inquiry, and even though a NASA report found that Hyde's company "ranked significantly lower than the other two competitors," the congressman kept up the pressure. Hyde got the contract, and within a year, Lott's mother, Iona, was put on the Hyde Security Services payroll.

Eight years later, Hyde and his wife were accused of improperly billing the government to the tune of tens of thousands of dollars. The Hydes worked out a plea bargain in 1992, but then attempted to renege on it after investigators began asking them questions about "influence peddling by a public official," according to court documents. The "public official" was widely believed to be Lott.

In the end, a federal judge upheld the plea-bargain agreement. "The Hydes refused to give up anything on Lott," says an official in the Justice Department's public-integrity section. "They took it and allowed the statute of limitations to expire," this source says.

The case has one more twist. John Batson, the NASA inspector who led the investigation, was abruptly transferred from Bay St. Louis, Mississippi, to Pasadena, California. He claimed he was being punished for having reported, among other things, that Lott's mother performed "less than substantial services" for the Hydes. During an administrative appeal, Batson said he had been told by NASA authorities "not to go within 500 miles of Lott's mother if you know what's good for you." He lost the appeal and was sent 1,500 miles from his Mississippi home.

The Son King

(*George* magazine, December 1997)

Members of Martin Luther King's family were embroiled for years in controversies over the use of Dr. King's legacy. In early 1995, I had gone to Atlanta to do a long piece for the *Globe* on a fight between the family and the National Park Service. I returned nearly three years later to expand on the Kings' unseemly quarrels in a freelance piece for *George* magazine.

While there, I was told by Dexter King's close associate that I was now considered "the enemy" and that family members would not see me. I thought that put me in pretty good company, with such writers as Cynthia Tucker, Taylor Branch, and David Garrow, and the filmmaker Henry Hampton, who had all been blacklisted.

In 2008 Dexter was sued by his siblings, Bernice and Martin King III, who accused him of using funds from the King estate "for his own benefit." The suit was settled out of court. In 2012 Bernice King took over as CEO of the King Center, but the battles over rights to King's words continue.

It was a strange scene last March when Dexter Scott King, the youngest son of the Reverend Dr. Martin Luther King Jr., shook hands with convicted assassin James Earl Ray. Live, in front of CNN cameras, Dexter professed his belief in the innocence of the aged man who has been imprisoned for twenty-nine years for Dr. King's murder. It was stranger still when Dexter went back on TV three months later and suggested that President Lyndon B. Johnson was part of an elaborate plot to kill his father. But then, these are strange times for Dexter King and his family.

Once revered as the last blood link to the civil rights prophet, the King family has seen its credibility shaken by its blessing of Ray. Yet the alliance with the killer is just the latest in a series of audacious moves that 36-year-old Dexter King has made since taking over the family's power base, the Martin Luther King Jr. Center for Nonviolent Social Change, in Atlanta. He has turned his father's crusade for racial justice into an enterprise that some say only exploits his father's name. Dexter's initiatives include selling the preliminary film rights for Dr. King's life story to director Oliver Stone, exacting fees from media that use his celebrated "I Have a Dream" speech, and contracting with Time Warner, Inc., to market books, recordings, and CD-ROMs of Dr. King's speeches.

Many of Martin Luther King Jr.'s admirers are troubled by the new direction of the King legacy, fearful that money may be the sole motivation behind these projects—including the bid to win freedom for Ray, the small-time thief convicted of shooting King on a balcony of Memphis's Lorraine Motel on April 4, 1968. While covering the South for the *Boston Globe*, I was in Atlanta following Dexter's meeting with Ray, and heard of widespread suspicion in the city's black community that the Kings' involvement in the case was simply designed to hype the possible movie. "Why declare interest now?" one prominent Atlantan asked me before providing an answer. "Their main interest is to whip up interest in the Oliver Stone project."

Dexter's June appearance on the ABC newsmagazine *Turning Point* bolstered these beliefs. In a colloquy with anchor Forrest Sawyer, Dexter pinned his father's murder on the same forces that were shown as plotting President Kennedy's death in Stone's movie *JFK*.

"Whom does the King family blame for Dr. King's death?" Sawyer asked.

"I am told that it was part and parcel army intelligence, CIA, FBI. . . ." Dexter replied.

"Do you believe that Lyndon Johnson was part of the plot to kill your father?"

"I do."

CHARACTERS

"Why?"

"Well," Dexter said, "based on the evidence that I've been shown, I would think that it would be very difficult for something of that magnitude to occur on his watch and he not be privy to it."

The curious case of the King legacy has almost biblical overtones, steeped as it is in blood and martyrdom, peopled with disciples and skeptics, and filled with promises of redemption and accusations of betrayal. The history of Martin Luther King Jr. maybe forever confused by it.

Americans have an abiding fascination with famous families. Some members of those families handle celebrity well; others crumple under the pressure. Since the death of Martin Luther King Jr. members of his family have struggled with their inheritance as bearers of the dream. King's widow, Coretta Scott King, has quietly devoted herself to protecting her children—none of whom have married—and preserving her late husband's memory. In the years since his death, she has continued to live in their modest brick home on Sunset Avenue in Atlanta, where his clothes are said to still hang in the closet. Though Coretta King has occasionally endorsed political candidates, she has largely retreated from civic life.

Dexter's older brother, Martin Luther King III, 39, served as a Fulton County commissioner before a defeat in 1993. He is now chairman of Americans United for Affirmative Action and lives with his mother. The two King daughters, Yolanda Denise, 41, an actress in New York, and Bernice Albertine, 34, an Atlanta minister, have expressed no interest in running the King Center, according to family friends. So the legacy has been handed to Dexter.

Tom Houck, an Atlanta political pundit who worked for Dr. King and has been a friend of Dexter's since he was a child, told me that Dexter was put in charge because "Coretta realized that of all the kids, Dexter was the one who would move the family forward." Dexter King attended his father's alma mater Morehouse College, in Atlanta, but never graduated. Atlanta newspapers have reported that he left the school in 1981 for undisclosed "medical reasons." In interviews, Dexter has refused to discuss his departure.

Since Dexter usually avoids the press, only a little is known about

THE SON KING

him. He is a vegetarian who lives in a fashionable condominium near downtown Atlanta, reportedly draws a $132,300 salary from the King Center, and drives both a Mercedes-Benz and a Lexus. He is often seen in the company of beautiful women. One of the figures Dexter admires most, Houck says, is Ted Turner, the swashbuckling Atlantan who founded CNN.

The contrast between father and son is particularly striking to those who covered the civil rights movement in the 1960s.

Three decades later, on the day in January 1995 that Dexter was formally installed as president of the King Center, I interviewed him. At the time, the Kings were embroiled in a dispute with the National Park Service over a project in Atlanta's King Historic District. They were also litigants in lawsuits involving the use of King's words.

Dexter and I met in a large room at the center. We sat in straight-back chairs facing each other, like adversaries in a chess match, but we had a pleasant conversation. The son bears a strong physical resemblance to his father—the same soulful eyes, the neat haircut and mustache, and the modulated speaking style. His father would gesture as he spoke, but Dexter kept his hands on his knees as he earnestly explained his family's reasons for trying to obtain fees for the use of King's writings and recorded speeches. His father, he pointed out, had copyrighted much of his work. "We have a responsibility to follow the conduct my father did," he said. "In death, his work has become so much more valuable."

Dexter acknowledged that the King Center, a combination of museums and archives, needed money. Congress had rejected a request to triple the center's annual allocation of $535,000, and several major Atlanta businesses had cut back contributions because of discouraging physical conditions at the center and visitor complaints that there was nothing to see. Despite the financial pinch, Dexter said, "I don't believe we should be blatantly commercializing the legacy. We're not starting a business called Martin Luther King, Inc."

But when I returned to Atlanta last spring, I discovered that the King legacy had become a booming business. Dexter had purged several of his father's old associates from the board of directors of the

King Center, I learned, and was now taking his counsel from Phillip Jones, an aggressive young promoter who had parlayed their friendship at college into a business called Intellectual Properties Management, Inc., which zealously manages the King legacy.

I remembered Jones from my 1995 visit. At the time, he was functioning as Dexter's de facto spokesman. He was a smooth, fast-talking man—he and Dexter had formed a college partnership as music promoters—and he persuaded a reluctant Dexter to talk with me.

When I contacted the King Center this year, I was told that Dexter was busy and would not be available for at least a month. So I telephoned Jones, an ex–New Yorker who in the 1980s went by the music biz moniker P.J. Blue. He quickly recalled that I had quoted critics of the King family in a piece I had written some three years ago for the *Boston Globe* about King's legacy.

Jones described it as "the most unbalanced article I read on that issue," and added, "I assume you are the enemy." Jones argued that Dexter is the ideal person to carry King's dream into the twenty-first century. "He is a new paradigm," Jones said, who would move the message from the "feel the spirit!" school of King's generation into a high-tech world.

He sounded doubtful about the older ministers who faithfully preach King's words. "Those people don't have a clue how to get the message out on CD-ROM." One of the people ousted from the board of the King Center in early 1995 was John Lewis, a 57-year-old veteran of the civil rights movement who is now a Georgia congressman.

"I don't know where Dexter is taking things," Lewis says. "It all sounds commercial. I don't know what it is, but it's not civil rights."

Last January, a growing murmur of complaints over his handling of his father's history prodded Dexter to write an op-ed for the *Atlanta Journal-Constitution*. He claimed the King estate does not charge nonprofit groups for the use of King material and defended the fees charged to others. "Because my father owned no real property, his intellectual property is especially important as an asset," he wrote. "Criticizing his family is criticizing him."

Joseph L. Roberts Jr., the senior pastor of Ebenezer Baptist Church, where Dexter's father, grandfather, and great-grandfather preached, cites a lack of mission at the King Center. "There is no specific plan of action," he argues. "The center has little comment to make on very heavy issues of nonviolence."

During the Kings' fight with the park service, which also involved plans for an addition to the church, Roberts said that the family was "high-handed, dictatorial, and undemocratic." He was ousted from the center's board when Dexter took over. Friends say Dexter no longer attends Ebenezer, his family's spiritual home. "The family is a tight circle, and they've drawn their wagons together," Roberts says. "They are exercising power and control based on paranoia."

Coretta Scott King first named Dexter president of the King Center on April 4, 1989, but he resigned within four months. He quit, Jones told me, because the center was "poorly managed." Dexter, however, told the *Journal-Constitution* that he left because his mother was unwilling to give up control.

Five years later, Coretta King reinstalled Dexter over the objection of some members of the center's board, who doubted his ability to assume such a role. This time, she made it clear that Dexter would have complete authority, and this time Dexter brought Jones with him.

The Kings' battle with the park service has typified their public activities since their formal association with Jones began. Over the years, tourists visiting the historic district had expressed dismay over the meager collection of King memorabilia on display at the center. So the park service negotiated with the city of Atlanta and Ebenezer Church to obtain property across the street from the center to build a new visitor's space. Participants in the talks say family representatives sat in and raised no objections.

But the negotiators were startled in late 1994, the year that Jones's company was contracted to manage the King estate, when the family suddenly challenged the proposal and tried to claim the land for an interactive museum. After the park service proceeded, the family banished the service's tour guides from King's birthplace at 501 Auburn Avenue, as well as from the nearby King Center. "We feel strongly that the heritage of the civil rights movement is too important to be controlled by a governmental agency that has only superficial familiarity with the internal dynamics of our freedom struggle," the family said in a statement.

John Lewis finally helped broker a settlement, and the park service got its visitors center, a handsome facility featuring old film from the days of the movement. A row of statues commemorating the 1965 Selma-to-Montgomery march appear to be walking toward King's tomb, visible in the distance through a giant window.

The King family is now scouting out a new location for its interactive theme park. But the park service fight isn't the only area where Jones has aggressively marketed the King legacy. Jones is involved in a lawsuit filed by the estate against CBS, which used the "I Have a Dream" speech in a documentary series for home videos, demanding that CBS pay $100,000 for each copyright infringement and turn over a portion of the profits the tape has earned.

Jones's company also struck the recent deal with Time Warner, which he estimates will earn the King estate $10 million a year. "Hell, if I didn't do what I'm doing," he told me, "we wouldn't have a collection of Dr. King's speeches available." (Prior compilations have been incomplete.)

Jones also holds the title of associate producer for the prospective film about King by Stone's company, Illusion Entertainment Group. A source close to Stone says the filmmaker began negotiations with Dexter several years ago. Jones later became involved and now has a role in planning. Thus far, Stone has paid the estate between $20,000 and $50,000 for a preliminary agreement for the use of King's work, the source says, and the figure could rise to several hundred thousand dollars if the movie is made.

Some critics point out that the Kings' embrace of Ray dovetailed with their negotiations with Stone, suggesting that the Kings hoped to boost interest in a movie and, as a result, boost their profits. The deal was apparently in the works before last March, when Dexter showed up at a prison hospital in Nashville for his televised encounter with Ray.

Dexter looked uneasy as Ray, beaten down by age, illness, and three decades of incarceration, moved feebly to a chair. They shook hands and exchanged a bit of awkward talk about Ray's health—he is said to be dying from cirrhosis of the liver—and the villainy of the late FBI director J. Edgar Hoover.

Then the visitor looked squarely at Ray. "I just want to ask you for the record: Did you kill my father?"

"No," Ray responded. "I didn't."

Thus assured, and despite eight rulings by state and federal courts to the contrary, Dexter declared that he was satisfied of Ray's innocence and promised that his family would "do everything in our power" to clear Ray's name.

If we are fascinated by the children of famous men and women, it must also be said that we hold them to high standards. And in fairness to Dexter, from the time he was seven he has had to live with the loss of his father and an understandable belief that forces greater than Ray were responsible for Dr. King's death.

In his memoir of the movement, *An Easy Burden*, Andrew Young writes of trying to comfort Dexter in the days after his father's death. He recalls that Dexter asked, "This man didn't know our daddy, did he? Because if he had known Daddy, he wouldn't have shot him. . . ."

Doubt over Ray's guilt was an article of faith among many of King's bereaved followers, according to Hosea Williams, one of the civil rights leader's trusted lieutenants. "The majority of us were more than convinced that Dr. King was murdered by J. Edgar Hoover's FBI circle or the Klan," Williams says. "I never believed Ray pulled the trigger. He was just a redneck, white-cracker boy with a lust for cheap sex, gambling, and alcohol."

James Lawson, the Southern Christian Leadership Conference (SCLC) minister who appealed to King to come to Memphis in 1968 to aid an ill-fated sanitation workers' strike, has long championed Ray's cause.

Young, who was present when King was shot, recently said he still felt the assassination was part of a conspiracy and that "the FBI might be involved in some way." This suspicion doesn't come out of the blue: Efforts by J. Edgar Hoover to destroy King's movement have been well documented over the years. The FBI director once publicly branded King the "most notorious liar" in the U.S. and wrote President Johnson that King "is an instrument in the hands of subversive forces seeking to undermine our nation."

FBI files from the now-defunct COINTELPRO espionage operation, released after a 1975 congressional investigation, revealed that the agency had taken vigorous steps to sabotage King. When I spoke with Dexter in 1995, long before he came to Ray's defense, he talked of his father's sense of being embattled. The FBI, Dexter said, "called him a tax evader, a womanizer, and finally they threatened him."

"Dr. King was no angel, but he was no whoremonger," says Hosea Williams. "He ran from women more than he chased them." Williams recalls that King summoned his aides to a retreat off the coast of South Carolina a few months before his murder. "He told us they were going to get him. He told us that black folks would never be free till we controlled our fair share of the economy. He told us, 'Don't be surprised when they get me.'"

Many of King's aides believed specifically that Ray must have had help in obtaining a false passport with an alias and escaping to London, where he was captured two months later.

To dig into these doubts, a House Select Committee on Assassinations conducted an extensive investigation, concluding in 1978 that although Ray was probably aided by racist associates, he was the man who shot King. But neither Ray's original confession nor the additional evidence collected during the hearings satisfied some King followers.

Nearly two decades would pass before interest in Ray's case was revived. The impetus came from William F. Pepper, an American attorney who practices in London and now represents Ray. In 1995, Pepper published a book on Ray called *Orders to Kill*. It traced an alleged conspiracy to kill King that involved Mafia figures, the FBI, army intelligence, and a mysterious rogue agent named Raoul.

James Lawson, who now preaches in Los Angeles, endorsed *Orders to Kill* and asked Atlanta colleagues to encourage the Kings to read it. "A lot of people accepted the guilty plea as the final word," he explains.

Dexter read the book and "made his decision," Lawson says. Before Ray died, he wanted answers to "multiple questions."

Reached in London, Pepper says that he had no contact with the Kings until "a member of the family read the book and the family made a decision to come out for Ray. After they made the decision, they were in touch with me."

The Kings' initiative set off a series of meetings that would have been unimaginable just a few years ago. Coretta and Dexter King appeared on Ray's behalf at a hearing in Memphis last February to try to reopen the case. Jerry Ray, the killer's brother and a former ardent segregationist himself, told me he enjoyed meeting the Kings.

When Dexter flew to Nashville for his prison meeting with James Earl Ray, he was picked up at the airport by Jerry Ray and Pepper. "We had a real good conversation," Jerry told me. He said he praised Coretta King's speech-making talents and told Dexter she should give lessons. "Dexter got a kick out of that. We got along real good. I told Dexter I never asked to meet with them before because I knew they were going through pain. I paid their family respect. And there was mutual respect. Dexter told me he felt the same way."

The Kings seem committed to winning Ray's freedom. The family is said to have underwritten ballistics tests on a rifle linked to Ray and identified as the weapon that killed King in an effort to disprove his guilt. Conducted this summer, the tests were inconclusive.

"Dexter really wants to put some closure—that's the word he uses with me—on the case," says Tom Houck. "Particularly before his mother passes on. He wants to know why his father was shot and who was responsible."

Taylor Branch, the author of a magisterial history of King and the civil rights movement, *Parting the Waters*, fears the Kings' intervention in the case will lead to false revisionism. "I think this is a very, very dangerous matter that they're toying with," he says. "It will unravel the one bit of certainty—that James Earl Ray pulled the trigger for racial reasons—and I think the last thing we'll get is closure."

As part of his offensive, Dexter has made several other extraordinary assertions on television. On the CNN show *Crossfire* in April, he declared that Raoul, who was supposed to have controlled the conspiracy to kill King, "has been located." Dexter warned that "for fear of his safety, security, the fact that he might flee before being brought to justice, it's very clear that this information has to be guarded."

David J. Garrow, whose 1986 biography of King, *Bearing the Cross*, won a Pulitzer Prize and exposed many of the FBI's attempts to subvert King, was also on the show. Garrow contended there was no doubt Ray was the gunman. After one exchange, Dexter suddenly said, "Mr. Garrow, I have been told and I am now more than ever convinced, is an agent for the national security and intelligence forces."

When I spoke with Garrow later in his office at the Emory University Law School in Atlanta, he characterized Dexter's allegations as "so loony it makes the most casual viewer say, 'What's wrong with him?'" Garrow, who once aided the family during an unsuccessful attempt to recover papers that King gave to Boston University, said, "I think there are two dimensions to Dexter's position—an appetite for conspiratorial worldviews and an incredible defensiveness to public criticism. Coretta King always wanted to view the world as divided between those who are on the family payroll and those who are dangerous. History shows he's his mother's son."

"Dexter's sorted out in his mind," says Houck, "you're either for me or you're against me." As Dexter goes about his business, his commercial efforts have been made largely in the name of the family estate rather than the King Center. According to those who are familiar with the arrangements, the income that accrues from the lawsuits, the movie, and the Time Warner deal will go to family members, with Phillip Jones also getting a substantial portion.

The King Center, meanwhile, continues to struggle. Located in a complex of brown brick buildings adjacent to King's tomb, the center has a small museum and operates a handful of educational programs. To reduce the center's deficit, the staff has been cut drastically since Dexter took over.

The center houses many of King's papers, as well as other invaluable archives from the civil rights movement—the records of the SCLC and other organizations. Yet historians have been effectively barred from the library for several years, and scholars lament that the records are deteriorating. Garrow says that the library's roof leaked and rodents prowled the stacks.

Jones acknowledged, this spring, that the archives had suffered water damage and had been handled badly before Dexter took over. He confirmed that library access was limited; there had been thefts of documents by visitors purporting to be historians, he said. Not only that, he explained, but "you don't make money from archives."

By July, he seemed to have found a way. The *New York Times* reported that Jones was negotiating with Emory, Stanford, and Boston University in an effort to transfer the center's valuable collection to a school. Jones, apparently, was savoring the prospect of a bidding war. "There seems to be a competitive spirit involved in this that we didn't anticipate," he said. The King family's plans for an interactive museum called King Dream Center were also still on the drawing board.

The *Wall Street Journal* reported this year that consultants had proposed a 90,000-square-foot "edutainment" complex that would charge a $10 admission fee. The study suggested that the King Dream Center, with 3-D displays and a simulated freedom march, was capable of generating an annual $3.2 million profit, money that could bail out the King Center.

Jones says he is still seeking corporate sponsors for the project. One executive contacted by Jones had talked about his desire to create a high-profile persona for himself. "I had a bad sense the meeting was all about him" and had little to do with the Kings, said the executive, who asked not to be identified.

Meanwhile, Dexter King told the *Wall Street Journal* that if the King Dream Center proved profitable, he would fund other groups to take over the work the King Center once attempted. The paper quoted Dexter as saying, "We're not in the civil rights protection-of-right business."

Jones argues that Dexter has been unfairly criticized in the press for pursuing payments from newspapers, historians, and televisions producers who used King's words. He contends that the Kings have moral as well as legal rights to the words, a position supported by a

1982 decision by the Georgia Supreme Court. The Kings brought the suit against a firm specializing in funeral accessories that sold busts of King.

The court concluded that the King estate had the right to market King's legacy and to prevent others from "unauthorized exploitation." The King family, the court wrote, could not be denied the opportunity to make money off his name "merely because Dr. King chose not to exploit or commercialize himself during his lifetime." Even critics say the Kings are justified in blocking tawdry attempts to exploit King's name; it is the family's fierce hold on his speeches and writings, they argue, that is so disturbing.

After Henry Hampton, producer of the acclaimed television documentary *Eyes on the Prize*, used footage of the "I Have a Dream" speech, the King estate demanded payment. Hampton told me he offered the estate $100,000 to avoid a public fight, but they wanted more—"an enormous amount of money," he said. "They seemed to have the notion that millions of dollars were available."

The dispute, which was eventually settled out of court for less than $100,000, kept PBS from re-airing the show during Black History Month in 1993.

Jones told me that Hampton's firm, Blackside, Inc., had been "self-righteous and arrogant" and that the action had been taken against Hampton because videos of *Eyes on the Prize* were being sold in stores around the country.

The same rationale is being used in the estate's suit against CBS, which featured the "I Have a Dream" speech in a nine-hour documentary, *The 20th Century with Mike Wallace*, which is being sold as home videos for $99.95. CBS used its own footage of the speech in its video, but because the network is using the speech for a commercial purpose, copyright lawyers say it is a debatable issue that has yet to be resolved by the courts.

The vigilance enriches the Kings, but to many it cheapens Dr. King's memory. As John Lewis argued at the outset of the controversy, peddling the "I Have a Dream" speech is "like selling the Gettysburg Address. Dr. King's legacy shouldn't be up for sale like soap."

Remembering Abu Jihad

(*Boston Globe Magazine*, May 29, 1988)

Abu Jihad's assassination, trumpeted in the West as an appropriate end
to the life of a "terrorist," provoked me to write this essay. I intended it
as a meditation on the differing definitions of "terrorist" and "freedom
fighter" in the Middle East. Journalists in the region don't win many
fans. The piece triggered a wave of criticism from the *Globe*'s readers
and complaints that I was a member of the Palestine Liberation
Organization, masquerading as a reporter.

The news that Khalil Wazir had been assassinated was not really surprising. He had lived with death and war for years, and even his nom de guerre, Abu Jihad, had the ring of violence. In the most popular English translation, the name was said to mean "father of the holy war." In fact, the more literal interpretation of the Arabic noun *jihad* is "struggle."

To the extent that he was known in the Western world, Abu Jihad had a reputation as Yasser Arafat's cold-blooded deputy, a man who deployed commandos of the Palestine Liberation Organization on murderous missions into Israel. On the morning after Abu Jihad was cut down in mid-April in Tunisia, David Brinkley referred to him on his Sunday morning TV show as a "terrorist leader."

Actually, Abu Jihad played by the rules in the Middle East, and the rules there are cruel and vengeful. It is a region where a terrorist today can be a statesman tomorrow. Menachem Begin and Yitzhak Shamir, for example, led what were branded as terrorist organizations during the battle for independence in what would become Israel. Scores of Arab civilians and British soldiers died as a result of bombings and murders by the Jewish underground during the 1940s. And many Jews died, too, at the hands of Arab guerrillas who sought to deny the Jewish homeland.

The life and death of Abu Jihad is a metaphor, an embodiment of the Middle East cliche "the cycle of violence," in which one outrageous act quickly begets another. His assassination was carried out with such efficiency that it was immediately assumed to be the work of an Israeli strike force exacting revenge for an earlier attack in Israel. But Abu Jihad also had deadly enemies in the Arab world. All his life was a struggle—"the armed struggle," as he liked to call it.

When I first saw him, it was during the battle for Tripoli, in northern Lebanon, in 1983. Rebel soldiers from his own ranks in Al Fatah, supported by the Syrian army and other dissident PLO factions, had attacked Arafat's last stronghold in the region in an attempt to overthrow him. Abu Jihad was loyal to Arafat, and as PLO military commander he directed the defense of Tripoli.

He dressed in fatigues to lead his irregular army and referred to his men, armed with AK-47s and dressed in jeans and scruffy army hand-me-downs, as "fighters." Not soldiers or guerrillas or commandos, but fighters. Arafat was there, too, and had put aside his kaffiyeh, the checked Arab headdress, for an olive-drab British field commander's cap and matching sweater. Imperiled and under fire for days, both PLO leaders were generally courtly, and sometimes good-humored, when they dealt with reporters. It was as if they were showing the flag by proving that they were still alive. "We shall die hard," Arafat vowed at one press conference.

When a Palestinian refugee camp at the battlefront on the outskirts of Tripoli fell to the opposition, Abu Jihad's fighters retreated into the city, using tactics reminiscent of their defense against the Israeli army in West Beirut the year before. It was classic guerrilla warfare. The civilian population was transformed into a hapless shield for the PLO, at the same time that the congested urban setting was turned into a menacing battlefield for conventional armored battalions and infantry who would have to resort to street fighting to flush out the PLO.

Just as the Israelis had done in Beirut, the Palestinian insurgents and their Syrian allies put Tripoli under siege and hammered the city for days with artillery fire and rockets. It was a lurid battle. The city was wreathed with black smoke from an oil refinery that had been shelled and was burning out of control. The floor of a room at the Islamic Hospital was turned into a makeshift morgue, strewn with blocks of ice and the bodies of little children and the elderly who were killed in the bombardment. When that room was filled, the hospital began keeping the bodies in plastic sacks in a refrigerated truck.

The wards were filled with wounded PLO fighters, and when Arafat visited the hospital, they hailed him by chanting Arafat's nom de guerre, Abu Amar, which means "father of the revolution."

Under attack by their own brothers, the cause of the Palestinians never seemed more hopeless. The PLO leaders claimed that they were desperately trying to arrange a cease-fire. "We are saying yes. They are opening fire," Abu Jihad told us one afternoon as rockets shrieked through the skies. Plenty of the rockets were outgoing, launched by his fighters from the roof of a parking garage in the heart of the city.

After several weeks, a truce was reached, and the PLO fighters were allowed to evacuate the city by boat. Abu Jihad was being driven into exile again, just as earlier he had been forced out of his native Palestine, out of Gaza, out of Egypt, out of Jordan, out of Beirut, and out of Damascus.

It would be more than a year before I would see him again. By that time, the PLO had made peace with King Hussein, who had expelled the Palestinian guerrillas from Jordan during the bloody Black September showdown in 1970. As a gesture to the PLO, Abu Jihad was being allowed to live comfortably in Amman, the capital of Jordan.

Only days before my visit to Amman, Fahd Kawasme had been murdered there. Kawasme, a Palestinian moderate, had been the mayor of the West Bank city of Hebron until the Israelis deported him. In exile in Amman, he was elevated to the fifteen-man executive committee of the PLO. His assassins, who were never caught, were believed to be members of the Palestinian rejectionist front, which was operating out of Damascus. Already there were talks of a joint Jordanian-Palestinian negotiating team that might be prepared to talk to Israel, and the rejectionists were prepared to go to any lengths to block a dialogue.

Amman is ordinarily a sleepy, overgrown town in the Jordanian highlands where, on clear nights, one can imagine seeing the refracted lights of Jerusalem on another mountaintop about fifty miles away. But there was fear in Amman during this period. When I met with Mohammed Milhem, another exiled West Bank mayor who had also just been elected to the PLO executive committee, his home was guarded by many gunmen, and every time he heard a noise outside, Milhem would peek through an opening in the curtain to assure himself that no one was making a move on his life.

Meetings with Abu Jihad were usually arranged through Lamis Andoni, a courageous Palestinian journalist who worked for the English-language *Jordan Times* and was later disciplined by the Jordanian government for her contacts with the PLO. For my first appointment, a sleek Mercedes appeared at the Amman hotel that caters to journalists, and two armed Palestinians escorted us to Abu Jihad's home.

The understanding with Hussein, if I recall correctly, permitted PLO bodyguards to carry sidearms but no automatic rifles or heavy equipment. The king, remembering 1970, did not want another civil war when relations between himself and the PLO deteriorated, as they were doomed to do. Besides his own bodyguards, Jordanian soldiers kept watch outside Abu Jihad's house, and visitors were frisked before entering the sprawling one-story structure that was almost palatial.

I would have many meetings with him there. He was a handsome man—52 years old when he died—with a mustache, receding hairline, and doleful eyes. Abu Jihad always entertained visitors in his spacious living room, with the sofas covered in velvet and the floors with rich rugs. Invariably, he was dressed in an expensive leisure suit, either forest green or deep brown. He always wore Gucci shoes and silk socks, and his demeanor was more like a friendly banker's than a guerrilla commander's.

His political leanings might have been Marxist, but he liked to live well. Once I was on the same commercial flight with him from Amman to Cairo. He sat in the first-class section. Several of his bodyguards, carrying satchels full of guns, sat in steerage with me.

At Abu Jihad's home, the chatter of his children could usually be heard from other rooms, and conversations were constantly interrupted by telephone calls. In the tradition of Arab hospitality, any meeting with Abu Jihad began with coffee or tea and candies. Arabs are not as direct as Westerners, so conversations with Abu Jihad began with small talk about health and mutual acquaintances before edging into more sensitive areas.

At that first meeting in Amman, I reminded Abu Jihad that I had covered the PLO war in Tripoli, and from that time on it seemed that I enjoyed a special cachet with him—as a fellow survivor of an ordeal. I'm not sure he ever learned my name, for my name is as strange to an Arab tongue as Khalil Wazir is difficult for me to pronounce properly. But he remembered my face and always referred to me as "my friend," trilling the first two consonants in the word "friend."

His English was heavily accented, and he would emphasize the "w" in the word "sword" when speaking of the "sah-whoord of vengeance." But he was quite open and articulate in his comments.

Sometimes we would be joined by his wife, a striking woman with light-colored hair. She was a fierce Palestinian nationalist and wore a replica of the Palestinian flag on her blouse as if it were jewelry. She was La Pasionara of the Palestinian movement, supervising the PLO program of welfare for families of Palestinian "martyrs" and prisoners in the occupied territories. Although her given name was Intissar, she had taken her own nom de guerre, Umm Jihad—"mother of the struggle."

Commentators who do not follow the Middle East carefully sometimes confused Abu Jihad with Abu Nidal, another Palestinian who broke with the PLO years ago to form his own group, which raised terror to an art form. The Abu Nidal group is believed responsible for many car bombings and assassinations. Both Arafat and Abu Jihad were said to be on his hit list. It was Abu Nidal's men—not the PLO—

who gravely wounded the Israeli ambassador to England in 1982, an action that gave the Israeli defense minister at the time, Ariel Sharon, the provocation to invade Lebanon and push the PLO up the coast to the edge of the sea in Beirut.

There was speculation when we met with Abu Jihad in early 1985 that Abu Nidal had died. He was curious, too, and reported that some of his compatriots had either claimed to have attended the funeral or to have seen Abu Nidal's grave. Like so many stories in the Middle East, the rumors proved false, but Abu Jihad was always a useful source to cross-check tales of Palestinian intrigue.

Another time, Abu Jihad was asked about reports that Abu Maizer, a Palestinian leader who had defected from Arafat's organization and was living in Damascus, was responsible for the hijacking of an Egyptian airliner to Malta. Abu Jihad laughed contemptuously. "Abu Maizer," he said, "is afraid of a frog."

Abu Jihad was constantly under pressure from his adversaries in Damascus, the breakaway factions of the PLO. They included George Habash's Popular Front for the Liberation of Palestine, Nayef Hawatmeh's Democratic Front for the Liberation of Palestine, and two other wildly radical groups—Abu Mousa's rebel force that had fought Arafat in Tripoli, and Ahmed Jebril's Popular Front for the Liberation of Palestine–General Command.

With talk circulating in the region about peace negotiations involving the United States, Israel, Jordan, and a PLO-approved slate of delegates, the Damascus groups sneered at Arafat's weakness and willingness to bargain at a table over the land that was once called Palestine. To demonstrate that they would never accept Israel, the rejectionists had been sponsoring all sorts of raids on the Galilee region. They came at northern Israel by air, with Katyusha rockets and commandos sailing on motorized hang gliders. They came by sea, in rubber dinghies. The guerrillas were usually intercepted and killed by vigilant Israeli guards, but the operations persisted.

With the peace process allegedly proceeding, Arafat's mainstream PLO was being discouraged by Arab moderates from mounting any new attacks on Israel. But Abu Jihad believed it was necessary to launch an offensive to demonstrate that the organization had not yet given up on the "armed struggle."

In May 1985, it was reported that an Israeli gunboat had sunk a vessel named *Ataviros* filled with PLO fighters somewhere in the Mediterranean, many miles out to sea from Israel. More than twenty Palestinian guerrillas died, and several were captured. The Israeli military reported that the ship had been embarked on a terrorist mission. It all sounded curious, but this, of course, was the Middle East.

The next time I saw Abu Jihad, I asked him about it. "Oh, yes," he said. "This was my operation." He went on to explain that the ship was supposed to penetrate Israel's coastal waters and land on a beach south of Tel Aviv. The commandos were under orders to then hijack a bus and drive to Hakirya, the Israeli defense ministry on the eastern edge of Tel Aviv. There they were to attack the heavily guarded complex, presumably inflict many losses on the Israeli army, and humiliate the Jewish state on the thirty-seventh anniversary of its independence.

The concept would have sounded like something out of a Mel Brooks comedy had it not been so deadly. Israel patrols its shores relentlessly. Its citizens are so security-conscious that untended bags of trash on streets are reported to police as potential bombs. To think that a small gang of commandos, with little familiarity with the landscape, could make it safely to the defense ministry, much less breach its walls, strained the imagination. But Abu Jihad was proud that his men had died trying. "They were discovered by luck," he said. "It failed, but another operation will take its place."

In the course of our conversations during the time that he lived in Amman, he learned that I lived in Jerusalem. Western journalists, diplomats, and U.N. officials based in Jerusalem do not advertise that fact in Arab nations. When they talk about Israel among themselves in places like Beirut and Damascus, they refer to the Jewish state in code. Israel is "Dixie," the land to the south. In Jordan it was safe to say that I came from "the West Bank" or "Al Quds," the Arabic name for Jerusalem. "Ah, my friend," Abu Jihad said to me once, "you must go to my home, my village in Ramleh. The lemon trees I planted there as a child must be grown now. Go there, and bring me a picture of it."

It is striking how many Palestinians in exile remember the citrus trees in their old hometowns. Many claim to be the rightful owners of lush groves in what is now Israel. At any rate, I didn't own a camera, never took the photo for Abu Jihad, and he never pressed me for it.

Abu Jihad was vilified in Israel as an archterrorist whose goal in life was to kill Jews. He saw his war against Israel differently. "Ramleh is my home," he told me. "We have a right to make military operations there." He drew much of his inspiration from the Algerian revolution, which succeeded in ending French colonialization a quarter-century ago. "In any struggle in all parts of the world under military occupation, people have the right to resist. It happened in Algeria under the French, in South Vietnam while peace talks went on for months. In any revolution, it's a part," he told me in August 1985 on the day the United States was pulling back from its promise to talk to a joint Jordanian-Palestinian delegation in Amman. "As we have no agreement to create peace, therefore nothing will stop." His military operations, he said, would go on.

Young Khalil Wazir was a child when his family fled Ramleh during the first Arab-Israeli war in 1948. He settled in the squalid refugee camps of Gaza, which was then under Egyptian control. When he was 19, he was arrested by Egyptian authorities for laying mines in the area. After serving some time in prison, he emerged to conduct his first successful strike against the Israelis. He led a team of guerrillas that blew up several tanks filled with precious water for agricultural purposes in Israel.

According to accounts of his personal history, he attended law school at Alexandria University, where he met Arafat and Salah Khalah, who is called Abu Iyad, the other member of the founding trinity of Al Fatah, the dominant wing of the PLO that was formed in 1964.

For more than two decades Abu Jihad directed the PLO's military operations against Israel. He once told me of the difficulty in smuggling weapons and explosives into Palestinian hands in Israel and the territories because of the strict security at Ben Gurion Airport and the onerous searches that Palestinians must endure at the Jordan River crossing between the West Bank and Jordan. Attempts to slip materials in bags of coffee and flour or in false heels of shoes were usually foiled, he said. Abu Jihad was delighted to report that sometimes he was successful in smuggling arms into the country via PLO sympathizers posing as tourists on El Al, the national Israeli airline.

Israel was most vulnerable by sea, he believed. Some of his fighters once stormed a Tel Aviv beachfront hotel in a suicide mission and killed several Israelis.

Abu Jihad was also blamed for a notorious raid in 1978—it is remembered in Israel as the coastal bus hijacking—when Palestinian commandos infiltrated by sea and captured a crowded bus near Haifa. The Israeli army overwhelmed the hijackers, but by the time the drama was over, thirty-five passengers had been killed.

Israelis still shudder when they recall another grisly event, in Nahariya—a picturesque seacoast town just below the Lebanese border—when a handful of PLO guerrillas sneaked into town and held hostages at an apartment building. A terrorized mother, hiding in a closet, unwittingly smothered her infant rather than have the baby's cries give away their position.

The impact of the Holocaust is so heavy upon Israel that the Jewish state will never accept a blow without striking back.

Each time that Abu Jihad's fighters hit, Israel retaliated. In the years leading up to Israel's 1982 invasion, Israeli warplanes bombed Palestinian refugee camps in southern Lebanon and other installations, in Beirut, where the PLO military infrastructure was based. Israeli military communiques described the activity as raids on "terror bases," but those who were left dead were often children and civilians. More sad, innocent victims.

The struggle between terrorists and counterterrorists has been going on for years. After the murder of the Israeli athletes at the 1972 Olympics in Munich, the Israeli secret service, the Mossad, fanned out across Europe to hunt down those responsible. The Munich massacre was believed to have been led by a man named Ali Hassan Salameh. The Mossad, thinking they had found Salameh, killed the wrong man in Norway, but Salameh was eventually blown up by a car bomb in Beirut. The Mossad, of course, never publicly acknowledged any of these activities, but the incidents are part of legend in Israel.

And Abu Jihad's death in Sidi Bou Said, a lovely suburb of Tunis, where the villas are all white with aqua trim, was hauntingly similar to the Israeli commando raid in Beirut fifteen years earlier, when three PLO leaders were killed shortly after Palestinian guerrillas attacked Israelis on Cyprus.

There is so much blood on so many hands as they grapple for the land that is now held by Israel, a land that is like a rose on a stem of thorns—beautiful, but dangerous to touch.

Abu Jihad may have been celebrated as a terrorist, but atrocities have abounded on both sides since the Jews began trying earlier this century to reclaim what they consider their homeland. During the Jewish underground's fight against the British, Begin's Irgun movement was responsible for the bombing of the King David Hotel in Jerusalem in 1946. The operation succeeded in destroying the British headquarters there, but the final death toll was 91: 41 Palestinians, 28 British, 17 Jews, two Armenians, one Russian, one Greek, and one Egyptian.

In April 1948, a joint force of Irgun fighters and members of the Stern Gang—another radical Jewish group in which Shamir was a partisan—massacred scores of Palestinians in the village of Deir Yassin, which is not too far from Ramleh. Arabs claimed that nearly 250 men, women, and children were slain. Israeli historians put the figure at 116. Before he realized the extent of the infamy, Begin issued an order of the day to his followers: "As in Deir Yassin, so everywhere, we will attack and smite the enemy. God, God, Thou hast chosen us for conquest."

Although his past is shadowy, Shamir is believed to have gone on to Europe after Israel's war of independence to serve as a hit man for the Mossad before returning to enter Israeli politics.

It has been reported that Shamir, as prime minister, and other high officials in the Israeli government authorized the daring attack on Abu Jihad in Tunisia, although there is no official acknowledgment. According to accounts, the squad of several men and a woman, who was said to be filming the operation with a handheld camera, first executed—with a gun equipped with a silencer—a driver sleeping in a car outside Abu Jihad's house. They then killed two bodyguards. When Abu Jihad investigated the noise, he was riddled with machine-gun fire. It was reported that he suffered seventy bullet wounds.

The last time I saw Abu Jihad was shortly before he was ordered out of Amman in 1986, after negotiations between Arafat and Hussein had broken down.

There had been a portent of the collapse in relations between Jordan and the PLO in the fall of 1985. At a time when Hussein was urging Arafat to renounce violence, a flamboyant operation was undertaken by members of Force 17, an elite PLO unit that was originally formed to protect Arafat and other key PLO officials. They captured and murdered three Israelis on a sailboat docked at the harbor in Larnaca, the Cypriot seaport, on Yom Kippur, the holiest day of the Jewish year. The PLO claimed the victims were members of the Mossad.

In a spectacular reprisal, Israeli warplanes flew two-thirds of the way across the Mediterranean to bomb the PLO headquarters in Tunis. When it was revealed that the air raid killed many civilians, world sympathies shifted to the PLO. Just as quickly, the PLO managed to dissipate the good will when a gang of terrorists, under the direction of Abul Abbas, an Arafat loyalist, commandeered the cruise ship *Achille Lauro* and murdered one of its passengers.

Hussein furiously summoned the PLO leadership to Amman to demand an accounting. Arafat, fearing that his plane might be intercepted by the Israelis, drove for hours overland from Baghdad to attend the summit meeting with Abu Jihad and his other chief deputy, Abu Iyad. It was their final gathering in Amman.

Arafat, in what became known as the Cairo Declaration, in November 1985, pledged to limit PLO operations against Israel to military targets inside Israel and the territories. But it was too late for Hussein and far too little for Israel. Officials in Jerusalem reacted with scorn to Arafat's promise. "This means he is going to give a discount," said an Israeli foreign ministry spokesman at the time. "He'll kill Jews, but not Jews in Europe."

Abu Jihad seemed more penitent. The murder of Leon Klinghoffer, a passenger aboard the *Achille Lauro*, had been "a mistake and a tragedy for our side," he told me. "We are educating our fighters. There will be no kidnappings, no dealings with civilians."

To avoid mindless violence, he said, every PLO strike would have to be sanctioned by the organization's military council. The *Achille Lauro* affair, he said, "is a lesson to all of us, even to Abul Abbas." He promised that only "those criminals who are tools of Syria and Libya like Abu Nidal" would order attacks outside Israel and the territories in the future.

Throughout the conversation, Abu Jihad was smiling and pleasant, and the cries of his new baby, whom he named Nidal, could be heard from another room. But he seemed to know that King Hussein could not be mollified, and that his refuge in Amman was slipping away from him.

Hussein had permitted a former PLO military intelligence officer, Atallah Mohammed Atallah, to set up headquarters a few blocks from Abu Jihad's home. Atallah, whose code name was Abu Zaim, claimed he was going to replace Arafat "democratically" through the internal politics of Al Fatah. Abu Jihad dismissed him as a "clown," but it was obvious that his rival's presence was pestering him.

In the summer of 1986, a few months after Hussein made a formal break with Arafat, Abu Jihad was expelled from Amman. He joined Arafat for a while in Tunis, then moved to Baghdad to help establish PLO training camps there. When I was in Baghdad a year ago, I tried to call him but was told he was away. Later, he resurfaced in Tunis. Like Arafat, who sleeps in a different bed—often in a different state—almost every night for security reasons, Abu Jihad was a man without a country.

The popular uprising by Palestinians in the West Bank and Gaza was spontaneous when it began last December, but the PLO—which is outlawed in the territories—moved quickly to take control of events. The irony of an analogy with the story of David and Goliath, which is an important part of Jewish history, was not lost on PLO leaders such as Abu Jihad, and Israeli authorities said he was orchestrating events.

He was said to have encouraged the young Palestinians to restrict their weapons to stones against the might of the Israeli army. Even as the Palestinians were being shot to death—sometimes two and three a day—by the Israeli army, they were finally winning world sympathy as unarmed underdogs fighting a military occupation.

But in the third month of the uprising, three PLO commandos infiltrated the Negev Desert and hijacked a small Israeli bus near Dimona—where an Israeli nuclear facility is located. Three Israelis were killed, and the Palestinian guerrillas all died when Israeli soldiers stormed the bus. Given the adverse publicity that the incident brought upon the Palestinians, it appeared to be a tactical error.

Abu Jihad was said to have insisted that it was a legitimate military operation, but the decision may have cost him his life.

An hour after midnight on April 16, he took up his gun for the last time when he heard the intruders at his home, but he was never able to fire a shot.

He could not be buried in the land where he was born, but Syrian president Hafez Assad—who has been a critic of the mainstream PLO and a supporter of the insurgency against Arafat's leadership for five years—allowed Abu Jihad's remains to be buried in a cemetery for martyrs in Damascus. Although he did not attend the burial, Arafat met with Assad a few days later to begin efforts to end their feud. If the rapprochement holds, it will be Abu Jihad's final legacy.

Abu Jihad will be remembered as a martyr by the Palestinians and as a terrorist by the Israelis. I believe he would prefer to be remembered as a father, a soldier of the revolution.

Ma'assalame, Abu Jihad. Farewell, and go in the peace you never knew in your lifetime.

Outlaw Minister

(*Boston Globe*, July 18, 1993)

Staff writers were rarely pigeonholed at the *Globe*. The editors had
no hesitation assigning a "black story" to a white reporter—or vice
versa. So it was not unusual for me to get assignments such as this
one, spending days in the company of a fiery man conducting a street
ministry in a tough neighborhood of Boston.

For much of his short life, Selven Brown ricocheted around the streets
of Dorchester until he went to an early death, another errant brother.

But to Rev. Eugene F. Rivers 3d, who tried to draw the troubled
young man into the fellowship of his Azusa Christian Community,
he was a lost child of God, and when Brown died of an overdose the
other day at the age of 27, he became in Rivers's mind another symbol
of the failure of Boston's black community.

Rivers spoke at the funeral, lashing at Brown's friends, the prosti-
tutes and pimps and pushers who filled the pews in their baddest suits
and dresses. "All of you who are whoring and speed-balling and snorting and sniffing and shooting up," he shouted at them, "are guilty of a
sin against black people and a sin against God."

It was another audacious volley in Gene Rivers's holy war. Since
establishing an outpost in the gritty Four Corners neighborhood of
Dorchester in 1988, he has conducted an unconventional ministry,
challenging the criminal element among his own people and criticizing the black establishment.

The city's most prominent black figures are the subjects of his fiercest scorn. He dismisses elected officials as "pathetic" and he mocks mainstream ministers as caricatures of the pious, fried chicken–eating clergymen with fancy Cadillacs and a reputation for servicing the women in their flock.

Rivers is the quintessential outlaw minister, and as the streets of Dorchester are convulsed by spasms of violence again this summer, he is emerging—to the consternation of traditional ministers—as a strong new voice in the city.

Following this month's shooting of 9-year-old Eric Shepard, Rivers called upon black religious leaders to "put their bodies where their rhetoric is" and for black professionals to join the struggle to eradicate drugs and crime.

His is an unorthodox mission, moving the church to the street in an effort to teach blacks discipline and self-reliance.

After working with Rivers to quell racial unrest in South Boston this spring, Father Thomas McDonnell of St. Augustine's Catholic Church says he is convinced Rivers has "a valid ministry. It may go unrecognized, but Mother Teresa worked in Calcutta for thirty years before anyone noticed her."

The 43-year-old Rivers operates in an outrageous variety of guises: the brilliant philosopher whose Harvard education has been burnished by street smarts; Jesus Christ as played by Eddie Murphy, mixing Christian precepts with comic profanity; Che Guevara reincarnated, complete with sly eyes and scraggly beard, a revolutionary theoretician using Four Corners as his own Sierra Maestra; a black Martin Luther, harassing the religious hierarchy. Sometimes he performs as primitive con artist, hustler, and agent provocateur.

Rev. Peter Gomes, minister at Harvard's Memorial Church and longtime campus chaplain, calls Rivers "probably the most remarkable undergraduate I've encountered in twenty-three years." He adds: "He's more than an intellectual hustler, but whenever I'm talking to Gene I have a feeling he's taking you to the cleaners. I always check my wallet."

Rivers has a more startling description of himself. "I've been a hoodlum, a thief, a gang member. I've been locked up," he says, pacing in his office on the top floor of a Dorchester three-decker. "I come from an outlaw tradition. Jesus was an outlaw and a revolutionary. That's why they killed him."

Rivers was born in Boston in 1950, but his parents divorced and he grew up with his mother in Philadelphia. He says he was "drafted" into a gang in junior high school when classmates stuffed his head into a toilet bowl. "I was told it was either join a gang or get it," he says.

As a teenager he "became immersed in the Pentecostal church," he says. "I'd do street-level evangelical work with the gangs." However, he says he was later excommunicated from the church "for being a radical black nationalist."

It led, he says, to "the most depressing period of my life," a time of spiritual disillusionment and criminal behavior. He moved to New Haven in 1973, where he "sold drugs—reefer—for a while." He also supported himself by "hustling welfare checks in three states, Philadelphia, New York, and New Haven, with multiple identities."

He was reading voraciously, the radical works of Fanon, Marcuse, and Chomsky. "I became a congenital book thief," he says. "I must have stolen $24,000 worth of books."

By 1976 he had attracted interest among Ivy League intellectuals, and came to Cambridge under the wing of Harvard professor Martin Kilson. He left behind a daughter, now 17, the product of "a relationship I couldn't terminate." That summer, he was arrested for stealing a book from the Harvard Coop.

"I decided God's telling me something," he says. So he resumed his spiritual quest. It took him to Twelfth Baptist Church, a pillar of Boston's black establishment. After a few months, he says, he was told by Rev. Michael Haynes: "You need to find another fellowship. We can't minister to you."

Haynes chuckles at the memory when asked about Rivers. "He was very stimulative in his questions and challenges. He had a lot of strong opinions about how churches should go. He was of a Pentecostal bent, and at the time he might have been teaching things that present a conflict to Baptists."

Rivers attended other churches, but found little comfort. He went to Harvard, but failed to complete his degree requirements. He was locked up after a street brawl in Manhattan in 1983, worked as an orderly at McLean Hospital in Belmont for a few years, and was ordained a Pentecostal minister in 1987.

Why is he making these confessions? "Because I think there is a rare Christian tradition that needs to be rehabilitated—to tell the truth," Rivers says.

It also demonstrates, he says, his empathy with the young people he wants to reach and establishes his place with other outcasts of society: Jesus, the Black Panthers, and Malcolm X.

Even the ministry he named Azusa, after the Los Angeles street where the first black Pentecostal church was formed, "is about outlaws," Rivers says. "We're a bunch of intellectual guerrillas." His congregation is so small that he has no church building. The Azusa community is composed of about twenty adults and holds its Sunday services at Freedom House in Roxbury.

Although most of the members were educated in the academic aeries of Harvard and MIT, they practice their religion with the demonstrative passions of the Pentecostal movement. Most of them settled in Dorchester to answer a religious calling, to live and work among the poor and the lawless.

The ethos, Rivers says, comes out of the early civil rights movement, when churches were the wellspring for social activism and the Student Non-Violent Coordinating Committee conducted its own ministry in the forlorn regions of Mississippi.

Although his congregation is small, Rivers is increasingly conspicuous because of his knack for attracting news coverage. He acknowledges that he deliberately began "playing the media" after he felt threatened in his neighborhood, concluding that if he had a higher profile he was less likely to be murdered.

He and his wife, Jacqueline, a Jamaican he met at Harvard, have two young children, Malcolm and Sojourner, and live in the heart of high crime. On their first day in Dorchester, Rivers says, he saw a youngster stroll past his home with a loaded pistol. The next day, his house was stoned.

A couple of weeks later, a drug dealer named Selven Brown made menacing moves against Rivers and his wife with a motorcycle. It was an odd start for a friendship that led to Rivers's introduction to the local gangs. Some of the "dudes," as Rivers calls them, refer to him as "Farrakhan" because he occasionally wears a bow tie, as does the Nation of Islam leader.

Rivers says the police were suspicious of his attempts to meet with gang members. "The police put out the word that I was running drugs," he says, "and they told the dealers I was a snitch." He appealed to his friend Jamie Bush, a nephew of President Bush, to ask then–U.S. Attorney Wayne Budd to intervene.

Budd confirms that he was approached by Bush, met with Rivers, and eventually determined the problem was resolved.

"He's mended his fences with the police," says Bernie Fitzgerald, the chief probation officer at Dorchester District Court. "He's in this courthouse more than any other minister as an advocate of kids in trouble, and he's had a positive effect on the neighborhood. I think when he first came down here, he was sort of like Father Flanagan. You know: 'There's no such thing as a bad boy.' He realized there are some bad boys."

Three summers ago, a gang shooting on the street ripped random holes in Rivers's house, where hundreds of books are piled on the floor. The shots also "murdered our church van," he says. He feels he gained credibility "because we didn't cut and run." Several black ministers from Boston's most venerable churches came to their gadfly's home in a gesture of concern. Rivers says sarcastically, "They really came to see if The Nigger was dead."

Despite the risk, he has persuaded several of his followers to join him in Dorchester. "This is a lifetime commitment," says Alan Shaw, a Massachusetts Institute of Technology scholar who directs an Azusa youth program in computer training. His wife, Michelle, is a neighborhood lawyer with a Harvard degree. They have been in Dorchester with Rivers for five years. Shaw says they will be there "until God calls us elsewhere."

Sometimes it seems like a losing battle. The loss of Brown was especially painful. The Azusa community had prayed with him and sponsored a year for him at a distant school to escape Dorchester's treacherous environment. After he returned, he drifted away. His death, Shaw says, "was a real setback."

At an Azusa Bible study group meeting at the Shaws' house last Wednesday night, the subject was "spiritual warfare," but the talk quietly turned to Brown.

Rivers's wife sighed sadly. "We should not be disheartened," she told the group. "God intends for us to persist."

Because he occupies the "front line," Rivers is contemptuous of his colleagues who preach to hundreds every Sunday under stately, vaulted ceilings, supported by gowned gospel choirs.

Rivers prefers the Pentecostal spirit, where believers shout in praise of the Lord and speak in tongues. "The black Pentecostal church," he says, "is the source of my intellectual revolution. It turned my life into a holy war."

Silber's Tortured Odyssey

(*Boston Globe*, February 11, 1990)

John Silber was one of the most combustible personalities I've known. After I was assigned to write a profile of the scholar-turned-politician, I spent about three weeks in Austin, Washington, New York, and New England interviewing people who had dealt with him. Then I had two extraordinary interviews with Silber in which he was brilliant and combative.

The day after the story was published I arrived at the office, thinking my portrait of the ornery candidate would croak his campaign. My pal Mike Barnicle, a *Globe* columnist, was more perceptive. "You just got the guy elected," he told me. With high unemployment and a dispirited economy, Silber was playing to the mood in Massachusetts, the same way Howard Beale's shouts of "I'm mad as hell and I'm not gonna take this anymore," had resonated in the movie *Network*.

Silber won the Democratic primary, but later antagonized legions of women voters by insulting a popular anchorwoman on camera and lost the general election. My article had little to do with the ultimate outcome.

In the end, Silber won my grudging respect, and he and I wound up on civil speaking terms. We exchanged long-distance greetings through mutual friends in the years before his death in 2012. But I voted for his opponent.

Anger hovers in the air, like the mythical Furies beating their wings, in John Silber's presence.

For as long as people have known him, Silber has been smoldering over what he perceives as false gods, sophistry, ignorance, and insult. In the face of scorn, he has compared himself with Hector, Coriolanus, and Galileo; and he holds other victims of society—Jesus Christ and Socrates—as heroes.

His academic career spans four decades of conflict and controversy. In conducting his personal war in the name of educational excellence, his critics say, he has waged a campaign of intellectual terrorism.

The halls of Boston University and the University of Texas are haunted by students and teachers he has humbled. Silber has a compulsion to make strong and provocative remarks, however impolitic, as if he considers it a form of honesty to speak his mind. He has offended blacks, Jews, feminists, and homosexuals with statements they feel are insensitive. He refuses to retreat from his own words and considers them educative tools in a philosophical debate.

As president of BU—a school he described as "big and ugly" and bereft of creative firepower when he was hired in 1970—Silber purged the faculty of professors he terms "second-raters." He is fond of classical metaphors and compares his task with Hercules's cleansing of the Augean stables. He also has battled the BU student body and board of trustees over the years. He once said he had survived the fights "because I've been right so much of the time."

And as he takes leave as president of BU to pursue the Democratic nomination for governor of Massachusetts, Silber has no intention of moderating his manner. An outspoken "outsider," as he sees it, he clearly hopes to draw strength from the anger that exists in the state this year against the political establishment.

BU has been transformed from a nondescript institution to one that last year attracted President Bush and French president Francois Mitterrand to its commencement exercises. But in the process, the campus along the Charles has become part of Silber's cult of personality.

Few figures in Massachusetts summon such thunder, arouse greater passions, or engender more hatred.

Before coming to Boston, Silber's experience at the University of

Texas was just as explosive. Norman Hackerman, who was president of the university when he appointed Silber dean of the college of arts and sciences in 1967, said that he chose Silber because the school "had a stodginess that had to be shaken out of it, and Silber was the man who could do it."

Within two and a half years, Silber replaced twenty-two of twenty-eight department chairmen. When his ambition and thirst for power became too obvious, he was brought down like the men in his pantheon of heroes.

At the time, his sympathizers depicted him as a force of light snuffed out by a retrograde board of regents. Twenty years later, the picture of Silber at the University of Texas has darkened like an old photograph. He emerges in some contemporary accounts as a willful and vainglorious administrator. Colleagues and acquaintances from his Austin days now characterize Silber as a "madman" and a leader who took on a "sinister edge" when he became dean.

He is also remembered there as a stern and demanding teacher. Some of his students responded to his challenges; others were broken by him and wept in his classrooms. A former student said that as a philosophy professor at the University of Texas, Silber "specialized in humiliating 18-year-olds."

"That," said Silber last week, "is a lot of revisionary horseshit."

Silber is proud that he does not "speak plastic."

Over the years, Silber has been subjected to drugstore psychology. According to one theory, his feelings about his right arm, deformed at birth at elbow length, have caused him to be so combative. Or: his German father imbued him with authoritarianism. Or: his immersion in philosophy has led him to use withering Socratic methods that often have turned normal conversations into arguments.

According to Silber, his childhood environment was shaped by strict, loving parents and a grandmother who helped teach him to read and write. He was one of two sons. His father was a German immigrant, who left Berlin in 1902 to use his skills as an architect in the New World. His mother was an American schoolteacher. They made their home in San Antonio.

Silber, who was born in 1926, grew up during the Great Depression. His father was a proud man, and when his work ran out, he refused to take lesser jobs. He applied to the public schools to teach mechanical drawing, Silber said, but because he had no political connections he was refused. The family subsisted on his mother's $810-a-year job, moving from their comfortable two-story home to a series of smaller houses.

As a child, he has said, he fought schoolmates who taunted him about his arm. He does not hide his physical handicap; his shirts and suits are tailored to expose the knot of flesh.

Silber does not accept simplistic theories about his psyche.

After Silber graduated from San Antonio's public schools, his life became a "wandering trail," he said, an intellectual and spiritual journey that ultimately led to a career as an educator.

He veered from Trinity University in San Antonio following his freshman year to Northwestern University, in Evanston, Ill., only to abandon music school there when he realized he was "an amateur." He went back to Trinity and graduated with a degree in philosophy and fine arts.

At Trinity he also met and married his wife, Kathryn, and they have been together for more than forty years. They have seven grown children—six daughters and a son—and four grandchildren.

The young couple moved to New Haven, where Silber enrolled at Yale Divinity School and considered becoming a minister. He left after a year for the University of Texas Law School and dropped out there following one semester because of "financial distress."

Silber earned money by selling "night snacks" to students. He "developed a passionate antipathy to sorority people who, on a cold day when you'd be hauling those drinks and sandwiches and things around to the dormitories late at night, they'd pay you by dropping the damn money in the bucket of ice."

Finally, the Silbers returned to Yale, where he received a master's degree in philosophy in 1952, followed by a doctorate in 1956. He wrote his dissertation on the German philosopher Immanuel Kant, who has been a major influence in his life. His study of Kant convinced Silber that man's will is free of extraneous forces; that logical conclusions can be reached through the power of thought.

Silber's theological quest was especially intense. He became skeptical of religious claims as a boy, he said, after hearing on the radio "some crazy fundamentalist fulminating on how godless evolution was."

He was brought up as a Presbyterian, in the austere faith of John Calvin. At Yale, he said, "I began to have intellectual difficulties with certain aspects of Presbyterianism. The Calvinist notion of predestination just seemed to me to be a form of madness.

"Terrible things were said about God," he said. "If John Calvin had said about a human being and attributed to a human being the virulence that he attributed to God, I think that no one would have accepted that view as satisfactory at all."

He also described as "arrant nonsense" and "a hatred of life" St. Paul's views that "it is better to marry than to burn, but it is better not to marry." When he discussed this with his Presbyterian minister, he was told "it wasn't my job to argue with St. Paul, but my job to believe him. I checked out as far as that minister was concerned from that day forward."

As a 21-year-old divinity student, he took over a Baptist congregation in Connecticut when the minister he had been assisting quit. "I helped him leave because at the end he had asked me what I thought of his sermons and I would tell him," he said. "They were awful. They were really bad."

To help pay for divinity school, he sang in the choir of a Jewish reform synagogue, where he found "the music was wonderful and the sermons were excellent." He considered converting to Judaism.

"I thought about it, and then found out that the racism of Jews is quite phenomenal," he said. "If you are goyim considering becoming a Jew, you are going to be second-class in that synagogue, and I didn't have any interest at all in moving into that congregation as a second-class citizen. I also thought that Judaism made a great mistake in not recognizing Jesus as one in the line of the great Hebrew prophets."

In 1959, after Yale, while he was studying at the University of Bonn on a Fulbright scholarship, Silber said he discovered that his father was Jewish. He knows nothing of the Jewish background. In fact, his father had become so assimilated in the United States that a stained glass window in the First Presbyterian Church in San Antonio is dedicated to his father's mother. "If she had been a practicing Jew, I don't believe my father would have done that," Silber said.

The ground for Silber's turbulent reign at BU was prepared at the University of Texas. He was lured back to his home state from a teaching post at Yale to join the university's philosophy department in 1955.

Stories of Silber the teacher vary according to the source.

His friend, Ronnie Dugger, publisher of the liberal weekly the *Texas Observer*, said, "There's something in him that's noble: the doctrine of personal excellence. He really believes it, and he wants everybody to aspire to it."

Willie Morris, another writer who was once part of the *Texas Observer* crowd, hailed Silber as an example of the renaissance that took place at the university in the 1960s.

However, Morris's former wife, Celia Morris, who studied under Silber, said he "picked on" women students. "He never mitigated this almost demonic deprecation of women," she said. "Any woman who had something to do with him has felt diminished."

Silber discounts her criticism. She turned against him, he said, when he refused to take her side in a poisonous divorce from Morris.

Laura Richardson, who was a philosophy student and a left-wing activist at the University of Texas during the 1960s, remembers Silber as "very arrogant . . . He would have temper tantrums. He thought he was a grandiose figure. He really believed he was an intellectual, hanging around with 17-year-olds. He never listened to anyone; he just bullied people with what he thought was the Socratic method."

Animosity toward Silber is fierce in some academic circles in Austin. Several sources there said that there is speculation over what they call "the great Silber fire" in Boston in 1972. There was a fire in the BU president's home, which his friends blamed on arson, in which Silber said his manuscript for a book on Kant was badly damaged. His adversaries in Texas suggest that the manuscript never existed.

Silber became furious when the subject was raised with him in an interview on Wednesday. "They're lying sons of bitches," he said. "That pisses me off. That's ridiculous." He had the reconstructed manuscript, which appeared to be several hundred pages long, delivered to his campaign headquarters to establish that his enemies were spreading falsehoods.

If Silber was exacting as a teacher, he was even more severe as an administrator, said several of his former associates in Austin. He became chairman of the philosophy department in 1962 and was named dean of the vast college of arts and sciences with more than 20,000 students in 1967.

"Academic politics? He practiced it ruthlessly," said Standish Meachem, the dean of the college of liberal arts, who now occupies Silber's old office at the University of Texas.

Meachem was acting chairman of the history department when Silber was dean. "I had to deal with a madman," he recalled. "Somewhere there's a screw loose."

While Silber was carrying out his first purge of the faculty, "A lot of people were very afraid of him, and I was one of them," Meachem said. "I'd come here in fear and trembling."

Celia Morris, who went on from the University of Texas to become a well-known feminist and writer, is less forgiving. "As John Silber got more powerful, the cheerfulness got lost," she said. "It was chilling when he started getting more power; there were feisty battles and real challenges. A sinister edge came to it."

And as he flexed his power, Silber came into conflict with Frank Erwin, the chairman of the board of regents, in a struggle that had national repercussions.

In the beginning, Silber was considered a loyal agent for Erwin, one of the most formidable men in Texas. Erwin was a product of the Democratic organization controlled by former President Lyndon B. Johnson and former Gov. John Connally. He was also the epitome of a University of Texas booster; his clothes and his Cadillac carried Texas colors—orange and white.

"They were twins in their own way," said Hackerman, the former president of the university. "Erwin and Silber both had the same attitude: It's my idea, so it must be good."

The clash was as inescapable as the plot to a Greek tragedy, and it has been misrepresented over the years as a struggle between liberals and conservatives.

Erwin died in 1980, but one of his closest confidants, Ben Barnes, said that Erwin was disturbed over Silber's tendency to testify on behalf of the university on matters that "Frank thought were on his turf." Barnes, who was lieutenant governor at the time, was asked whether Silber had become "too big" for Erwin's comfort. "I guess that was in the back of his mind," he said.

Silber said that the issue that was used as a device to remove him as dean was a contrived one—the division of the college of arts and sciences that would eliminate his job.

Silber, who opposed further expansion of the university, said he actually ran afoul of Erwin over the university's building scheme. Silber had invested in a privately built dormitory adjacent to the campus. He said he sold his interest in the property when he became dean, though, to avoid a conflict of interest.

Silber said in an interview last week that he had a confrontation with Erwin before he was fired. "You and your friends are buying up land all around the university and building high-rise buildings around it as condominiums or as apartments," Silber said he told Erwin. "As long as you push the size of this university, you can guarantee yourself a huge profit. Don't you see that as a serious conflict of interest?"

Silber said that Erwin "looks over his half-glasses and shakes his head at me, and he says, 'John, you aren't ever going to understand.' He says that in a very friendly way: 'You're never going to understand. Where there's no conflict, there is no interest.' That ought to be in Bartlett's famous quotations because that is a wonderful quotation. That is the quintessence of cynicism. He wasn't embarrassed, he wasn't ashamed, or anything else."

Despite the emotional climax to their disagreement, the two men remained friends until Erwin's death. Silber said he admired Erwin "because the man is so direct." Erwin cut him down, Silber once said, "just as Achilles met Hector."

For four hours last week, Silber discussed his career in two long interviews with a *Globe* reporter, talks in which he was alternately contentious, mocking, and philosophical. At 63, he looks ten years younger than many people his age, and his voice is strong. It carries traces of Texas; *where* is pronounced "whur" and *at all* is broken into "a-tall." Anger seeps into the conversation when he discusses his relationship with some of the institutions in Boston, including the *Globe* and Harvard University.

"The *Globe* thinks it's nice to try to write me off as some goddamned racist," he said. Tapping his skull with his finger, Silber said, "I've got a shit-detector that can figure that out."

Silber's record on civil rights in Austin was highlighted by his efforts, as early as 1957, to integrate the university opera company and local theaters. He refused to speak at segregated halls on campus unless the topic was integration.

But as dean, he refused to accede to the demands of a black group, Afro-Americans for Black Liberation, calling them "impossible . . . unreasonable . . . racist . . ." His sharp attacks on bilingual education and "ghetto language" as self-defeating practices brought fire from minorities. He became fully engaged in battle with the student left after he came to BU and he called in the Boston police to put down a demonstration against Marine Corps recruiting on campus.

He began to be perceived in some circles as a reactionary, a label he is unwilling to accept, just as he refuses to be pigeonholed as a conservative.

In the summer of 1984, the day after Rev. Jesse Jackson's speech to the national Democratic convention, Silber was interviewed by David Luberoff, a reporter for the *Tab*, a weekly newspaper circulated in the Boston metropolitan area.

"The words were the words of Jesse," Silber told Luberoff, "but the voice was the voice of Adolf Hitler . . . Now get old Jesse Jackson at the end, speaking in a high-pitched voice just like Hitler. That's insane. It's electrifying. You can feel him grip an audience."

When he was asked about the remark last week, Silber reinforced his language instead of trying to defuse the statement. "It's demagoguery," he said of Rev. Jackson's speech.

Asked whether he did not recognize the potential to antagonize black voters, Silber said, "It's not in my interest to lie." He said parallel tape recordings of a Jackson speech and a Hitler speech would prove his point.

"Now I think there are excellent black politicians," he said. "I see no reason to place Jesse Jackson on a pedestal. I have said that if I were president of the United States, he'd have a place in my cabinet, because every president needs someone to write bumper stickers."

"You think in order to run for governor of Massachusetts I'm going to take a dive on that? That's the difference between me and a plastic-speaking politician."

In an age when college presidents are diplomatic and often more skilled in fund-raising than scholarship, Silber stands out as an unconventional, pugnacious administrator.

The school has been the scene of unrelenting controversy since he came here. From the police raid against antiwar protesters to the decision to allow BU to manage Chelsea's public schools, Silber has been in the forefront of storm and change.

He minimizes the turmoil on campus today, and said, "The idea of opposition that I have among the faculty is a myth."

In 1976, by a three-to-one ratio among those voting, the BU faculty called for Silber's ouster. Ten of the university's fifteen deans also urged his dismissal. A confidential report prepared that year by a subcommittee of BU's board of trustees observed that Silber had "the vision to see the importance of securing top-flight educators," but it also found evidence that he was "his own worst enemy. His modus operandi has served to alienate most constituencies at BU at the precise moment when the need for cooperation and mutual trust is great."

Silber averted another firing by cultivating support among the trustees, a lesson he had learned from his Texas experience. Armed with a vote of confidence, he moved to seal his power.

Arthur Metcalf, a Route 128 entrepreneur and Silber ally, ascended to become chairman of BU's board, and Silber's opponents among the trustees were relieved or quit. In a gesture of resignation a decade ago, several of the trustees attended a dinner at Boston's Somerset Club with Hans Estin, the former chairman who had hoped to replace Silber and had failed. They passed out T-shirts bearing the acronym BUST—for Boston University's Sacked Trustees—and slipped the shirts over their formal clothes.

The renegade deans were also dispersed. By 1984, when the National Labor Relations Board ruled that the American Association of University Professors was ineligible to serve as a bargaining agent for the faculty, Silber had at last succeeded in breaking the teachers' union. The rout of his adversaries was virtually complete.

One of the last battlegrounds is the College of Communication. In 1987 Silber installed H. Joachim Maitre, a right-wing emigre from East Germany, as dean of the college. Maitre replaced Bernard Redmont, who had opposed the school's decision to sponsor what was called the "Afghan project." The program was financed by the U.S. government in order to train the mujahedeen, or Afghan rebels, to use propaganda in their war to drive out the Soviet Union's army of occupation.

It is in keeping with Silber's policy. He has written, "No university worthy of the name can pretend to be value-neutral in the assessment of the United States and the Soviet Union."

After Redmont objected to BU's participation in the Afghan operation, unfounded thirty-five-year-old allegations about his "Communist sympathies" were leaked to the student newspaper.

"It's interesting to see" Silber "yell about McCarthyism, because that's what he specializes in," said Bernice Buresh, who quit as an associate professor in the journalism school. When she spoke out against the project at a panel discussion at BU in 1987, Maitre appeared in the audience, wearing a mask.

"They act like schoolyard bullies," she said of Silber's followers on the faculty. "How did this bunch of thugs get in this place?"

One of Silber's few setbacks occurred in 1987, when BU lost a sex discrimination suit brought by Julia Prewitt Brown, an instructor in the English department, who had been denied tenure. Silber, who has been scolded by feminists for language he uses about women, was grilled on cross-examination and testimony was introduced that he had referred to the department, in which one-fourth of the tenured faculty were women, as a "damn matriarchy." The school was ordered to pay Brown $215,000.

Silber has also antagonized gay groups at BU by drawing analogies between homosexuality and bestiality.

Still, Silber said he is proud of his record at the university. "Since 1980 we've made spectacular progress with the recruitment of 800 new faculty members. They didn't come because they're intimidated. They didn't come because I'm repressive. They didn't come because I resemble Adolf Hitler. They came because this is one of the most exciting and challenging institutions to be at."

As he moves into politics, Silber will be judged not only by his stewardship at BU, but by his brusque personality and pungent views.

In the rancorous political climate of Massachusetts today, Silber's scorched-earth rhetoric could be an elixir for the state's angry voters.

"I'm an outsider because I've got the perspective of a person who's never made his living on the back of the taxpayer," Silber said. "And I know just how outraged the taxpayer can get."

Part VIII

Southern Gothic

Holier Than Thou

(*Boston Globe*, November 13, 1991)

In the fall of 1991, I was covering Bill Clinton's campaign in New
Hampshire when I got a call from the *Globe*'s national desk. David
Duke, an erstwhile leader of a Ku Klux Klan unit, had just won his way
into a runoff for governor of Louisiana with the flamboyant playboy-
politician Edwin Edwards. Somewhat apologetically, I was asked if I
would be willing to set aside the presidential campaign for a couple of
weeks and go to Louisiana to report on the story there. I made plane
and hotel reservations for New Orleans before they could change their
mind. The story proved to be as colorful as promised, and I wished
that A. J. Liebling, the author of my favorite political book, *The Earl of
Louisiana*, had been alive to write about it. Edwards ultimately prevailed
and served a fourth term as governor. But there would be an epilogue:
within a few years, both Edwards and Duke would ultimately serve
time in Federal prison.

BATON ROUGE, La.—In a state where evangelical Protestant beliefs
clash with traditional Catholicism, it was probably inevitable that religion would create a major schism in the sulfurous race for governor
of Louisiana.

As the contest between the Republican, David Duke, and the Democrat, former Gov. Edwin Edwards, began to veer out of control in the
closing days of the campaign, the two candidates have compounded the political burlesque by challenging each other's credentials as
Christians.

Duke was fighting off questions yesterday about his claims to be a born-again Christian after one of his own aides charged that Duke was a "neo-Nazi, Ku Klux Klanner, and non-Christian" who had lied about his church affiliation.

Meanwhile, the Duke campaign continued to distribute leaflets claiming that Edwards had "mocked the crucifixion." Duke contended that Edwards "basically said the Bible was a lie," in connection with doubts Edwards expressed in 1984 concerning Christ's resurrection.

Louisiana politics has long been divided by a religious fault line between the southern half of the state, which is predominantly Catholic, and northern Louisiana, where strong strains of Protestant fundamentalism influence voting behavior.

Edwards, a Catholic, overcame upstate prejudices in 1971 when he became the first Cajun elected as governor. But in the days since the two men wound up as competitors in a runoff election, slated for Saturday, Duke has sought to stir conservative, Protestant suspicions.

On New Orleans television Monday night, Duke displayed a 1984 photo of Edwards at a satirical press club dinner in Alexandria, La., that showed Edwards standing with his arms spread and splotches on his palms and chest. At the time, Edwards was governor and was under attack by many newspapers. As Duke described it, Edwards made a crucifixion pose vivid by smearing "catsup on his shirt."

"If these skinheads knew anything about the Bible, they'd know Jesus was not stabbed in the chest," Edwards fired back at a news conference at his Baton Rouge headquarters. He said Duke's views were "totally alien" to Christianity.

Yet Duke, who has been cultivating the conservative, fundamentalist vote, insists he is a staunch Christian. In public appearances, Duke says he has been persecuted in the campaign, an apparent allusion to Christ's travails. "Christ has been a powerful force in my life," he said. "He's given me strength."

However, the Duke campaign was shaken on Monday night by the departure of Bob Hawks, Duke's state coordinator. Hawks, a former Tennessee legislator, told reporters: "The straw that broke the camel's back, relative to Duke's claim of Christianity, was when we went to a Christian TV station in West Monroe, Louisiana. During the program, Duke was asked what church he belonged to, and after hesitating for at least a twenty-second delay, he named some Church of Christ, which later proved to be untrue."

Duke suggested that Hawks had been "planted in my organization to discredit me"—part of an elaborate Edwards plot, Duke said, that includes plans to import "people from outside to act like Klansmen" and disrupt the election.

Duke's chief adviser, James A. McPherson, speculated in an interview yesterday that Hawks was "offered five thousand bucks or something to do this" by an Edwards supporter. "While Hawks was our coordinator, he was not the campaign theologian," McPherson said. "He has no more weight to talk about David's religion than the janitor."

Edwards ridiculed Duke's contention at a rally last night. He said that Duke had met Hawks at a Ku Klux Klan meeting in Memphis six months ago.

"He could have been an escaped rapist or child molester," Edwards said. "But Duke said, 'You can have any job,' and the fool came down here." Edwards said he had no connection with Hawks. "The people we planted in his campaign have not yet been identified."

The *Times-Picayune* of New Orleans had reported earlier that an "Evangelical Bible Church," which Duke said in a Nov. 2 debate he attends, does not exist.

Questioned during a TV appearance about the discrepancies, Duke professed to be "a born-again Christian." He added: "I go to evangelical Bible worship . . . You don't know where I go to church." He said he wanted to protect those with whom he worshiped from intimidation.

To buttress his claims, Duke is depicted kneeling in a prayerful position inside a church in sequences of a slide show that is presented at his nightly political rallies.

At a rally for Duke on Monday night at the Livingston fairgrounds, in a Protestant, piney-woods belt of the state, the Duke campaign produced Jim Rongstad, who identified himself as an ordained Lutheran minister without a congregation. Rongstad, wearing a hairpiece that resembled a pecan pie, said he had come to vouch for the "authenticity of David Duke's Christianity."

As the audience, which had been rattling the wooden building with war whoops, was hushed, Rongstad said he "began my search for the truth" with Duke a year ago, wondering: "Was this gentleman for real? Could a leopard change his spots? Could he be genuine? Is he too good to be true?"

Rongstad said he and Duke "have prayed together; we have shared the Scriptures together." He concluded, "If you're going to vote for Duke, you're doing the right thing."

In an interview, Edwards said he understood that Catholic priests had been telling parishioners that the church "was very concerned about the philosophy of my opponent, about his race-baiting and anti-Semitism."

But Edwards said he was not troubled that religion had been injected into the campaign. "I'm comfortable," said Edwards, who has always seemed to enjoy his playboy image. "I'm a practicing member of the Catholic Church. I know I'll be judged by my maker who knows all my thoughts. While I'm not a perfect person, I know I'll not be held accountable for the thoughts I might have had."

Cultures Clash in Jones County

(*Boston Globe*, February 23, 1994)

Mississippi's Jones County seemed an unlikely place to harbor a
lesbian colony, and after Camp Sister Spirit was established on a
remote hillside there, some nearby residents not only failed to extend
Southern hospitality, they terrorized the occupants. When I went to the
embattled camp, I was not exactly welcomed with open arms by the
lesbians or the locals. But one of the camp's founders sat me down in a
"fire circle" to explain their movement, and I eventually got comments
from Baptist opposition.

Camp Sister Spirit did not exist for very long, but the controversy
triggered a Congressional hearing in Jackson led by the openly gay
Rep. Barney Frank of Boston, one of the wittiest politicians I know. I
invited Barney to dinner afterwards, but the congressman told me he
was booked on an early flight and wanted to get out of town before
nightfall.

OVETT, Miss.—Late last July, after the Mississippi sun had withered
the green of spring, Brenda and Wanda Henson, a lesbian couple,
bought an abandoned pig farm in the rolling pine woods of Jones
County and began to transform the property into Camp Sister Spirit,
a feminist retreat.

"I didn't anticipate this kind of backlash," Brenda Henson admitted
Monday.

By choosing to locate the camp in this rural, fiercely conservative
region, the women set off a storm, and it is hard to imagine a greater

clash of American cultures than the struggle here between lesbian activists on the crest of change and followers of a deeply fundamentalist faith.

Over the past three months, Camp Sister Spirit has become the target of a campaign orchestrated by the powerful Southern Baptist Convention to oust them from Ovett, a farming hamlet where churches outnumber stores and prohibition is still enforced.

The formal opposition to the women has consisted of mass public meetings, a bid to buy the Hensons out, and an impending lawsuit that is expected to brand Camp Sister Spirit as a public nuisance.

Since the battle was joined, Henson said, Camp Sister Spirit also has been subjected to bomb threats, crank calls, explosions and gunshots in the woods, and the grisly scene of a slain female dog draped over the camp's mailbox along with two sanitary napkins.

An air of incipient violence hangs over the camp, where the Hensons, who consider themselves married, and six other lesbian "caretakers" live. They have been joined by a few sympathizers, including a couple of men. One is Wanda Henson's son from an earlier marriage. Although the camp is armed with shotguns, rifles, and a stack of metal baseball bats and ax handles, Brenda Henson said, "I don't feel safe here at all."

The Ovett dispute led Attorney General Janet Reno to dispatch a team of federal civil rights mediators to Mississippi last week to tackle for the first time a case involving charges of harassment of homosexuals.

Hours after the federal officials left the camp Friday, Henson said, intruders came. "We heard shots and voices in the woods. We hollered and told them to get off our land. Wanda shot a rifle in the air and they cut loose with an automatic weapon." No one has been hurt, but the sheriff's office has repeatedly investigated incidents.

Rev. John Allen, the pastor of the First Baptist Church in Richton and a leader of the opposition to the camp, said he disapproves of harassment. "But in my view, these women are a threat to the community."

Rev. Allen said that Richton, the town nearest Ovett, once tolerated two homosexuals who ran a florist shop and provided flowers for his church.

"This is not about people being homosexual, per se," Rev. Allen said. "This is about a group of people who have endorsed the radical agenda of the National Gay and Lesbian Task Force. They have told us: 'We are here to educate you.' They want lesbian role models in schools. Their most odious endorsement is to reduce the age of consent for young people. These people are radicals who have come to change this community."

Paul Walley, a prominent young businessman and attorney in Richton who is representing the opposition, said the Hensons espouse "an aberrant lifestyle that is opposed to God's plan" as well as Mississippi's sodomy law.

Walley regards the Hensons as provocateurs in southeastern Mississippi. Camp Sister Spirit, he said, "is not Walden Pond."

The camp is tucked off a country road marked by an occasional mobile home and ranch houses, a mile from Ovett's general store, where a clerk said, "We've been told not to comment. Our lives could be in danger."

The women of Sister Spirit painted lavender swatches on the pine trees to mark the approach, but barbed wire, a locked gate and several menacing "No Trespassing" signs bar the uninvited.

Sitting on a chair inside a ceremonial "fire circle," Brenda Henson talked of how the camp's mission has been misunderstood.

"We've even been accused of dancing naked around the fire. It's been too damned cold to do that. . . . We are not a lesbian organization," she said. "We are lesbians who are human rights activists. We want to set up an education center with intensive study courses on weekends on issues like racism, anti-Semitism, and jobs for women. There is a lot more fear about our human rights work. Feminists teaching feminism is more scary to the good old boys than lesbianism."

The Hensons once ran a feminist bookstore on the more tolerant Mississippi Gulf Coast. After it evolved into a women's crisis center,

Brenda Henson said, they decided to move the operation to the country.

They settled in Jones County, she said, simply because of "cheap land—120 acres for $60,000."

They have had problems from their immediate neighbors, she said; otherwise, the people of Ovett have been generally hospitable. "This is not about Ovett. This is not about the state of Mississippi," she said. "This is about Southern Baptists."

Rev. Allen chuckled when he was told later of Henson's allegation. "There are a lot more than Baptists involved. There are Methodists, Pentecostals, and Holiness. We all object to the immoral lifestyle." He acknowledged that the Southern Baptist Convention was lending its support to the movement to get Camp Sister Spirit out of Jones County—"but not in a Nazi fashion."

As the legal battle heated up, Walley, the lawyer representing the opposition, was accused recently of "supporting this sort of KKK mentality" by the camp's attorney, David R. Daniels.

"We've tried to handle this as Christians and gentlemen," Walley said. He added that he offered to give the Hensons their $60,000 back and pay for their improvements if they would leave.

"We're not trying to drive them off the land," Walley said, "although I'd love for them to pack up and leave. We just want to stop the construction of a 180-bed retreat they're talking about."

Henson said her plans were constantly exaggerated by the Baptists. She was asked if she could be driven off the hilltop property. "In a hearse," she said.

The Night I Met Elvis

(*Oxford American* magazine, July/August 2000)

Since my mother made me wash off his autograph and I never saw
Elvis again, all I have are distant memories of an encounter six high
school kids from Summit, Mississippi, had with the rising rockabilly star
nearly six decades ago.

In the fall of 1955 Elvis was a lesser star in Sun Records' orbit. He
played second fiddle to another performer, Carl Perkins, and often
shared the spotlight with Johnny Cash. When the Sun troupe barn-
stormed through southern Mississippi in September of that year, Elvis served as a warm-up act before Cash took the stage.

To a tenth-grader, the Sun road show had greater appeal than the
one-elephant circuses and cheesy carnivals that drifted through town,
but the engagement fell on the same night as our football game. Since
Summit High School was small, every able-bodied boy, however un-
coordinated, was pressed into duty. Still, the prospect of seeing a live
rockabilly performance enjoyed a higher priority than our gridiron
contest. Following the game (which we lost to Cathedral High of Natchez, 41–6), we dressed hurriedly, met our dates, and rushed a couple
of miles to the McComb Auditorium, where we watched through an
open window as Johnny Cash sang the last number of the night.

Disappointed that we had missed most of the show, we three couples squeezed back into the car, drove farther south, across the Louisiana line, into the embrace of "wet" Tangipahoa Parish, where we
were able to buy a bottle of cheap wine. Emboldened, we returned

to the auditorium, hoping we might meet the recording artists. The roadies were loading equipment onto a trailer rig when we arrived.

As far as we were concerned, Johnny Cash had been the star of the show. He had already departed, we were told, but a pleasant fellow, introducing himself as D.J. Fontana, the drummer for Elvis, volunteered the information that Presley was still around. Our dates begged to see him.

Out of the darkness, the 20-year-old singer materialized. He had slicked-back hair, sideburns, and looked as unprepossessing as a mechanic. Yet he represented our first brush with celebrity, and we were excited by the chance to talk with him. Leaning into a rear passenger's window, Elvis carried on most of the exchange with the girls. I remember that he was totally unaffected, indeed charming.

Butting into the conversation, I asked Elvis if he were driving his pink Cadillac. One of his records, "Baby, Let's Play House," had lyrics—rewritten by Elvis—that included the line "You may drive a pink Cadillac, but don't you be nobody's fool."

"I wrecked it up the road," he said. (I learned years later from his biographer, Peter Guralnick, that Elvis's dream car, the pink Cadillac, had actually caught fire and burned en route to a performance in Texarkana in June.) "But I got a new one, a nice yellow one," Elvis told us, pointing to a gleaming Cadillac with tail fins as imposing as God.

Our encounter with Elvis lasted no more than ten minutes, and before he left, he used a red ballpoint pen to autograph each of our forearms. When I got home, well past my midnight curfew, a scent of alcohol did not help as I pled my case. I explained to my mother that we had been delayed by a meeting with "this famous singer." As evidence, I produced my arm, where the words *Elvis Presley* glistened in red script. Mother said she had never heard of Elvis Presley and told me to go in the bathroom and scrub off the stuff.

Rowdy Lunch a New Orleans Tradition

(*Boston Globe*, October 17, 1994)

One of the pleasures of being a journalist involved an expense account. Luckily, I retired from the *Globe* before budgets were severely cut, an industry-wide move that eliminated the days of first-class air travel (on long flights), distinctive hotels (if available), and fine dining (if it could be found). Based in New Orleans for much of the 1990s, I was constantly called upon for unusual stories. So I thought of Friday at Galatoire's, perhaps my favorite restaurant in the world, and I treated myself and a couple of friends to a long, liquid lunch there. To try to relate the place to a New England audience, I compared it to Locke-Ober, the grand old Boston fixture that closed in 2012. After publication, Arnold Chabaud, the maitre d', told me that tourists from Boston began to show up there. Though Galatoire's has been remodeled since this piece was written, I'm delighted to report that it retains its charm, that Arnold still holds forth there, and that its Friday lunches are as lively as ever.

NEW ORLEANS—There is a book called *Dinner at Antoine's,* and a tourist attraction known as "Breakfast at Brennan's," but nothing in the world of New Orleans's venerable restaurants quite compares with Friday lunch at Galatoire's.

Once a week, it is as though *Animal House* relocates at Locke-Ober. A sense of exuberance and abandon overtakes an elegant old eating house, and just as much as Mardi Gras, Friday lunch at Galatoire's symbolizes New Orleans's reputation as the "City That Care Forgot."

For ninety years, Galatoire's has occupied a place at the head of Bourbon Street, serving as an outpost of civilization in that raunchy strip. It has been kept in the same family, just as generations of New Orleanians have handed down the tradition of dining there.

Sunday is a family day. Grandparents, parents, and children often take over long tables after Mass, feasting on shrimp remoulade, crabmeat Yvonne, and pompano amandine amid leisurely ambience. Friday is something else.

The cognoscenti arrive early, because Galatoire's does not take reservations. Doors open at 11:30 in the morning, so the queue starts along Bourbon Street before 11: a lineup of women in fashionable dresses and glittering jewelry, of men in tailored suits and ties.

A camaraderie develops while they wait; many already know one another. Some cross the street to a carry-out bar to bring back Bloody Marys in plastic go-cups. Celebrities are sometimes annoyed, for they must stand and wait on the sidewalk like ordinary mortals. But among most of the growing group, there is a happy spirit of anticipation. They chatter about rival restaurants, favorite waiters, and the best dishes in town. In other cities, they may talk of their sports franchises; in New Orleans, they talk of their restaurants.

Arnold Chabaud, the genial maitre d', works the line, assuring early arrivals of a table, warning latecomers of a wait. It is not a large restaurant. The first twelve or thirteen groups are sure to be seated, he says. It is problematic for the next three or four groups. If you are more than twentieth in line, he says, "forget it."

The most difficult days, he says, are the Fridays before Christmas and Mardi Gras, when entrepreneurs earn $100 or more to maintain places in line overnight.

On other Fridays, the clientele is willing to endure long waits. A few weeks ago, dozens were still waiting outside at 2 p.m. when a couple emerged from Galatoire's warning, "It's a zoo in there."

Actually, it is a party, conducted in the splendor of one of the city's landmarks. Waiters encourage mass serenades of "Happy Birthday." There is laughter. Loud stories are told. A young woman takes a flute from her purse and suddenly launches into a recital of Mozart. Women wind up in men's laps. Cigar smoke curls to the ceiling. Once, on the occasion of a rare snowfall, a Galatoire's regular remembers a snowball fight.

Entire law firms are known to empty for the afternoon for lunch at Galatoire's. Elderly widows, wearing flowery Old South hats, drive in weekly from surrounding parishes.

Chabaud estimates that 65 percent of the Friday crowd is local. "Some of the same groups come every Friday," he says. Why is Friday so popular? "Maybe nobody wants to go back to work."

Last Friday, as the restaurant filled, the pleasant murmur of conversation slowly built to a loud buzz, boisterous and buoyant. According to Chabaud, "The difference on Friday is that there is more jubilation. You are through with the week. Of course, the alcohol may affect the character."

There is never a rush to turn tables at Galatoire's. The establishment recognizes the markup on wine, champagne, and liquor is more profitable than the price of a piece of fish. Glasses that are quickly emptied are just as quickly refilled.

Service is loving. Many of the waiters, moving gracefully in tuxedos, have worked here for decades. A woman recently broke their ranks. She, too, wears a tuxedo.

Although Galatoire's is brightly lit, with white tile floors and rows of chandeliers and old ceiling fans, dark curtains close off outside forces. It becomes a retreat, complete with revelry.

Friday's crowd included the queen of the Garden District real estate trade as well as a kingmaker trying to complete arrangements for a new casino.

At 2:45 p.m., Philip Carter, a local businessman, looked up from his platter of soft-shell crabs and wondered, "Who is working in New Orleans?"

Sound and Fury over Elvis

(*Boston Globe*, July 4, 1995)

As soon as I heard about a squabble over an Elvis conference at Ole Miss, I called Bill Ferris, the director of the Center for the Study of Southern Culture, who assured me the story would be worth a trip to Oxford. It turned out to be a prototypical Southern tale that made me think: two of the most important figures in twentieth-century American culture had birthplaces within fifty miles of Oxford. The conference went off as planned and drew mixed reviews. (A keynote speaker passed out on stage, and there were other odd happenings.) It failed to become an annual event at Ole Miss, but I still have a purple poster for the conference hanging in my office on campus.

OXFORD, Miss.—Some faculty members at the University of Mississippi, novelist William Faulkner's alma mater, were all shook up after English professor Vernon Chadwick devised a course that equated Herman Melville's South Pacific adventures with Elvis Presley's Hawaiian movies.

So when the school's Center for the Study of Southern Culture decided to sponsor the first annual International Conference on Elvis Presley this summer, a week after the 21st annual Faulkner and Yoknapatawpha Conference, there were more suspicious minds.

While classicists shuddered at the prospect that Oxford would be overrun by Elvis admirers bound for Memphis for the annual August vigil on the anniversary of the singer's death, Mayor John Leslie vetoed a $7,000 appropriation the town board granted to support the

Elvis conference. The town has provided funds for the Faulkner conference for years without controversy.

The council is scheduled to decide tomorrow whether to override the mayor's veto.

There are all sorts of subplots in the squabble, and not the least of these is a brewing cultural war over the legacies of Mississippi's greatest native sons, Faulkner and Presley.

In the quaint old college town of Oxford, the model for Jefferson in Faulkner's mythical Yoknapatawpha County, it is a little like a feud between the landed gentry and the redneck arrivistes, the Compsons and the Snopeses.

"Faulkner belongs to us, but we really have no ties to Elvis," Leslie said in an interview. The mayor called the request for $7,000 to provide programs for the 350 participants expected at the Elvis affair "excessive." He said he was encouraged to withhold the funds by many townspeople, including "old ladies in book clubs." Besides, he added, "I'd be insulted if Memphis State wanted to have a Faulkner conference."

But William Ferris, director of the Southern Culture center, said the mayor has offered "no substantive reason" to oppose the Elvis conference. "Politics has fallen to a new low here. It's approaching a skit on *Saturday Night Live*."

Ferris, who has built the center into a major institution at the university known as Ole Miss, said there is a "class-based tension at the heart" of the struggle.

"Here you had a poor kid whose dream was to come to Ole Miss and play football," he said, referring to Presley's boyhood days in nearby Tupelo. "But he was from the working class and couldn't get in. Blacks were not allowed here back then, either. Faulkner came from the privileged, educated elite, and this was his school. There is a deep and enduring division between the powerful elite, whose literary canon is represented by Faulkner, and the working class and blacks whose values are represented by Elvis."

Even though the Presley conference, scheduled for Aug. 6–11, is attracting serious scholars, Elvis's followers have become "a class-based stereotype of the working class," Ferris said, and there is a feeling that "we don't want them on the streets of Oxford."

If that is the case, there is special irony because in Faulkner's lifetime perhaps half of the white male population of the Oxford area looked like the characters who shoot Peter Fonda and Dennis Hopper at the end of *Easy Rider*.

Despite the class cleavage, Faulkner and Elvis are bound by more than their roots. Coming from a society where work clothes were de rigueur rather than haute couture, both men dressed outlandishly. Elvis favored sequined jumpsuits. Faulkner wore tweedy suits, a bowler, and carried a walking cane. He was thought of as something of a fop in Oxford and was called "Count No Count." Elvis, of course, had his own royal nickname, "The King."

Both men went to Hollywood to seek fortune. Both returned to the South and turned ordinary homes into artifacts of their fame. Rowan Oak in Oxford and Graceland in Memphis, the city where Elvis moved as a youth, are now shrines.

Faulkner won the Nobel Prize in literature. Ferris believes that Elvis's cultural impact is still unappreciated. "Elvis is the most important figure in popular music in the century," he said. "He was a transitional figure between traditional pop music and rock 'n' roll, and he bridged black and white musics. In many ways, he invites comparisons with Faulkner."

Ferris and Chadwick, who created the Melville-Presley course that is known on campus as "Melvis," developed plans for an organized consideration of Elvis. The first annual International Conference on Elvis Presley is called "In Search of Elvis: Music, Race, Religion, Art, Performance."

When Ferris announced the conference, he described Elvis as "probably the most famous Southerner of the 20th century," quoting the *Encyclopedia of Southern Culture* that he edited. The keepers of Faulkner's flame did not accept that appellation.

Chadwick said he met similar resistance when he conceived "Blue Hawaii," a course that compares Melville's trilogy of Polynesian novels with three Elvis films: *Blue Hawaii, Paradise, Hawaii Style*, and *Girls!*

Girls! Girls! Members of the English and philosophy departments "thought it was inappropriate," he said.

"When I proposed a book concept to get a grant, I scandalized the process," Chadwick said. The graduate school officials who dismissed the Elvis project "spoke out of ignorance," he said. "It's a good example of prophets not appreciated in their own land."

With or without Oxford's money in the decision expected tomorrow, the Elvis conference will go on. It has received a $60,000 grant from Graceland, and private interests in Tupelo, forty-five miles away, have committed $15,000.

Calling the conference "a significant economic asset as well as an academic exploration," the *Northeast Mississippi Daily Journal* urged Leslie to reconsider. The mayor said he doesn't read the Tupelo paper.

Chadwick suggested that the mayor was opposing the Elvis conference because Chadwick's sister ran against him in the last town election. It is a theory worthy of Faulkner. As Chadwick said, "Faulkner explored small-town people, their petty grievances and jealousies."

"Slave Labor" in Louisiana

(*Boston Globe*, June 23, 1996)

Louisiana produces many cases of political corruption, and in my third year in New Orleans, I got a tip about a story that sounded scandalous. Outside of the *Baton Rouge Advocate*, very little was being written about the use of prison labor at the notorious state prison in Angola, so I began pursuing leads and wound up with many documents and much inside information which did not reflect well on the prison management. While I was working on the story, the warden, Burl Cain, invited me to go hunting with him. I told Cain it would be prudent for me to stay out of range. My *Globe* story was published and picked up by other papers, but nothing ever happened to advance the investigation. I did succeed in getting another message from the warden, who was accustomed to favorable publicity for his tender treatment of condemned prisoners on their execution day and for staging an annual rodeo for prisoner-cowboys. Cain said I should not bother to show up at the gates of Angola again. I had no plans to do so.

BATON ROUGE, La.—First, cries of "slave labor" came from the dreaded state prison at Angola, but those plaints were merely the prelude to a greater scandal that exudes the essence of Louisiana, a state with a moral code that invites plunder and profiteering by anyone with a political connection.

Plans to put prisoners to work for private contractors quickly grew from a chicken-boning operation to a scheme to take more than a million cans of rejected evaporated milk and tomato paste and relabel them for sale under other brand names.

Although the relabeling operation at the Louisiana State Penitentiary at Angola was aborted last fall after a prisoner's complaint reached a federal judge, the chicken plant at another Louisiana prison is still bustling and is said to be saving millions of dollars in wages for a businessman with ties to former Gov. Edwin W. Edwards.

Prison Enterprises, the state agency responsible for the contracts, has been rebuked by a legislative auditor, who contends the state is not being "adequately compensated" for the use of prison labor. The federal judge, whose jurisdiction over the troubled prison system was reaffirmed by the Fifth Circuit Court of Appeals last week, subjected Department of Corrections officials to a scathing review of the business activities during several days of hearings last fall.

And investigations are being carried out by the FBI, the Food and Drug Administration, the U.S. attorney in Baton Rouge, and the East Baton Rouge Parish district attorney.

Yet some of those cooperating in the investigations—who asked that their names not be used because they fear retaliation by state officials—believe that nothing will ever be done.

"This is a Louisiana situation," said a former ranking officer in the Department of Corrections. "The governor's friends make money. You lay out the problem, but nothing ever happens. Somebody always puts the kibosh on the investigation."

In this case, however, there is extraordinary documentation of two "cooperative endeavor agreements" between Prison Enterprises, an arm of the Department of Corrections, and private contractors that shows state prisoners were paid negligible wages to relabel cans and debone chicken for businesses that set up shop at state prisons.

Although some of the evidence has been sealed by court order because of the FBI intervention, hundreds of pages of court transcripts, state records, and copies of correspondence reviewed by the *Boston Globe* reveal a questionable pattern of business operations behind the prison gates.

Sources involved in the case say the arrangements can be traced to Burl Cain, the warden of the Angola penitentiary, an affable man with friends in high places. Cain is the brother of State Sen. James David Cain. He is also an ally of Edwards, who left office earlier this year.

In an interview, Cain described his relationship with Edwards as "not really close." He said the only meal he recalls with Edwards was "the time we ate at Chris Steak House and I begged him to appoint Richard Stalder secretary of corrections." Stalder was once Cain's deputy. By helping place his associates in leadership positions inside the Department of Corrections during the Edwards administration, Cain became de facto head of the department, sources say.

Cain first helped set up the chicken processing plant while he was warden at Dixon Correctional Institute at Jackson, earlier in the decade. According to a 1994 report by the legislative auditor, the venture cost Prison Enterprises $234,500 during a fourteen-month period surveyed, at the same time a private contractor was using prison labor to process nearly 8 million pounds of chicken thighs at a projected labor savings of $3.3 million.

After he was promoted to Angola, the prison featured in the film *Dead Man Walking*, in March 1995, Cain was instrumental in establishing the can relabeling operation that was characterized in court as "fly-by-night" by an attorney representing the prisoners.

"All of this is incredibly connected," said a federal official involved in the investigation. "It's a web, and you don't know who are the spiders."

U.S. District Court Judge Frank Polozola subsequently fined Stalder, the department secretary, and Cain $1,000 each for contempt for failing to produce records, and the judge ordered state prison officials to attend courses on constitutional rights because they took punitive measures against an inmate who reported the operation to the federal government. So far, Polozola's order has been blocked by appeal.

Cain said he had been "totally persecuted by a federal judge" whose opinions "are formed by his friends, who are my political enemies."

Cain called the allegations against him "crazy" and said, "If we'd done something criminally wrong, we'd be doing more than a day in class."

Under the agreements, private contractors paid the state $220 for each eight-hour shift of eighty to ninety inmates deboning the chicken thighs at the Dixon facility. A similar $220-a-shift contract was later set up for fifty-five to sixty inmates at the relabeling plant at Angola. The state paid the inmates four cents an hour.

Cain said the relabeling plant replaced a defunct program he described as "illegal as hell." In the earlier activity, he said, Angola inmates disassembled old telephones while the phone company paid only $100 a month into an "inmate welfare fund."

Owners of the chicken and relabeling operations testified that Cain was not a partner in either enterprise. In 1992 questions of ethics led Cain to back away from a contract with Controlled Recycling Equipment Inc., that would have paid him a 5 percent commission on all deals he arranged. The company was trying to hire Dixon inmates to run a recycling plant, and Cain was the warden there.

The latest troubles developed after David Miller, a close friend of Edwards's top assistant, Sid Moreland, signed a contract in 1992 to take over a failed crawfish-picking operation at the Dixon prison and use prisoners to debone chicken thighs.

Operating under the name Crawfish Unlimited, Miller bought millions of pieces of chicken from B.C. Rogers Poultry Inc., a producer in Morton, Miss., and shipped it to Louisiana in cans for processing. After the inmates deboned the chicken, the same cans were allegedly used to ship the poultry back to the Mississippi company under a different label, Jackson Farms, used by Miller.

Crawfish Unlimited "would buy from us and we'd buy it back," said Jack Rogers, general counsel for B.C. Rogers. He said Miller approached the company about the deal and the agreement was made because the poultry producer faced a severe labor shortage in Mississippi.

"They do it that way because it's cheap labor. It's essentially slave labor," said a source familiar with the situation at Dixon. "The inmates work in a big, noisy, cold room, cutting up buckets of chicken. They have incredible problems with their hands. The prison system calls it a school to train inmates, but it doesn't sound like a school to me."

Moreland, who held a powerful position in Edwards's office, said Miller, the chicken entrepreneur, had been unfairly criticized. "The boy took all the risks by himself. He built the program. That chicken plant is the only successful enterprise in the prison system of the state of Louisiana."

According to Moreland, who is now a private attorney in Baton Rouge, "Edwards never gave out a contract to Miller. He never lifted a finger to help him." He predicted that Miller would be "tremendously vindicated" by a forthcoming report by the legislative auditor that is researching the case.

Daniel Kyle, the legislative auditor, said his findings were not ready for release. The report will eventually address two questions, he said. "We want to see if there is exploitation of inmates, and if the prison operations represent unfair competition for private enterprise."

According to testimony in federal court here last fall, Cain and Miller were deeply involved in setting up the can-relabeling plant at Angola a year ago.

During the hearings before Polozola, Cain testified that Moreland, the governor's aide, came to the prison "a time or two. He thought it was good for industry to come into the state." Moreland, in an interview, denied that he had ever visited Angola to check out the plant.

The operation began to unravel after a convicted murderer, William Kissinger, wrote the U.S. Department of Health and Human Services last July, charging that inmates were being forced to work in an illegal operation that was "shrouded in secrecy." Kissinger, an inmate counselor, was writing on behalf of other convicts who complained of "slave labor" conditions.

The matter was referred to the Food and Drug Administration, which contacted the Louisiana Department of Health and Hospitals. An inspector for the state's food and drug unit began an investigation at Angola last Aug. 30. At that time, a copy of Kissinger's letter was turned over to prison officials. Kissinger was immediately transferred to an onerous job on a farm line for punishment.

After the case came to the attention of Polozola in September, there was a flurry of paperwork. The company finally established a checking account, and the state, which had not bothered to bill Louisiana Agri-Can for the prison labor, sent its first—and only—bill for $4,400 for inmate work performed during July.

Laurie MacDonald, vice president for corporate and brand affairs for Nestlé USA, said in a telephone interview that she was surprised to learn that the company's Carnation evaporated milk and Contadina tomato paste wound up at Angola. It was originally sold to Bilmart Marketing Salvage Co., a California firm.

She insisted the products were still wholesome. Nestle did not want its brand names associated with the goods, she said, because "they didn't meet our standards." There was "cosmetic rust" outside the cans of Carnation milk, she said, and tomato solids in the paste were insufficient to be marketed under the Contadina label.

Although officials inspecting the goods at Angola said that shipments were labeled "bad" and original expiration dates on the cans had passed, MacDonald said nothing was expired when the Nestlé USA shipments were sold to Bilmart, the company that passed the products on to Louisiana Agri-Can operation at Angola.

In a letter to the manager of the Louisiana food and drug unit, Lloyd Hockel, a quality assurance manager for Nestlé, wrote that 21,043 cases of Carnation milk were sold to Bilmart in August and September 1995 "on the condition that the Carnation label would be removed and replaced with a label bearing a Bilmart trademark."

At Angola, the old Carnation milk was given a new brand name, Pot o' Gold. The tomato paste was renamed Veronica.

When the Corrections Department attempted to send some of the milk for consumption at other prisons and a state school for the deaf, officials at the institutions refused to accept the shipments because they felt the product was tainted.

Bohemia's Last Frontier

(*The Nation*, October 3, 2005)

The water stopped a block from my Creole cottage on Burgundy
Street, where I lived for ten years and which I still own. So when the
Nation asked me to write an essay about New Orleans in the days after
Katrina, it gave me another opportunity to express my fondness for the
city.

If the restoration of New Orleans fails as miserably as its rescue, the
nation will have lost not only a cultural treasure but an important
enclave of progressive values and Democratic strength in the Deep
South.

From the time French explorers claimed a clearing for a settlement
along the massive river three centuries ago, New Orleans existed as a
place distinctly different from the rest of the country. There was nothing remotely Puritan about its early years. A strong hint of the pagan
could be smelled in the air, and in modern times the city became a
refreshing detour off the Bible Beltway. While the rest of the region
exercised piety, New Orleans honored tolerance. In New Orleans,
wine, women, and song were not synonymous with sin; gay people
found refuge; and racially mixed couples were acceptable at a time
when there were laws against miscegenation in neighboring states.

New Orleans was not without the racial tensions and urban problems that grip other American municipalities. Its public schools had
deteriorated badly, presenting an image as shameful as its gang-in-
fested housing projects. In the days since Katrina struck, the world

has been exposed to New Orleans's saddest and seamiest side: the inequities that trapped the poor in neighborhoods vulnerable to flooding, the distrust that troubled relations between blacks and whites. New Orleans was always a poor place; that's why the blues resonated so clearly here. Yet a dogged live-and-let-live spirit helped the city transcend its difficulties and persevere as one of the last resorts for romantics.

Though a polyglot army of pirates and militiamen fought a famous battle a few miles down the river at the end of the War of 1812, New Orleans was not known to be bellicose like its sister cities in the South. The city surrendered without a fight at the beginning of the Civil War and endured its occupation with characteristic elan. Residents painted the visage of Union General Benjamin Butler on the bottom of their chamber pots and dumped the morning contents on the heads of Yankee soldiers from the same balconies where their descendants would fling Mardi Gras beads a century later. That was the extent of the resistance. New Orleans did not suffer from the hardcore Confederacy complex that contributes to the South's conservatism. The city got over the war and went about the business of growing as a cosmopolitan port.

Yes, the city harbored slave markets in the first half of the nineteenth century. But even before Emancipation, New Orleans had a bourgeois class known as "free gentlemen of color." Many came from the Caribbean, spoke French, and supported a network of educators, musicians, and writers. After Reconstruction, African Americans and Creoles gained a foothold in New Orleans more rapidly than elsewhere in the South. Well before the Voting Rights Act of 1965, blacks voted in large numbers, encouraged by the quirky populist regime of Huey Long, which controlled Louisiana during the Depression. The city's black society sent out two sons, Maynard Jackson and Andrew Young, who became mayors of Atlanta. By the mid-1970s the black majority had gained political supremacy in New Orleans as well, resulting in a succession of black mayors that continues to this day.

Disgruntled whites shuffled off to suburbs in Jefferson and St. Tammany parishes, and their departure left the city increasingly in the hands of blacks and whites unperturbed by racial fears. When David Duke, the wizard of a faction of the Ku Klux Klan, wound up in a runoff for governor of Louisiana in 1991, he was rejected overwhelmingly in New Orleans, where 87 percent voted for the eventual winner, Edwin Edwards. A year later, the city's vote provided Bill Clinton's margin of victory in Louisiana.

Politics in New Orleans has been a byproduct of a way of life that grew out of the city's history. While much of the South was being settled by Calvinistic Scots-Irish immigrants, New Orleans developed as home for a mélange of ethnic backgrounds. French and Spanish flags flew over the city before the Louisiana Purchase in 1803. Slavery brought thousands from Africa. Then came the Irish and Italian laborers, German businessmen, Greek restaurateurs, and merchants from the Middle East. By the beginning of the twentieth century, New Orleans stood as a largely Roman Catholic island in a sea of Southern Baptists. A strong, stable Jewish population provided more leavening. The Rev. Jimmy Swaggart might prosper down Airline Highway in Baton Rouge, but New Orleans was hostile territory for the tent revivalists and braying fundamentalist demagogues.

From its site in the deepest part of the South, New Orleans acted as an anti-Montgomery, offering an antithesis to the Southern stereotypes of redneck sheriffs, moonlight, and magnolias. And it stubbornly resisted modern homogenization. New Orleans was a city of idiosyncrasies, sweeping from the palatial mansions along the St. Charles Avenue streetcar line to the rundown bungalows and shotgun houses in the working-class wards. Much of the architecture in the fabled French Quarter either reflected a Spanish influence or consisted of Creole cottages built in the Caribbean style. Despite its name, the Quarter was actually a residential neighborhood for Sicilian families for most of the past century, until it was discovered by artists and writers and antiestablishment characters such as Ruthie the Duck Girl, an elderly woman who kept a duck on a leash and cadged drinks in the corner bars.

In *Faulkner*, Joseph Blotner's biography, the author writes of how the aspiring Mississippi novelist and others were attracted to New

Orleans after World War I. These "young artists in revolt and champions of the arts" were reacting, Blotner says, to H. L. Mencken's scornful 1917 essay "The Sahara of the Bozart." They felt Mencken's theory could be disproved in New Orleans.

The South, Mencken had claimed, was a cultural wasteland. "In all that gargantuan paradise of the fourth-rate," Mencken wrote, "there is not a single picture gallery worth going into, or a single orchestra capable of playing the nine symphonies of Beethoven, or a single opera-house, or a single theater devoted to decent plays, or a single monument that is worth looking at." Yet in New Orleans there were museums and orchestras and theaters. And the city nurtured writers, from Kate Chopin and Lillian Hellman to early Faulkner and Sherwood Anderson and, later, to Walker Percy and Richard Ford. Tennessee Williams called the French Quarter, the neighborhood he chose as home, "the last frontier of Bohemia."

Before the storm New Orleans hosted two literary festivals, one linked to Faulkner, the other to Williams. The latter featured a contest for those who felt they could shout "Stella!" the loudest, a slightly refined example of street theater.

New Orleans could be raunchy. The striptease joints on Bourbon Street were tolerated for tourists' sake. But New Orleans preferred its own kind of spectacle, using the slightest excuse for a parade. St. Patrick's Day. St. Joseph's Day. Anybody's birthday. Hundreds of transvestites in outrageous drag marched every Labor Day in connection with an event called "Southern Decadence Weekend." To tweak the wealthy barons of Uptown, who bankrolled Mardi Gras through their private krewes—as they called the organizations responsible for the lavish carnival floats—commoners organized a rump parade called the "Krewe of Barkus." It involved several thousand hounds of all descriptions parading through the French Quarter. Most famously, New Orleans turned a religious event into a bacchanal, spending the two weeks leading to Lent in revelry as boisterous as the celebrations in Venice and Rio de Janeiro. Lent, when it came, was not observed faithfully, abstinence not being in the New Orleans manner. Bars were open 24/7 and drinking permitted on the street. The city actually had an ordinance requiring bartenders to furnish plastic takeout containers known locally as go-cups.

The celebrities in New Orleans were chefs, men and women who enjoyed a higher place in the city's pantheon than sports figures, political leaders, or television personalities. New Orleanians talked about eating like Bostonians talk baseball. Visitors might have known about Antoine's and Commander's Palace, but locals knew Mandina's and Casamento's. The native cuisine was Creole—not to be confused with Cajun—and many of the ingredients came from the nearby Gulf. There was nothing bland about it. Even the lesser dishes were unique: the gigantic muffuletta sandwiches built with cold-cut salami and ground olives, the po' boys bulging with fried oysters, the Lucky Dogs that gave sustenance to millions of late-night drunks. (Oh, that Ignatius J. Reilly, the purveyor of Lucky Dogs in *A Confederacy of Dunces*, could see his city now.)

As much as New Orleans loved good food, it moved to music. Gospel. Folk. Funk. Blues. Rock 'n' roll. Jazz was born here, and when someone died here there was no better sendoff than a jazz funeral beginning with soulful dirges and ending in an explosion of colorful umbrellas and an upbeat version of "When the Saints Go Marching In." New Orleanians appreciated good music—Mencken be damned. They were connoisseurs of the improvisation or the backbeat. They knew that Kermit Ruffins blew his horn on Thursday nights at an out-of-the-way spot in the Bywater section; that Aaron Neville sang carols a cappella at a church on Christmas Eve on Rampart Street.

Suddenly, the sounds are silent, the streets still, the people dispersed. Merriment has given way to lamentations, and no one knows when the good times will roll again.

Index

Burt, Richard, 93–94

Bush, George H. W., 289, 292; opposed by Bill Clinton, 125, 143–45, 150; ridiculed by Hunter S. Thompson, 213, 217–18, 223–24

Bush, Jamie, 289

Butler, Benjamin, 329

Byrd, Isaac, 5

Caddell, Patrick, 101

Cain, Burl, 322, 324–26

Cain, James David, 324

Cairo Declaration, 282

Callahan, James, 108

Calvin, John, 295

Camden, Maine, 90

Camp David Accords, 173

Camp Sister Spirit, 309–11

Capital Hotel (Little Rock), 148

Caplan, Thomas, 122

Carey, Hugh, 97

Carmichael, Stokely, 54–55, 61, 235

Carnation milk, 327

Carr, Oscar, 49

Carroll County, Miss., 246

Carter, Amy, 75, 109, 110

Carter, Billy, 76, 79, 81–89, 104; service station, 81–82, 85–88

Carter, Earl, 87

Carter, Hodding, 30–31, 62, 90–95, 106, 248

Carter, Hugh, 89

Carter, Jimmy, 31, 37, 189, 220; black neighbor, 74–77; brother Billy, 83–86; campaign in 1976, 69–73; challenge by Ted Kennedy, 96–98; criticism from Hodding Carter, 90–95; defeat in 1980, 100–103; victorious return home, 78–80

Carter, Lillian, 89

Carter, Lindsey, 14, 17–18

Carter, Philip, 317

Carter, Rosalynn, 79, 101, 105, 223

Carter Center, 104

Carter's Warehouse, 85, 87–88

Carville, James, 132–35, 140, 142

Casamento's restaurant, 332

Cash, Johnny, 313–14

Cass, Mama, 212

Cathedral High of Natchez, 313

CBS, 82, 87, 92, 135, 265, 271

Center for the Study of Southern Culture, 318–19

Chabaud, Arnold, 315–17

Chadwick, Vernon, 318, 320–21

Chancellors, 248, 256

Chaney, James, 25, 27

Chapel Hill Baptist Church, 59

Charlotte Observer, 31, 62

Chelsea (Mass.) Schools, 300

Cheney, Richard, 80

China, People's Republic of, 106

Chomsky, Noam, 287

Chopin, Kate, 331

Chris Steak House, 324

Christopher, Warren, 109

Church of the Nativity (Bethlehem), 178–79

CIA, 91, 93, 260

Citizens Councils (White), 5, 28, 30, 71, 254

Citizens Rights Movement, 194

Civil Rights Act of 1964, 15, 120

Civil War, U.S., 329

Clarion-Ledger, 7, 17, 26

Clark, Joe, 108

Clark, Joseph, 46–49

Clarksdale, Miss., 46

Clarksdale Neighborhood Center, 46

Cleckley, Franklin, 65

Cleland, Max, 135

Clement, Frank, 120–21

Cleveland, Miss., 47–49

Clinton, Bill, 211, 256, 305, 330; development as candidate, 113–27; primary in New Hampshire, 128–47; sex scandals, 148–56

Clinton, Chelsea, 136

Clinton, Hillary Rodham, 124, 128–30, 133, 136, 141, 146

Clinton, Roger, 118

Clinton, Roger, Jr., 119

CNN, 131, 135, 137, 259, 262, 268

Coahoma County, Miss., 30, 43

Coalition Program, 32

Cochran, Thad, 248, 253–54, 256

Code Four, 13, 16, 21–22

Cohen, Steve, 130–31

COINTELPRO, 267

Coldwater Attendance Center, 32

Coleman, J. P., 35–36

Coleman, Randy, 82

Colmer, William M., 252–53

Colonel Rebel, 36, 247

Colorado, University of, 221

Colorado College, 209

Columbia University, 215

"Comeback Kid," 147

Commander's Palace restaurant, 332

Compson family, 319

Confederacy of Dunces, A, 332

Congress of Racial Equality (CORE), 26, 55

Connally, John, 297

Conrad, Joseph, 224, 226, 230

Contadina tomato paste, 327

Continental Airlines, 219

Continental Hotel (Saigon), 220

Controlled Recycling Equipment, Inc., 325

Coriolanus, 292

Corlew, John, 246, 247, 249

Council of Federalist Organization (COFO), 42, 44–45, 55

Coxwell, Merrida, Jr., 5

Crawfish Unlimited, 325

Crossfire, 268

Cuomo, Mario, 131

Dahmer, Bettie, 15

Dahmer, Dennis, 17, 21

Dahmer, Ellie, 14–15, 20

Dahmer, Vernon, Jr., 13–14, 16, 18

Dahmer, Vernon, Sr., 12–13, 15–18, 20–23

Damascus Gate, 226, 228–30

Daniels, David R., 312

CPSIA information can be obtained at www.ICGtesting.com
Printed in the USA
BVOW04s0214010816

457375BV00002B/5/P